PRECISION
POOL

**Gerry Kanov
and
Shari Stauch**

Human Kinetics

Library of Congress Cataloging-in-Publication Data

Kanov, Gerry D., 1949-
   Precision pool / Gerry D. Kanov and Shari J. Stauch.
      p.   cm.
   Includes bibliographical references (p.) and index.
   ISBN 0-88011-897-0
   1. Pool (Game) I. Stauch, Shari J., 1962-   . II. Title.
GV891.K33 1999
   794.7'3--dc21   98-44031
                                                                CIP

ISBN-10: 0-88011-897-0
ISBN-13: 978-0-88011-897-2

Acquisitions Editor: Martin Barnard; **Developmental Editor:** Laura Hambly; **Assistant Editor:** Leigh LaHood; **Copyeditor:** John Mulvihill; **Proofreader:** Lisa Satterthwaite; **Indexer:** Sharon Duffy; **Graphic Designer:** Jeff Kenney; **Graphic Artist:** Denise Lowry; **Photo Editor:** Boyd LaFoon; **Cover Designer:** Jack Davis; **Photographer (cover):** Don Manning; **Photographer (interior):** Brian Ormiston, except where noted; **Illustrator:** Paul Harris; **Printer:** United Graphics

Human Kinetics books are available at special discounts for bulk purchase. Special editions or book excerpts can also be created to specification. For details, contact the Special Sales Manager at Human Kinetics.

Printed in the United States of America   15   14

Human Kinetics
Web site: www.HumanKinetics.com

United States: Human Kinetics
P.O. Box 5076, Champaign, IL 61825-5076
1-800-747-4457
e-mail: humank@hkusa.com

Canada: Human Kinetics
475 Devonshire Road Unit 100
Windsor, ON N8Y 2L5
800-465-7301 (in Canada only)
e-mail: orders@hkcanada.com

Europe: Human Kinetics
107 Bradford Road, Stanningly
Leeds LS28 6AT, United Kingdom
+44 (0) 113 255 5665
e-mail: hk@hkeurope.com

Australia: Human Kinetics, 57A Price Avenue
Lower Mitcham, South Australia 5062
08 8277 1555
e-mail: liaw@hkaustralia.com

New Zealand: Human Kinetics
Division of Sports Distributors NZ Ltd.
P.O. Box 300 226 Albany
North Shore City, Auckland
0064 9 448 1207
e-mail: info@humankinetics.co.nz

Our special thanks to the following people and organizations, who made finding all the answers we sought effortless and enjoyable!

Roger Griffis, 1998 ESPN Ultimate Nine Ball Champion, billiard columnist, and touring pro, Phoenix, Arizona

Cecilia C. Heiges, O.D., Vision Fitness Clinic, LaGrange, Illinois

Ewa Mataya-Laurance, author and WPBA touring pro, Charlotte, North Carolina

Vicki Paski, billiard columnist and WPBA touring pro, Grand Ledge, Michigan

Thomas C. Shaw, billiard author and columnist, Summerville, South Carolina

Harold L. Simonsen, Publisher, *Pool & Billiard Magazine,* Summerville, South Carolina

Special thanks also to friends and family members, including Laura Kanov, Vicki Paski, and Tom Shaw, who took the time to read our words and offer their valuable insight and suggestions to make *Precision Pool* the best it could be!

Contents

Preface

Whether you're a beginning player interested in learning more about pool . . .

An amateur who enjoys competing in local leagues and tournaments . . .

A dedicated semipro aspiring to break into the professional ranks . . .

A skilled student of the cue sports . . .

Or a professional seeking new insights . . .

We guarantee that *Precision Pool* will teach you things you've never had the opportunity to explore in any instruction book on the cue sports.

Not so long ago in pool's history, all those well-kept secrets and tips of the professionals were passed down by word of mouth from legends and mentors to aspiring players deemed worthy. As pool's popularity has spread, an avalanche of instructional material has become available to supply new demands. Unfortunately, even the most comprehensive works spend a great deal of time rehashing basic information. Pool is a sport, requiring that players be taught not just rules of the game and how the balls move around the table, but how the players themselves should move, how they need to think, how to become mentally and physically tougher than their opponents.

It's time for a fresh new approach to teaching the cue sports! We go beyond the normal realm of available material written on the sport, opening a whole new world for the men and women who wish to improve their knowledge and their skills. Our goal is that you really enjoy the learning process, so as to appreciate the artistry, sport, and sheer fun of pocket billiards!

Precision Pool is organized into 10 concise chapters, beginning with "The Shooter's Checklist," which explains the different kinds of equipment you will encounter, how to choose and maintain your own equipment, and the fundamental skills you'll need to master first: proper handling of the cue, proper stance, stroke, approaching the table, and establishing your own rhythm of play. Of the thousands of people we encounter in billiard clubs across the country, the vast majority could improve their games 100 percent just by learning the proper fundamentals.

Next, in chapter 2, "Aim and Vision," we let you in on the secrets of aiming, beginning with a unique section on finding the pocket center and adjusting for pocket movement. Perhaps the most often-asked question from our readers and fans is how to aim, and we've suggested the best and most popular options available. Then, in a special section completely unique to pocket billiard instruction, you'll learn how to improve your aiming accuracy with information on how your eyes work, optical illusions, perception, focus, and eye dominance—factors that can affect your aim, and quite often, your choice of aiming methods.

In chapter 3, "Cue Ball Control," we focus on the techniques and optimal results of using center ball, follow, draw, left and right english. In chapter 4, "Game Breaks," you'll learn how to develop a powerful break (one of the most important shots in every game) and the best breaks for each of the most popular cue games. Chapter 5, "Critical Shots," will teach you banks, combinations, and carom shots, along with stop, stun, and drag shots. Finally, we'll show you the advanced skills of executing kicks, jump shots, and massés—the crowd pleasers!

Next, in chapter 6, "Pattern Plays," you'll be able to use all your newfound skills in real game strategy, beginning with position and pattern play. Basic pattern types are discussed and diagrammed for the most popular games. Sound advice on how to look for patterns, natural paths around the pool table, and angles towards and away from the object ball are provided as keys to honing your own skills. Equally important, you'll learn in chapter 7, "Safety Play," when to recognize that a good pattern does not exist, and when a safety option is your best bet. Sample safeties are illustrated, and you'll learn how to create effective safeties.

Chapter 8, "Match Strategy and Tactics," will take you beyond pattern and safety play into actual game situations, including taking intentional fouls, winning games via the three-foul rule, and using an opponent's strengths and weaknesses to your best advantage. You'll discover a few secrets of team strategy, and how to find, enter, and compete in lucrative leagues and tournaments.

Chapter 9, "Mind-Body Toughness," transports you into that brave new world of billiard instruction that serious players have sought for years. Incredibly important to your high-performance pool game is heightening mental awareness. Part one of this chapter addresses the most practical methods of building concentration in your pool sessions, practicing mental imaging for runouts and pinpoint position play, building confidence in your skills, and playing pool effortlessly. We continue with your physical game, including exercises, stretching, and warm-ups to maximize your playing ability. Pool, like golf, tennis or bowling, is a *sport*, and these additional skills will furnish you with immediate improvement in your physical performance. And, it's a well-known fact that most pros go back to the basics when they're having problems with their own skills, so we've included a unique section that offers quick fixes for typical problems you might be experiencing in your game as a result of bad physical habits.

Finally, you can put it all together with chapter 10, "Practice Made Fun!" Included are several fun games that will maximize your practice sessions, without the dull repetition and monotony associated with practice "drills." Each exercise and game we've illustrated works specific target areas of your game. A sample one-week practice routine and goal-setting sections have been provided to stimulate your interest in continued participation.

Over one hundred million men and women worldwide have picked up a cue in the last year and played pool. Most of you are still looking for ways to improve your game. No matter what your current level of ability, no matter how far you wish to take your skills, *Precision Pool* will take you there faster!

How to Use This Book

Precision Pool first assumes that you have some working knowledge of the cue sports and the rules of today's most popular games like Nine Ball, Eight Ball, Straight Pool (also known as 14.1 Continuous), and One Pocket. If there are rules you are not familiar with, visit your local club or billiard supply store for a copy of the Billiard Congress of America *Billiards: The Official Rules & Records Book.* This comprehensive and inexpensive guide is updated annually with new rules variations and professional sports records, and it offers additional rules of less popular games to amuse you and your pool-playing friends.

The text has been carefully prepared in order of a player's necessary skill development. That means if you start with chapter 7, you'll be learning safeties that you won't yet have developed the skills to execute, and it's impossible to learn speed control in chapter 3 if you haven't taken the time to develop sound fundamentals in chapter 1. Take the time to read the book, at least once, from beginning to end before allowing yourself to skip around to those areas that most interest you.

You'll quickly find in your own practice and competition that there just isn't enough paper in this book, or a book ten times its size, to diagram each and every shot situation that you will encounter on your path to great pool playing. Nevertheless, we felt the need to arm you with as much actual situation play as possible. The compromise has resulted in diagrams of key shot and game situations throughout the book that you definitely will encounter in your own game and that will serve as a guide for you to expand your knowledge. And, in teaching you each new skill, we've accompanied the lesson with its practical application in an actual game situation. After all, it's of no use to you to have a great set of power tools if you don't know what they're useful for!

Where applicable, we've written about and illustrated situations for each of the most popular games mentioned above. If you are strictly a Nine Ball player, still take the time to read about Eight Ball, Straight Pool, and One Pocket. In most cases, a concept that is prevalent in one game will also be useful in other games.

Because of the nature of the sport, its confines and concepts, and its dual offensive and defensive characteristics, there will be similarities between games, as different as the format and rules may appear at first glance.

Chapter 10 offers a special section on practice techniques. While many new concepts and exercises are presented here, it will also refer to items mentioned throughout the book that are worth your occasional attention. While no individual can practice everything we've suggested every day, you will want to target certain areas of your game on certain days as you develop your skills. It's rather easy to compare this to a total body workout. On Monday you may target neck, shoulders, and triceps, on Tuesday thighs and abdominal muscles, and so on. In the same way, we've offered you a sample one-week "pool workout," allowing you to work specific target areas of your game, continue a regular practice regimen, and avoid boredom with the same old daily drills that tend to stagnate so many players' games.

Above all, we want you to have fun! This is a sport, a game, a form of recreation enjoyed by millions of people. But it can be a difficult and frustrating sport for untold millions—and you—if you're not enjoying it. Accept the challenges, embrace the difficulties, revel in the mastery of each new skill, no matter how trivial at first glance. There's not a professional player in all the pool circuit that will tell you they've mastered the art of the cue sports. What they *have* mastered is the love of pool, and the thrill of discovery in a sport that will endlessly challenge them for as long as they wield a cue. We wish the same for each of you!

Gerry "The Ghost"
Shari "The Shark"

Chapter ①

The Shooter's Checklist

Let's get started! First, you'll want to find the best places to play, practice, and improve your cue skills. The right place for you to play will depend on your skill level, geographical location, and budget. Once you've established your main "base of billiard operations," you can determine what type of equipment you will need. Armed and ready to attack your pool game, we'll begin by building a strong physical foundation with fundamental skills like stance, various **bridges**, the **stroke** (or **swing**), and timing. Even if you are already an accomplished player, a quick cross-check of your fundamental skills against the information in this section will enhance your cueing ability.

THE RIGHT PLACE TO PLAY

Pool is a unique sport. Although it is played indoors like bowling or basketball, the minimal area required for competition allows the sport to be played in a wide variety of venues. This flexibility has made cue sports one of the most popular recreational activities in the United States. It has also made for some confusion as to table sizes, games, rules, and where it is best to play, compete, and improve your game.

Though there are many choices of where to play, your preferences will most often depend on your level of skill. This is not unlike golfers who begin on municipal courses, and, as their games progress, seek the greater challenges offered by "championship caliber" courses. In pool, however, the jump to playing on better equipment in better clubs won't cost you an arm and a leg. Billiard club rates remain highly competitive, especially when compared to the escalating costs of other recreational activities—just take a look at the price of a movie ticket and a bag of popcorn!

1

Players today are usually first exposed to the game on a relative's or friend's home table. Naturally, as an individual's environment expands, so do the choices of where to play pool, and from these first experiences at home, an occasional game is played in the local bar or lounge. It is then that the first avenue for organized competition usually emerges. Not surprising, this is the atmosphere that changes the "person who plays pool on occasion" into the "pool player." Players begin to engage in weekly league play through their local bars, and soon after, many of them seek better equipment, bigger tables, and the open space and social climate of the billiard club, participating in club leagues and tournaments. A proud few will advance to the professional arena.

Many players, after a few years of regular visits to the billiard club, will come full circle with the purchase of their own home table. This offers them the flexibility of playing as often as possible and never having to wait for a table, along with the enjoyment of owning equipment purchased to their own specifications.

Other venues where pool has become quite popular include recreation centers, senior centers, and college campuses. In short, wherever people socially congregate these days, there's likely to be a pool table! This makes for tremendous variances in equipment you will encounter, but you will soon find the optimal place with equipment that best suits your own tastes.

EQUIPMENT

Specific equipment is essential to the game of pool. Without the pool table, proper lighting, cloth and balls, the pool cue, and some accessories, you can't play the game!

The Pool Table

The first (and biggest!) piece of equipment needed to play pocket billiards is the pool table. Pool table sizes include 7-, 8-, 9-, and 10-foot models, plus a hybrid called the oversized eight, $8^1/_2$, or big 8 (a model that now accounts for less than 1 percent of manufacturer sales). **Snooker** tables, gaining popularity in some areas of the country, are 12 feet standard, with 10-foot models now more widely available.

The purchase of a pool table today is easily the best buy in the recreation marketplace. A table costing a couple thousand dollars 10 years ago sells for virtually the same price today, despite increased material and labor costs. And, if you're in the market for a home table purchase, this is one piece of furniture that will grace your home for a lifetime.

The most popular size for a home table is the 4 by 8 model, which fits well into most large recreation rooms or basements. Remember, it's not just the size of the table you should consider, but the space you must have on all four sides—typically, a minimum of the length of a cue out from the table edge (60 inches or five feet). This allows extra space for the player to pull the cue back on the backswing, even when executing rail shots, while avoiding any obstacle such as a wall, post, or piece of furniture. Smaller tables were invented, naturally, to accommodate smaller playing areas, and even if your available space will not allow an 8-foot model, the 7-foot option is available, most often tagged with the nickname "bar table," or **bar box**. Actual bar tables are typically 7 feet long but come equipped with coin-operated mechanisms, an option you probably won't need, unless you're also in the habit of charging your guests for drinks.

Most billiard clubs will have a selection of 4½ by 9 professional-competition-sized tables, though 8-foot models are popular in the South. Older rooms, or upscale rooms with a selection of antique tables, may feature some 5 by 10 tables (which were the commercial standard until the late 1940s and early 1950s), along with carom tables (no pockets), and even the massive 6 by 12 snooker tables. If you frequent such an establishment, you will undoubtedly have an excellent opportunity to watch and learn the carom and/or snooker games from local aficionados of those disciplines.

A quality pool table will have a slate bed, and no matter what people may try to tell you, there is no substitute. Slate provides a consistent table surface, is heavy, durable, elastic, and will last forever. Most slate used in pool tables is imported from the Liguria region of Italy and bears an "OIS" (Original Italian Slate) mark. A few manufacturers have experimented with other materials and Brazilian slate has made a recent debut, but pocket billiards is laden with tradition, and the desire for Italian slate is no exception.

Table cushions are made of rubber, and this, along with the slate, is covered with billiard fabric. Materials throughout the rest of the table will vary depending on the manufacturer's preference of construction, stability, design, and decor.

Beyond the basics, there is a table to satisfy every individual's tastes, from traditional to contemporary, designed in every color of the rainbow, with billiard fabrics to match. Today, the average price customers pay for a pool table ranges between $3400 for a 9-foot model, $2300 for an 8 footer, and $950 for a 7 footer.

A billiard dealer can steer you in the best direction to make a purchase of a pool table. It's safe to say that such a purchase is still one of the best values around—a well-constructed table will outlast us all!

Billiard Lighting

Lighting over your billiard table is an often overlooked item. Nevertheless, proper lighting will ensure the maximum use of your equipment by preventing troublesome shadows and painful eyestrain. The best lighting for a pool table is fluorescent, versus traditional incandescent light bulbs. Fluorescent lighting is easier on eyes, and frankly, more economical. Since they will last much longer, fluorescent bulbs are definitely worth the initial cost difference you will pay. Manufacturers now offer fluorescent light bulbs for regular incandescent sockets. To prevent shadows on the balls, especially near the short rails of the table, billiard lights should extend the length of the table. This results in clearer visibility of balls and angles. Some billiard clubs have tried to cut costs with inferior lighting; try and choose a club with lighting that will allow you to play comfortably for the greatest length of time. Also avoid clubs where the lighting is recessed in the ceiling. You can trust that club owners who don't know enough to place the lights in closer proximity to the table probably don't have a reasonable amount of knowledge about your other equipment needs either!

Cloth and Balls

Once commonly called felt, billiard fabric is really a worsted or nonworsted wool or wool/nylon blend. Worsted wools (more expensive) consist of combed fibers and will result in the most consistent playing surface with the least "**pilling**." Pilling is when fibers loosen from the wool strands and form small cloth bits, or "pills," on the surface of the table.

While you can purchase billiard fabric in virtually any color to match your decor, we caution against anything that tends to quickly become harsh on the eyes. Reds, purples, and so on may be pretty to look at for a few minutes, but eye fatigue will soon set in, and you won't be enjoying your game as much, or as often. If you are playing in a club or lounge, cloth types and color choices will already be made for you. Since cloth must be changed more often, and on many tables for many customers, chances are that billiard fabric in public venues will be of a kind that is more durable, but less optimal for playing. Don't spend too much time worrying about this—it's best to learn to play in all sorts of conditions. And, the cloth that may be playing poorly today, due to excessive heat or humidity, may play great tomorrow. It's just one of those variables we have to live with. Look at it this way, your pool game will never be rained out!

Most billiard balls distributed and sold in the United States are from a single company, Saluc, located in Belgium, best known for balls manufactured under the Aramith name. Saluc produces over 900 different balls and exports them across the globe. While balls used to be made of ivory, composition, and clay, today's durable alternatives are predominantly composed of phenolic resins. Balls from Asia are made from polyester resins, making them less expensive to produce, with a quality level geared more toward limited home-table use.

Since phenolic resins are photosensitive, white portions of billiard balls often yellow with age, but this won't effect their playability. Balls should be cleaned to avoid buildup of chalk, dirt, and hand oils. Many people wax their billiard balls, and while this makes them look great, it can also cause some skidding as the smooth finish eliminates friction. Clean, but not too slippery, is the most desired condition by discerning players. There are a variety of cleaning products on the market for your equipment; consult your local billiard supply store for their recommendations.

The standard size of a pocket billiard ball is $2\frac{1}{4}$ inches in diameter, with a weight of six ounces. Manufacturers take great pains to keep a close watch on variances in weight, size, roundness, and balance so that you won't have to. You will, of course, run into unusual cue balls on coin-operated tables. These balls will be heavier, larger, or contain a magnet inside to keep the cue ball from arriving in the same spot as the object balls, allowing you to retrieve the cue ball on a **scratch** without inserting more coins.

The Pool Cue

Not so many years ago, a good, quality custom cue could cost as little as $100. But that was then, and this is now. American-made, wood, two-piece custom pool cues have become all the rage, and the collector's market has forced prices up and up. In addition, graphite and composite-material cues were introduced to the market several years ago, and have become more popular lately.

The beauty and quality of today's custom cues are more sought after than at any time in history. Pro shops, billiard supply stores, and magazine ads offer an amazing number of choices, and most cues are the best built and best playing available to any generation of pool players. Players with one cue are most often seeking to add to their personal collection. Add to this the new bevy of break cues, jump cues, and break/jump combinations, and you'll find that many cue cases are fast becoming a close cousin to the golf bag.

It is the limitless variety that makes cue buying and pool playing so exciting. A single manufacturer might produce a dozen lines, with half a dozen models in each line, all varying in color, **wrap**, inlay, **joint**, and so on. Some players are under the impression that the larger manufacturers will not make a custom cue, but all the large cuemakers we know are usually willing to create something to a customer's specs. (Figure 1.1 illustrates the parts of a pool cue.)

The following represent some of the specifications you will need to know regarding your cue's performance:

• Length: The standard length of a cue stick is 58 inches. Most cuemakers provide choices in length, with a range of 56 to 62 inches. The player's height is not as much of a factor as limb length, though height and limb length tend to correspond. If you are short, a long cue may feel cumbersome and unbalanced. If, on the other hand, you are tall or have long arms, you will tend to "run out of cue" with a shorter model. That means, simply, you will have to hold the cue too far back to achieve a proper stroking motion. If you're having this problem, seek a longer weapon.

• Weight: The most common weight range for cue sticks is 18 to 21 ounces, with the standard settling in at 19 to 19$^1/_4$ ounces. Players are divided over the desirable weight of the break cue. Some lean towards a heavier cue with the idea of putting more weight behind the stroke, while others prefer a lighter cue, claiming this allows more speed and flexibility in the stroke, resulting in more power. Many players still prefer to **break** with cues similar in weight to their regular playing cues.

• Balance: When speaking of the weight of cues, many players will also talk about balance—in other words, where the weight is on the cue. To test the balance point, you can hold the cue on one hand, palm up and flat, until it does not lean to either side. Most manufacturers advertise a balance point 1-2 inches above the wrap or 18 inches above the **butt**. This is partially a matter of personal preference, but a cue that is properly balanced will always feel natural to you, never awkward or "butt-heavy."

• Tips and tapers: 13 millimeters is the most common tip size, with ranges from 10 millimeters (predominantly snooker cues) to 14 millimeters. Too small a tip can result in a loss of control; too large a tip will not allow you to put as much spin on the cue ball. Cue tips are leather or one of the new varieties of synthetic materials on the market. The synthetics retain their shape better, but traditionalists prefer leather. Taper, without getting too technical, is the taper of the **shaft** from the tip back toward the joint of the cue. Depending on the manufacturer, these will vary, but settle into the 9-12-inch range, with the 10-inch pro taper being the most common.

• Joints and **ferrules**: You will find ivory quite often used in the ferrule and joint construction in older cues and in the artistic cues produced by today's

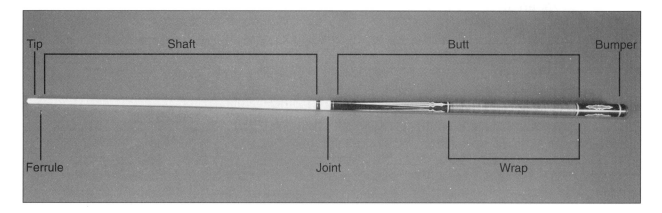

Figure 1.1 Parts of a pool cue.

select custom cue makers. While considered a prized material in cue construction, ivory is also more delicate. The newer plastics are more common, and usually more durable. Joint materials vary even more, with everything from steel to plastic to various animal horn. Steel may sound a little different to you, but we have cues in our collection with steel joints, plastic, and even buffalo horn—and they all play well. Again, this will be a matter of personal preference and your desire for the product of a certain cuemaker. Then, you'll hear about joint screws. There are big screws, short ones, wood to wood, and so on and so on.

Bottom line—does the cue feel good? Does it have a solid hit? Do you feel comfortable shooting with it? These are the questions that should first concern you.

Accessories

Billiard accessories are designed to help you play better, or make playing easier. Your local retailer or a billiard club with a retail section can offer you a selection of cue cases to shelter your cue; pocket liners to make the pockets on your pool table smaller and more difficult; **mechanical bridges** and bridge heads for hard-to-reach shots; cue papers and burnishers and cleaners to keep your cue clean and smooth; chalk and talcs; gloves to eliminate the need for messy talcs; **tip tappers**, shapers, and **scuffers** to maintain your cue tip; jump cues that make jumping the cue ball over impeding balls easier; break cues designed to improve your breaking ability; and so on. The list is endless.

Then there's the proliferation of instructional materials available in today's marketplace, on everything from building cues to playing One Pocket. In the recent past, knowledge of these skills were closely kept secrets, passed on to the fraternity of players and select manufacturers. But you can now benefit from the pool boom of the 1980s that brought about a tremendous increase in retail sales, and so an ever-increasing demand for educational materials. Many books and tapes now exist on the cue sports, and most have something of value to offer the aspiring player. Your best bet in selecting instructional materials is to check with better players in your area, talk to your local club owner (many show tapes in their clubs to get players more involved and even rent instructional tapes to patrons), or consult book and tape reviews in billiard publications.

There are even websites devoted solely to pool players. Pool & Billiard Online Expo (**http://www.poolmag.com**) boasts a dozen showrooms with everything from tables to cues to accessories to supply stores and billiard clubs. If you enjoy surfing the Internet, this is an ideal place to begin learning more about the sport and its equipment. The site also boasts live tournament coverage and instruction features.

Now you've chosen your equipment and you're ready to play pool. You know the object of the sport is to make balls (if you want to continue shooting). You also need to play **shape** for the next shot. However, before we go too far, there's no substitute for good fundamental skills. If your body doesn't feel comfortable, nothing else will either. These fundamentals, including stance, **grip**, bridges, swing, and rhythm/timing will turn your body into a solid foundation from which to manipulate the cue stick.

STANCE

One of the most important keys to playing well begins with how a person plants his or her feet, or rather, the back foot. The back foot placement—right foot for right-handed players, and left foot for left-handed players—is key. If your back foot is too close to the table, the body becomes cramped and cannot swing the cue freely. This often results in a crossover stroke, or jumping up on the shot, to get your body out of the way. If the foot is too far back, the body is bent too far forward. This too, will put you in an awkward position and restrict movement of your cue.

The following are 10 easy steps to find the proper placement for your back foot:

1. Stand up straight behind a shot at the table.

2. Line up the little toe of your back foot with the cue ball and object ball.

3. Hold the cue stick with your back hand (not your bridge hand).

4. Let your arms hang naturally down at your sides.

5. Place the tip of the cue stick about an inch behind the cue ball (see figure 1.2).

6. Pivot your back foot—that is, swing your heel in toward your body.

7. Step your front foot to a comfortable position.

8. Bend at the waist.

9. Lock or slightly bend the back leg.

10. Allow your front leg to bend slightly and be relaxed (see figure 1.3).

Realize that different body types will dictate different positions for comfort. For example, someone with short legs may have a closer foot position compared to someone with long legs or wide shoulders. It's most important that you listen to your body to find your own comfort zone. Shorter players will tend to lock the back leg. Taller or long-legged players will most often have to bend both legs, or else end up with a sore back.

These simple guidelines should put you in a powerful position to deliver the cue smoothly and deliberately. In fact, it is a process you will want to return to often during each playing session. Check your body position regularly until it becomes second nature. Spacing yourself properly behind your shot will prevent

Figure 1.2 Approaching your pool stance.

Figure 1.3 Bending into your stance.

many a bad habit later in your game. A relaxed leg position will allow you to make subtle subconscious adjustments in your aim (more on aiming in chapter 2).

Once you've established a comfortable stance, check the following:

• Are you balanced? A friend or partner can help you with this. If you lose your balance or stance when nudged from either side, you are not balanced. Remember, you're building a foundation; it's got to start out sturdy.

- Can you easily see the shot on the table? Check your head position. Your chin should be directly over the cue stick and everything, including your cue, chin, and swinging arm, should be in line behind the shot, as demonstrated in figure 1.4.

- Does your cue stick have room to swing freely? If the cue is hitting any part of your body in your follow-through, you will need adjustments.

- How low are you bent over? Bending over too far will, in most cases, restrict movement. We have observed in many players that a lower head position equates to aiming accuracy. But it also holds true that standing up a bit more offers more power in your delivery. Here's an interesting tidbit—watch the professional women play. Watch the pro men play. Notice any differences? Nine out of ten men play with their heads up higher in their stance, while the women tend to all play with their chins on, or nearly on, the cue. One exception on the women's pro tour is Vivian Villarreal. Not surprisingly, she's also known for having one of the most powerful strokes among professional women players.

- Is your swinging arm hanging naturally? Make sure your back arm is not turned inward or outward from the elbow and can deliver a smooth swing naturally, as in figure 1.5.

Figure 1.4 Front view of ideal stance. Notice that chin is directly over cue.

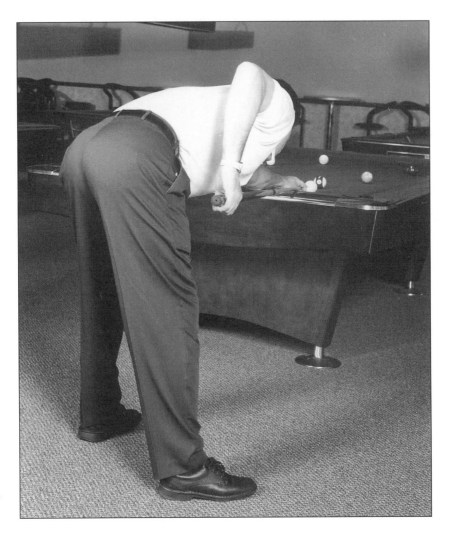

Figure 1.5 Back view of ideal stance. The swinging arm
should hang naturally.

You're also going to notice, especially among better players in your area and
pros playing on television, many variances to the physical outlines we are giving
you here. Let's get one thing straight right away. Yes, many professionals have
physical "quirks" that may not look right or pretty or "by the book." You'll see,
among other things, very low stances, sideways stances, cockeyed head positions,
sidearm swings, forward grips, and so on. Remember, though, in most cases they've
been playing that way for 20 or more years, 6 to 12 hours a day. In other words,
bad habits that were perhaps never corrected in the early years of play were *over-
come*, rather than corrected. Unless you plan to invest as much time into your
pool game as they have, it makes sense to learn proper body placement from the
beginning!

Now that you've developed your basic stance, it's worthwhile to note that you
won't always be able to use it! Certain shots, where the cue ball is more difficult to
reach, require a few variations, including stretching one leg behind you, or putting
one leg on the table. The rules are less strict here, as different body types will find
different comfort zones for stretch shots. See figures 1.6 and 1.7 for classic examples, then do a little experimenting on your own.

Figure 1.6 Stretching to reach a shot with one leg behind you provides a comfortable alternative stance for hard-to-reach shots.

Figure 1.7 Another stance alternative is one leg on the table. (But remember, in the rules of pool, the other foot must always be touching the floor.)

GRIP

Interestingly enough, very little has been written or discussed about the grip hand, perhaps because it is almost always behind your body, your line of aim, and the spot where most people assume the game is being played—on the table. Nevertheless, even tiny problems with your back hand and arm will translate to critical errors up front. Think for a moment about the sport of bowling. So much depends on the movement and proper coordination of the back arm as it swings back from the body, then comes forward to release the bowling ball. Now visualize your cue stick in the same way. Your back arm and hand are what really control your cue.

Unfortunately, players soon realize that control lies with the back hand, and seek to overcontrol, which becomes just as problematic. The solution is compromise. Develop solid fundamental skills in handling your cue properly, then let the cue stick do the work. That means, first and foremost, ease up on your grip. Frankly, we really hate to even use the word *grip*! Too often, people tend to automatically conjure up images of death grip or vice grip, feeling they need to strangle the cue—another cue-restricting problem to avoid at all costs! The word best used is *hold*.

Much has been written on *where* to hold the cue, mostly focusing on finding the balance point of your cue stick, then moving the hand back five to six inches (or more if you are a taller player). As not-so-tall players with long arms will tell you, this doesn't work. In fact, there is no steadfast rule for a spot to hold your cue behind the balance point. Instead, focus on the placement of your swinging arm in relation to the cue and the floor. The upper part of your arm, from your shoulder to your elbow, should be parallel to the floor. The lower part of your arm should be perpendicular to the floor, when in a relaxed position, as demonstrated in figure 1.8. If you need to move your arm back farther, or up closer to the balance point, do so. If you do not know where the balance point of your cue is, and feel that you need a reference point to start with, you can find the point 1-2 inches above the wrap or 18 inches above the butt, or hold the cue lightly with your index finger and thumb until, like a scale, the cue stick tips neither to one side nor the other.

On finesse shots, or shots where the cue ball and object ball are very close together, you will be using a shorter bridge, in which case you will need to move the grip hand closer to the joint of the cue in order to maintain your parallel position. In contrast, when the bridge hand is farther from the cue tip, your back hand will move backward, accordingly. (see figure 1.9)

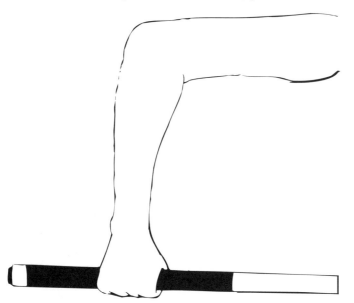

Figure 1.8 The ideal swinging position of the arm.

Figure 1.9 The top figure shows a shorter bridge with the grip hand closer to the joint of the cue. The bottom figure shows that when the bridge hand moves farther from the cue tip, the grip hand moves back accordingly.

To hold the cue properly, use your two middle fingers and the thumb. Then, wrap your index and little fingers around the cue. Your cue should rest gently in your grip hand and your hand should turn neither inward nor outward, but rather hang relaxed and in line with your arm from your elbow down, as shown in figure 1.9. Imagine you are holding a cream puff, which, if squeezed too hard, will ooze out filling. A light hold on the cue is crucial for a straight, smooth follow-through; this can't be emphasized enough. Just check out the pro golf tour, where there are very few calluses on players' hands despite the rigors of swinging a club at 120 miles per hour. A loose hold gives the professional golfer incredible results. What does that tell you? In the same way, a relaxed hold on your cue will give you incredible results.

Here's a test of whether you're holding the cue stick too tightly. Lay your bridge hand down in an open bridge on the table. If you can lift the front of the cue stick off of your bridge hand, using your grip hand, you are gripping too tightly. Figure 1.10 demonstrates this exercise. It may not be easy to stay loose initially, especially in difficult or tense shot and game situations. But remain steadfast in your resolve and work constantly toward the loose grip.

A simple way to practice loosening the grip is to hold a couple of pieces of chalk along with your cue stick. Shoot several shots holding both the cue and the chalk and you'll soon realize that holding onto the chalk with the cue in your hand forces you to relax your grip hand more, and that you still have control over your cue with the relaxed hold. Refer to figure 1.11.

Often, the fingers and thumb surrounding the cue aren't the only problem areas in a player's grip. The wrist should also be relaxed. In other words, the entire arm, from your elbow down through your fingers, should move freely and naturally. If you are forcing your arm to move, or forcing everything into a straight line, you

Figure 1.10 Is your grip too tight? If you can lift your cue off the table in this position, loosen up your grip hand!

Figure 1.11 Using chalk cubes to illustrate just how loose your grip should be.

are exerting force that just isn't needed, and that will actually work against the power of your stroke.

BRIDGES

Just as the stance is your foundation for balance at the table, your bridge hand will serve as a foundation on, or in, which to guide and support the front end of your cue stick.

Traditionally, the first bridge taught to students by astute instructors has been the closed bridge, with variations of the open bridge reserved strictly for cue ball positions on, or close to, the table rail. New theories have replaced tradition in recent years, and many professional players are leaning toward the open bridge in more and more shot situations (see figure 1.12).

The reasons for this choice center on two areas. First, it is easier to sight the shot without the distraction of an impeding knuckle, which is raised in the closed bridge. Second, when a player reaches a certain skill level, the closed bridge is no longer needed as a guide; rather, the emphasis in aiming and delivery is placed on the swinging arm. In the past, players typically first made an open bridge, before they learned the closed bridge from a local pro or teacher. Today, instead, players will learn the closed bridge, often switching to the open bridge when they are comfortable with their swing and delivery of the cue through the shot. Snooker players, who are shooting with smaller millimeter shafts at smaller balls into smaller pockets, almost always use the open bridge. (This makes a good case for the open bridge since the game of snooker requires great control and accuracy.) Closed bridges may be preferred in tight situations, where the cue ball and object ball are close together, or in certain

Figure 1.12 In the open bridge, the cue stick rests on top of the
bridge hand, guided by the thumb and forefinger.

finesse shots requiring extreme spin, and they help the amateur player learn to stay
down if he or she is having problems following through. But, on the other hand, too
many players begin to rely heavily on the closed bridge, and in fact will often move
the hand during execution of a shot in a feeble attempt to steer the cue stick from the
front. This very bad habit is more easily avoided with an open bridge, by not allowing
so much control in front that you become dependent or attempt to overcontrol your
cue. The best bet—learn to execute shots with all of the bridges we show you here;
then experiment with which works best for each of your typical shot situations.

The Open Bridge

Place your bridge hand flat on the table. Putting pressure on the palm of your
hand, slowly raise your knuckles above the bed of the table so the pressure is now
equally distributed between your fingertips and the palm of your hand. Spread
your fingers as far apart as they will go. Keeping your thumb next to your index
finger, allow the cue stick to rest between the thumb and first knuckle of the index
finger. You can raise or lower the center of your hand to keep the cue level for

Figure 1.13 By raising the hand, you can achieve follow with a level stroke.

Figure 1.14 By lowering the hand, you can achieve
draw with a level stroke.

draw (bringing the cue ball backward) or follow shots. Figure 1.13 and figure 1.14 indicate optional higher and lower hand positions with the open bridge.

The Closed Bridge

To form a closed bridge, place your hand flat on the table and spread your fingers, as in the open bridge. Then, form a loop with your thumb and index finger through which your cue will slide. When you form this loop, your hand will naturally raise

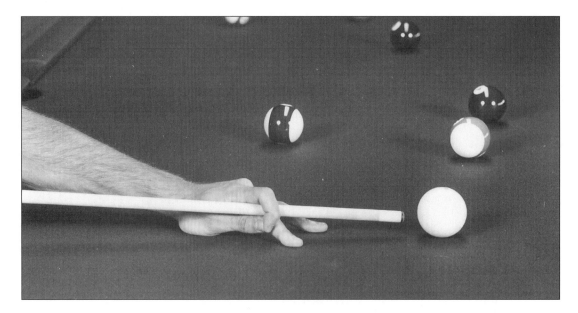

Figure 1.15 The closed bridge is formed by looping the
forefinger and thumb.

up on its side. The heel of your hand and your remaining three fingers will rest on
the table for support (see figure 1.15). This bridge, too, can be lowered or raised
by extending the fingers, or bringing them in closer to the heel of the hand.

Bridging Near the Rail

With a table bed surrounded by elevated rails, you will be shooting many shots
where the cue ball is on or near the rail, in which case you won't have room on the
table bed to make a normal bridge. There are several options for bridging on or
near a rail, illustrated in figures 1.16 to 1.20. You'll notice that the variations depend on the cue ball's distance from the rail, and whether you need to draw the
cue ball. Also note that in figures 1.19 and 1.20 the cue stick is elevated above
rather than parallel to the bed in order to hit lower on the cue ball. Do your best to
keep the cue as level as possible. If you must elevate the butt end of the cue, your
follow-through is very important so that you do not dig under the cue ball or **miscue**.

As shown in figure 1.16, holding the cue between the first two fingers allows
good control, but cannot be used if the cue ball is too close. The closed bridge can
also be used in bridging alongside the rail, as indicated in figure 1.17. As shown in
figure 1.18, if the cue ball is too close to the rail, use the rail itself to support your
hand and bridge with an open hand. The open bridge on the rail depicted in figure
1.19 may also be used if you need to elevate the butt end of your cue to impart
draw on the cue ball.

In some cases, you will find yourself in a position where object balls obstruct
the cue, making the use of a normal bridge impossible. In this case, you will also
need to elevate your bridge. Figure 1.20 illustrates an example of an elevated bridge.
Again, the back end of your cue stick will be elevated. For better control you should
try to keep your cue as close to center ball as possible with a short, smooth stroke.

Figure 1.16 A rail bridge formed by the forefinger and index finger.

Figure 1.17 This rail bridge can also be used alongside the rail.

Figure 1.18 Using the rail to support an open bridge.

Figure 1.19 Using an open bridge on the rail for a draw shot.

Figure 1.20 This elevated bridge allows you to shoot lower on the cue ball even if it's very close to the rail.

The Mechanical Bridge

The mechanical bridge is sometimes called the rake or usually just "the bridge." Knowing how to correctly use this piece of equipment is crucial for an all-around solid game. If a person isn't ambidextrous—that is, can't shoot pool with both hands—this tool comes in very handy to shoot those shots that can't be reached with a conventional stroke. Because you're giving up control of the cue stick with your bridge hand, most people feel uncomfortable at first with this equipment, but with a little time invested in perfecting the proper technique, it's not that tough!

When the need to use the mechanical bridge presents itself, simply place the head of the bridge approximately where you would normally place your bridge hand on the table for a standard shot. With your normal bridge hand, hold the butt end of the bridge firmly on the table. Place your feet at least shoulder-width apart, square to the shot. In other words, line up your belly button with the shot.

Place the tip end of your cue on the bridge head. With your normal swing hand, hold the very end of the cue stick with the back of your hand facing the ceiling. A very light hold, using only your thumb, index finger, and middle finger should be used—just enough to control the cue stick. Place the butt end of the cue stick in the middle of your chest, then raise the elbow of your swing arm about 90 degrees, or shoulder height. When using the bridge, you are actually swinging your hand directly away from the middle of your chest. Figure 1.21 shows the perfect body position when using the mechanical bridge.

Figure 1.21 The mechanical bridge is best used with
an adjusted body stance.

To begin practicing with the mechanical bridge, start out by hitting only the middle of the cue ball. As your skill with the bridge increases, try hitting above and below center. This will be more or less difficult depending on the type of bridge you are working with. Bridges with lower grooves can give you more control, while bridges typically found in clubs and lounges often offer higher than optimum grooves for the cue and will force you to elevate the back of your cue stick more, preventing better execution of draw shots. If this becomes a problem for you, speak to your local dealer or pro shop about a portable bridge head you can slip on to your own break cue or house cue.

THE STROKE OR SWING

One definition of stroke is "to hit or propel a ball with a smoothly regulated *swing*." Since we want to focus on the movement of the arm, we will hereafter refer to the stroke in pool and billiards as the swing.

You'll find that this is a big topic of discussion among pros and amateurs alike. People are always dissecting the strokes of top players, pointing out the grace or criticizing the irregularities. Again, trite as it sounds, different strokes for different folks. But, bottom line, they all have the same goal. Perhaps the most "irregular" strokes can be seen in many of the top Filipino players, most notably Efren Reyes and Jose Parica. So, you ask, how can they be top players? In their case, what appears to be an irregular stroke is in fact a warming-up of the arm. The arm and wrist are moved in a more dramatic fashion to loosen up the muscles in these areas—but on their final stroke, and through contact, they hit exactly where they want to hit the cue ball and stay loose to accomplish the optimal follow-through.

We're not telling you to emulate anyone's stroke. Again, the pros have played for years this way. What you can take from this is that developing a regulated but relaxed swing *will* increase your performance level on the pool table.

How does one develop a smooth, relaxed swing? There are several key elements. First, the movement of the cue stick must be level; keep your swing parallel to the table. Any upward or downward hit on the cue ball may translate into unwanted spin or bounce on the cue ball, which will hurt your accuracy.

Here's a quick step-by-step that you can use to find that parallel position:

1. Put your bridge hand on the table 18 inches in front of the end rail.

2. Securely make a closed bridge.

3. Let go of the stick with your back hand and allow the cue stick to come to rest on the end rail.

4. Your cue stick is now parallel to the table.

5. Resume your hold on the butt end of the stick without moving the cue out of its parallel position. You are now in position to deliver a level swing. Figure 1.22 illustrates this process.

Next, be sure you are not losing control of the cue in the back swing. For better control and accuracy, limit the backswing to 5 or 6 inches. Once mastered you may want to increase this gradually up to about 10 inches, depending on how

Figure 1.22 Find your parallel position with this simple exercise.

much power is needed in execution of a particular shot. Any more than this is analogous to golfer John Daly's past-parallel backswing—it may add to your game, but your timing will have to be perfect!

Right before you start your forward swing into the shot, you should allow a slight hesitation in your stroke. At this point of hesitation, you should actually be looking at the object ball. This is where your timing will come into play. It allows you that extra moment to zero in and look at the object ball just before you pull the trigger on your forward swing.

In your forward swing, visualize letting the cue stick stop by itself. Follow through, dropping your elbow as you do, and let the cue do the rest of the work. Your elbow will drop naturally. There is no set rule for this—much depends on where you grip the cue, the length of your swing, and so on. This keeps you relaxed through execution of the shot and prevents you from trying to overcontrol your stroke.

One of the most difficult things you may have to learn is to *not anticipate the hit.* Anticipation of the hit can create anxiety and doubt in your swing. You won't get a true hit unless you swing *through* the ball. Pretend it isn't even there. As you practice, note how far the cue stick travels after contact with the cue ball. If it's stopping at or just a few inches past where the cue ball was on contact, you need to work on your follow-through. Figure 1.23 illustrates the proper distance range of follow-through after contact.

Here's an excellent practice technique for your swing—play a few racks with your eyes closed. This may sound difficult, but in reality it's quite simple. Just get down on the shot, take your practice swing, close your eyes, then shoot through the ball. You will be amazed at the shots you can make with your eyes closed! This practice eliminates the hit anticipation and will force you to stay level and not twist or make any unnecessary physical movements as you swing through the ball. Not only can this help your swing, but it will help you to visualize each shot and, as a bonus, boost confidence in your ability.

Remember not to move anything but your swinging arm. Any movement of your head is going to distort your perception of the shot, and your subconscious may try to adjust your body's position or its action through the shot, which can result in steering the cue stick and missing the shot. Any movement of your body will make it more difficult to hit the cue ball where you had originally intended. Picture your body as a statue and your arm as the only moving part. You'll see the most common mistake on the part of amateur players is jumping up off of a shot, perhaps in anxiety, or in most cases, to watch the result of their shot. Have confidence that you've made the ball and that your cue ball is heading in the desired direction, and don't get up until you've followed through completely!

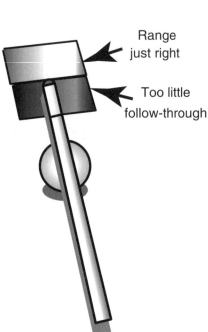

Range just right

Too little follow-through

Figure 1.23 Swinging through the ball requires proper follow-through.

Etiquette at the Pool Table

The dictionary defines etiquette as: "The manners and ceremonies established by convention as acceptable or required in social relations." In other words, every form of human interaction has unofficial rules to live by. Pocket billiards is no exception.

Let's first talk about your space around the pool table. When you go into the billiard club to play pool, you are actually renting the table and the space around it for a set period of time. By space we mean the area around the table a player needs to comfortably examine or execute any shot. Nothing is more irritating than to be looking over a critical table situation when suddenly someone walks between you and the table. A close second is when you're down on a shot and someone decides to walk by or bump the table just as you're ready to shoot. Give your fellow players a break by giving them space and courtesy. They're paying for it.

Playing with a friend or practice partner? Here are a few golden rules:

- Don't grab the chalk as you leave the table and your partner approaches. He or she will be needing it before you do. If you feel the need to chalk your cue while sitting in your chair, keep a piece there, or, if you must, attach it to one of those chalk-on-a-rope things you might still find at your local pro shop.

- When you use the chalk, don't place it facedown on the table. The residue is left on the table to be neatly wiped up by you and your partner's clothing; you'll both end up looking ridiculous.

- This applies to your more serious matchups: when a player makes a great shot, you don't need to make an immediate loud announcement of the fact. Chances are, they're probably looking, concentrating, and preparing for the next shot—don't interrupt their focus. Either wait until the end of their turn at the table and say, "Nice shot on the seven," or tap the butt of your cue lightly on the floor in the time-honored tradition of the legendary players.

Years ago they used to call sharking "gamesmanship." But in today's day and age there is no place for either term in our illustrious sport. It's bush league tactics, plain and simple. There are many forms of sharking: blowing your nose, roughing your tip with your cue tip shaper or scuffer, yawning loudly, standing in front of the shot, talking to friends while your opponent is shooting, dropping your cue on the floor—the list goes on and on. In short, any sudden movement or noise, or constant subtle moves and noises become, to those who know, sharking techniques. Those who don't know will catch on quickly, and you'll soon run out of practice partners.

If you have to resort to sharking techniques to gain advantage, we suggest you practice more or just concentrate on *your* game. If you try to shark your opponent and it does not work, it will only hurt your game and at the same time, harm your reputation.

Good sportsmanship goes beyond common sharking, to playing the game. Players know when they touch the cue ball by accident. Be honest—call the foul on yourself. It is amazing how "good karma" will come your way. A player also knows when he or she makes a **bad hit** on an object ball. Again, the short-term gain you might realize in such a situation *will* cost you in the long run.

A little honesty and integrity goes a long way on the pool table, just as it does in other of life's situations. When a situation arises and you are not sure of the most sportsmanlike response, use your common sense. Determine first how you would like to be treated, and then act accordingly.

RHYTHM AND TIMING

You've learned how to stand and bridge correctly depending on your shot situation. You've learned the importance of a relaxed grip and swing. Once these fundamentals are mastered, they will need to work in concert to produce effortless performance in your shotmaking and position play. This is where rhythm and timing come into play.

The Difference Between Rhythm and Timing

Players of many sports—Michael Jordan in basketball, Jack Nicklaus in golf, and Ted Williams in baseball, to name a few—can perform what seem to us to be superhuman feats. Each attribute their breakthrough performance to an episode of near-perfect timing and rhythm. Timing in your pool game refers to the actual steps you take in execution of the shot: your warm-up strokes, swing, hesitation at the backstroke, and so on. Rhythm refers to the overall cadence of your game as you move from shot to shot.

Each of us also has our own personal rhythm. Some people think faster, jumping from one idea to another. Their eyes tend to focus quickly on the object ball and get out of focus quickly as well. They have a quicker internal pace. Some of us maintain a slower pace, waiting for the object ball to come into focus, or waiting for that last ounce of doubt to leave our minds. Therefore, don't worry if you are geared toward one extreme or the other, or just in the middle. It makes no difference in the quality of your play whether your own personal rhythm is fast or slow. What *does* make a difference is that you remain consistent, and that you remain true to your own natural rhythm.

We have seen great players with no practice swings. They simply put a hand on the table and pull the trigger. On the other side of the spectrum, legendary players have used as many as 10 warm-up swings. But what they all had in common was the fact that *they did the same thing every time*.

Finding Your Own Rhythm and Timing

Here are a series of steps you can use to find your own rhythm and create good timing:

1. Line up as many balls as possible along the head string.

2. Get into your stance to shoot the balls one by one into the corner pocket.

3. First, look at your target (the corner pocket), then take three practice swings before you shoot the ball directly into the pocket.

4. If three swings feels uncomfortable, try two or four.

5. If those still do not feel comfortable, try one or five, and so on, until you feel natural in your approach and neither rushed nor too slow in your attempt to pocket the balls.

After you've established your rhythm using these steps, set up actual shots on the pool table, and practice maintaining the same pace on each and every shot. If you discover you are taking more time on more difficult shots, you need to scrutinize your shot before you are in your stance and swinging at the ball!

When you are looking for your rhythm, you may find that you are influenced by music playing in the background. In order to find the purest sense of your rhythm, it is best to first find it without any music. You will quickly learn, after you've found your rhythm, which music augments your game, and which interferes with it.

Of course, you won't always have a choice of music playing in the background, especially in billiard clubs. Some professional players have favorite tunes, which match their rhythm, to combat this problem. When they are playing in a match, they hum the tune (to themselves, of course) to maintain their own sense of rhythm, no matter what is going on around them. This has also proven to be a helpful practice when playing against a player whose rhythm is vastly different from your own. For instance, if you tend to play at a brisk pace, and are playing an extremely slow, methodical player, you will likely, when it finally becomes your turn at the table, jump up and shoot too quickly, as if trying to counteract the effects of the slower pace. Others will try and match the pace of the other player, trying to play slower, which can be equally damaging. Keeping your own rhythm in your head, even while sitting in your chair, will better prepare you when it's your turn at the table.

Once you have found your rhythm, timing comes into play. As Forrest Gump was so wisely told before he picked up a table tennis paddle, "The key to this game is to never take your eye off the ball!"

Lucky for them, table tennis players only need to look at the ball and where it's being directed. Pool players have it a little tougher. You have a cue ball, an object ball, a target pocket, and a target area of position where you want your cue ball to arrive. This gives you more items that can distract your attention from the task at hand. For proper timing, look at the object ball and its intended path *before* you get down on the ball. Also, decide where your cue ball will go before you get down on your shot. Once in your stance, you may need to briefly look at where your cue stick is approaching the cue ball, especially in situations requiring extreme english. Now it's time for you to use your own personal number of warm-up swings before you execute the shot. (For more advanced players, this step is second nature, requiring no thinking whatsoever.) Take a slight hesitation on your final backswing to help you focus on the target (the object ball) last.

The only time we would recommend looking at the cue ball last is in developing your power break, which will be discussed at length in chapter 4. Looking at the cue ball last in any other shot situation too often results in lost sight of your target, and poor follow-through, not to mention difficulty in controlling the speed of the cue ball.

You've found a place to play, selected your equipment, and learned the fundamental skills needed to manipulate your cue stick. Your shooter's checklist of these fundamental skills is worth checking back on regularly, as these skills will often be at the root of your success as a player. But for now, we're ready to move on to the fun stuff—pocketing balls with deadly accuracy!

Developing Your Preshot Routine

A consistent preshot routine is a simple, yet critical part of any successful pool player's game. It is so simple, in fact, that players often skip over it in favor of the more tangible aspects of the game. Imagine this. You are playing a match with a very talented opponent who has just run the last three racks. He finally missed a **combination shot** and leaves you a look at the next ball. Your first instinct is to jump out of your chair and shoot anything, just so you feel that you are, once again, part of the game. Before the urge to shoot overwhelms you, step back, take a deep breath, and think. This is where your preshot routine should kick in. It will bring comfort to your body and confidence to your mind, facilitating familiarity and consistency.

The preshot routine occurs in your mind. Analyze the table and the situation you are in. Playing pocket billiards is like playing chess—you can't think about just one move at a time. A successful strategy is a well thought out coordination of moves. Before going into your stance, you must have a plan. It could be a good plan, or a fair plan, but have a plan nonetheless. Indecision is a formula for disaster! Your plan will improve over time—thanks to trial and error, as well as remembering situations you've been in or seen others in, and the outcomes associated with each.

Your thinking will depend on which of the cue sports you are playing. Take Nine Ball as an example. Your opponent has just missed the 3-ball and you have a decent shot. The questions to ask yourself are, "Where are the 4-ball and the 5-ball?" "Do I have the skill and confidence to make the 3-ball and place the cue ball in good position to make the 4-ball, at the appropriate angle to get on the 5-ball?" In your mind, you follow the rack all the way to the 9-ball. You must think through at least three balls before you shoot even the first. When you can't, **safety** play should come to mind. Now, and this is critical, before you shoot that second ball (4-ball), you must have, again, thought through at least three balls. As burdensome or difficult as this may sound, it becomes easier and quicker with practice.

Strategy in Nine Ball is in some respects easier than in other cue games, because the table dictates your next shot. Other games don't afford such a luxury—the patterns are virtually limitless, and some patterns are better than others. That's where experience and knowledge of the different games come into play.

These steps are needed for a successful preshot routine:

1. Step to the table.

2. Review the pattern and the options that are dictated by the lay of the balls.

3. Decide where to put the object ball and where to put the cue ball.

4. Visualize the shot happening with all its related table activity.

5. Get down on the shot.

6. Concentrate on pocketing only the current ball.

7. Shoot the shot with confidence.

Keep in mind, these steps work best when you have first learned the proper fundamentals. Your stance, grip, bridge selection, rhythm, and timing should all be decided upon before you begin your preshot routine.

Chapter 2

Aim and Vision

Once you've mastered the physical fundamentals, you're ready to begin pocketing balls. This is where the sport gets really fun. There's nothing quite like that satisfying "thunk" of a ball falling into the pocket on a pool table! It's a feeling you'll enjoy each and every time you make a ball, for as long as you play the game.

A few ingredients are needed beyond your fundamental skills to pocket balls well. First, you must know how to find the center of the pocket, depending on which pocket you are shooting at. Surprisingly enough, some players consistently shoot for the wrong side of the pocket. They come to believe that their aiming skills are in question, when in fact they just aren't aiming in the right spot.

Second, you must learn how to aim. We'll show you a few basic methods and visualization techniques that have been used by virtually every player who has learned the game. Very few professional players can really tell you exactly what they look at when they pocket a ball; but they'll all tell you how they learned to aim when they were just starting out. Once you get to a more consistent playing level, you, like these pros, will come to rely less on certain aiming techniques and more on memory and feel. Your visualization skills will extend beyond the pocketing of the ball to the entire shot, including resulting position of the cue ball.

Finally, to maximize your aiming efficiency you must have a working knowledge of how your eyes work. While players may most often question how to aim, the problem usually lies not in their technique, but in their own eyes. Therefore we'll spend a little time and space to discuss perception, focus, and eye dominance—things that affect a player's aim and often choice of aiming method. We've even included a few exercises that can improve your own vision and aiming ability.

FINDING THE POCKET CENTER

There are six pockets on a pool table, one in each corner and one in the center of each long rail. This part you know. But as simple as it may seem, you would be amazed to find out how many players do not understand where the ball must hit a pocket to fall in! With a ball that is $2^1/4$ inches in diameter, and a pocket usually not much more than twice that size, it would seem to be in your best interest to learn this lesson, and quickly. There's no point in cheating yourself out of space to pocket a ball by shooting at the wrong location.

When finding the pocket from a location on the table, you must look at the opening from point to point. These "points" are defined as the extreme ends of each piece of cushion, as shown in figure 2.1. You can cheat yourself out of a much "bigger" pocket by aiming at the back of the pocket when it is not in your best interest to do so. That is, the *back* of the pocket is not necessarily the *middle* of the pocket. Rather, the pocket center depends on where you are shooting from on the pool table.

As you can see, we've also illustrated three examples of object ball position and where the center of the pocket is for each. Position A shows that when the object ball is sitting on the **foot spot**, for instance, the extreme back of the corner pocket *is* the target for the object ball. As the object ball sits on the table left of this spot, as shown by position B, the opening of the pocket moves to the right. The left point closes up and the right point opens, so that you can more clearly see the cushion inside that point. You can no longer shoot the ball at the back of the pocket, as described earlier. If you do, you will hit the cushion to the left of the pocket, and the object ball will bounce back out onto the table, rather like a basketball rebounding off the backboard, unless you hit the right spot. You must instead shoot the ball at the cushion inside the point, or where the cushion meets the pocket on the right side. As the ball moves farther left, you can see more of the cushion inside the points. Similarly, if you move the object ball to the right, as shown in position C, the optimal pocket opening shifts to the left. Thus, although the size of the opening is constant, the opening of the pocket "moves," and you must adjust your aim accordingly.

This same principle applies to the side pockets. If the object ball is straight in from side to side, the back of the pocket is the target. The difference with the side pocket is that, as the angle of attack becomes steeper, the opening actually gets smaller, as illustrated in figure 2.2.

Once you discover exactly where the pocket is in relation to the object ball, it's time to aim the cue ball at the object ball to send it into the correct opening of the pocket. Don't worry, it's less complicated than it sounds.

AIMING TECHNIQUES

There are so many different ways of aiming—from the ghost ball theory, to measuring your aim with your own cue, to the use of a variety of aiming practice devices. We caution you again not to get too caught up in methodology. Pick a system (or two) that works easiest for you. You may find that different aiming techniques work better under different circumstances or shots, so you don't need to limit yourself to just one. Each of the aiming techniques we will share with you involves some form of visualization, and will therefore be a matter of personal preference.

The Ghost Ball

This is the most common, and usually easiest to comprehend, method of aim training in pool. To employ the ghost ball method, simply visualize a line through the middle of the object ball to the pocket center. Then put an imaginary (ghost) cue ball at the spot where the actual cue ball must arrive behind the object ball in order to pocket it, as shown in figure 2.3. It won't be long before you will automatically line up correctly without having to consciously visualize the ghost ball. Your memory takes over, knowing that the cue ball must arrive in that exact spot.

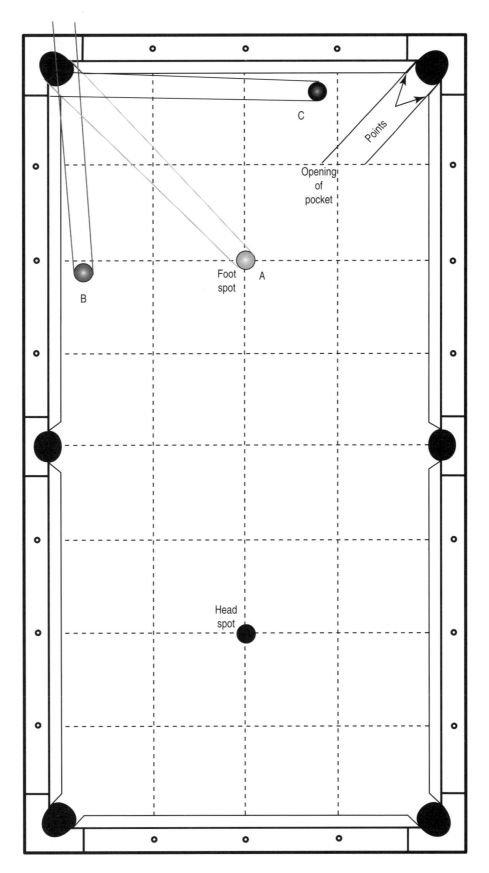

Figure 2.1 The pocket opening is not always at the back of the pocket.

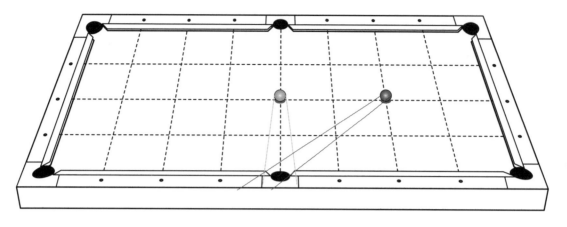

Figure 2.2 With the side pocket, as the angle of attack becomes steeper, the pocket opening becomes smaller.

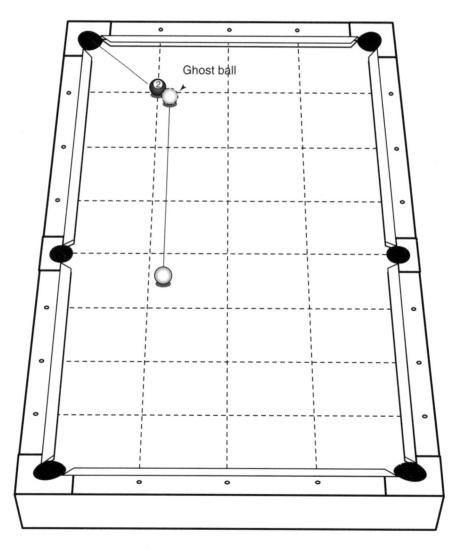

Ghost ball

Figure 2.3 Picture a ghost ball for aiming visualization.

Parallel Aiming

A method of aiming that was popular long ago was aiming with parallel lines, a system that immediately taught players that because both the cue ball and the object balls are round, you cannot aim directly at the contact point. To learn this system, it is easier to set up two striped object balls, as shown in figure 2.4. Set up the striped ball that will be your object ball with the stripe facing the center of the intended pocket. Your "cue ball" is then placed in virtually any place on the table that the shot can be made from. If you draw an imaginary line from the center of the cue ball parallel to the line from the center of the object ball to the pocket, you will see the exact spot on the cue ball that must contact the spot on the object ball to make the ball! Figure 2.4 shows the contact points for cue balls placed in three different locations.

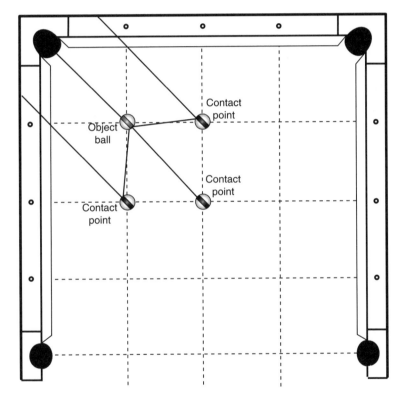

Figure 2.4 Parallel aiming can be learned with striped object balls.

Once you've shot a couple of these using a striped object ball as your cue ball, replace the striped ball with the real cue ball. You'll find it's not difficult at all to see this line, and it will give you an immediate sense of where the cue ball actually must be aimed to hit the object ball at its contact point.

The Railroad Track

For some players, it's easier to see the whole path of the cue ball to the object ball, rather than the final spot where it must arrive. Thus was born the aiming method known simply as the railroad track system. Line up the middle of the object ball with the pocket center, then visualize a set of railroad tracks running from the cue

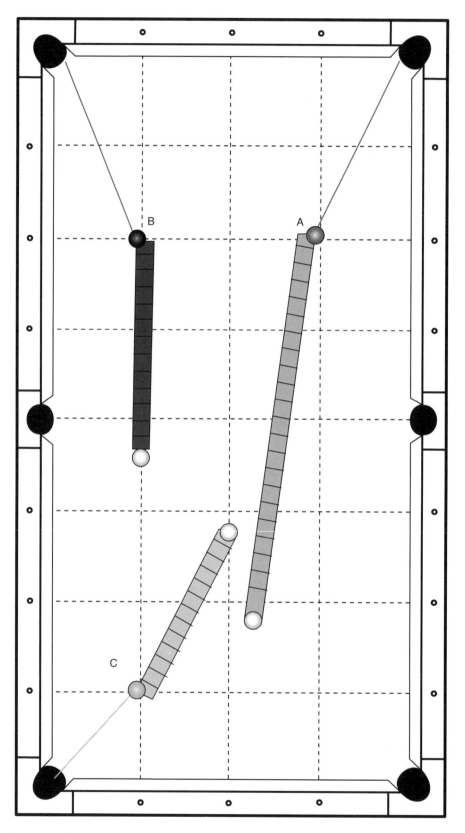

Figure 2.5 Shot A shows using the railroad track aiming method to cut a ball to the right. Shot B uses the same method, shooting a ball to the left. Shot C represents a straight-in shot.

ball to the correct point on the object ball. As illustrated in figure 2.5, to cut a ball to the right, simply line up the right side of the track with the contact point on the object ball, shown by shot A. For a shot to the left, the left-side track will be lined up to the contact point, as shown by shot B. If the shot is straight in, as illustrated by shot C, you split the tracks down the middle and aim that point at the contact point.

The Fraction Theory

The fraction method of aiming is a bit harder to explain but equally effective, and is employed by many players—even some professionals, who swear by its accuracy. Figure 2.6 illustrates aiming points resulting from various hits.

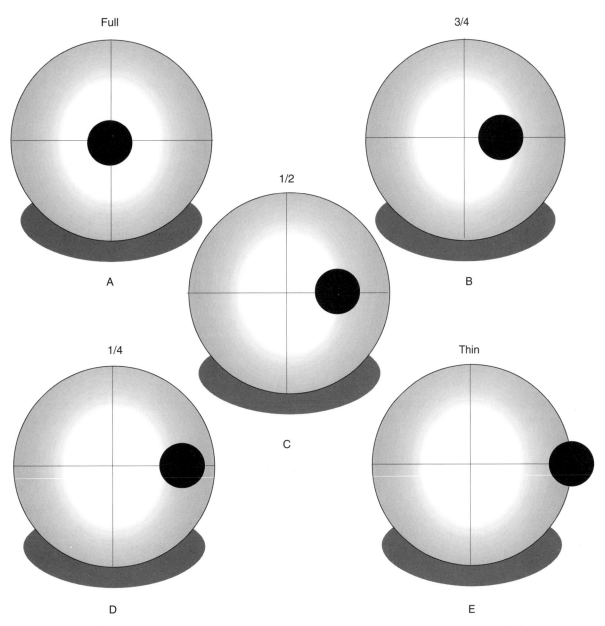

Figure 2.6 The fraction method of aiming shows aiming points resulting from various hits on the cue ball: (a) full-ball hit, (b) three-quarter-ball hit, (c) half-ball hit, (d) quarter-ball hit, and (e) a very thin cut.

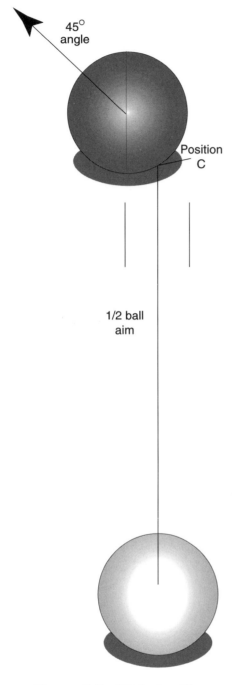

45°
angle

Position
C

1/2 ball
aim

Figure 2.7 With the 45-degree cut shot shown, you need a half-ball hit.

Say, for example, you have a straight-in shot. This shot requires a full-ball hit on the object ball (A). Now let's look at what would happen if you have a 45-degree cut shot to your left, as shown in figure 2.7. To find the fraction on your aiming point, you take the center of the object ball and, going from the center to the right side of the object ball, simply cut that side of the ball in half, resulting in a half-ball hit (aiming at the point illustrated by position C).

If the angle of your cut shot is greater than 45 degrees, you simply find the center of the object ball, the edge of the object ball, and go to a quarter-ball hit, as shown by position D. If you have a very thin cut shot, let's say somewhere between 80 and 90 degrees, you aim at the edge of the object ball, to the point shown in position E. A three-quarter-ball hit as shown by position B applies to lesser-angle (but not straight-in) shots. You can also visualize this as covering that fraction, or part, of the object ball with your cue ball, rather like phases of the moon. In other words, with a full-ball hit your cue ball covers the entire surface of the object ball, whereas a half-ball hit results in the cue ball covering half of the object ball.

While it can be a bit more difficult to understand initially, this particular aiming method gives beginners a great reference point to begin pocketing balls, after which it becomes easier to simply line up to the proper angle.

Measuring With Your Ferrule

After you get a rough idea of the fraction theory of aiming, you can expand on this knowledge with another technique, adding the variable of your own cue stick to make it easier to actually see your aiming point on the shot. After you find the fraction on the object ball, you line up the inside of your ferrule to your aiming point on the object ball. For example, figure 2.8 illustrates a shot with a half-ball hit to the right. First find the half-ball hit on the left side of the object ball that will send it to the right. Then, as you're looking down the shaft and ferrule of the cue stick as it makes contact with the cue ball, you aim the right side, or inside (going into the hit on the object ball), of the ferrule to the half-ball hit, cutting the ball to your right. If you are attempting a half-ball hit to your left, you find the halfway distance and line

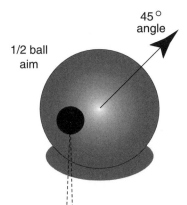

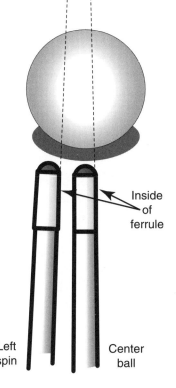

Figure 2.8 Adding your cue stick as a measuring device to the fraction aiming method.

up the left side of your ferrule to that point on the object ball.

This method works well on longer shots, can work wonders on thin cuts, and also helps aim with english. As we've also shown you in figure 2.8, even with left english on the cue ball, you will keep the inside of the ferrule to the half-ball aiming point on the object ball.

Advanced Tips and Tricks

For most players, the above theories will set them well on their way to more consistent shotmaking. As we've talked about, eventually you won't use a particular theory as much as you will employ your own muscle memory. Nevertheless, even the pros resort to little tricks to keep them focused on their contact point, especially in situations where a tough shot demands total focus on making the shot, regardless of resulting position. This is commonly referred to in pool lingo as "**cinching** the ball."

Most of these techniques involve extended visualization. For example, don't just visualize the contact point on the object ball, or ghost ball, or the railroad track to the object ball, but visualize a track all the way to the pocket. Or, as illustrated in figure 2.9, visualize the tip of your cue extending to a reference point all the way to the rail beyond the shot, forcing you to follow through in a straight line to the contact point.

Many players, once they've learned a bit about shotmaking and have built up a memory for their aiming points of reference, will check their stroke and follow-through by playing with their eyes closed. Not all the time, mind you. We don't want you groping your way around the table. But you can check your aim and swing by lining up a shot, taking a few warm-up swings, and closing your eyes before you let the cue stick swing through the shot. The results of this exercise may astound you; if you trust in your ability, you will make these shots without using your eyes in the final swing!

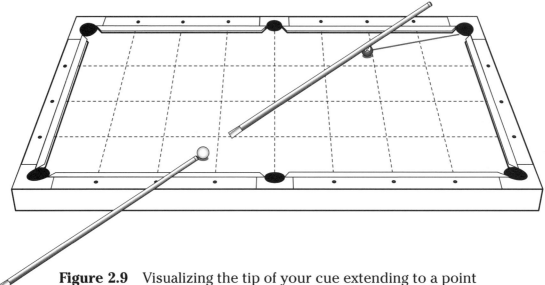

Figure 2.9   Visualizing the tip of your cue extending to a point beyond the shot helps you to follow through straighter.

HOW VISION AFFECTS YOUR AIM

We've always found how the eyes work fascinating—how they actually see, perceive, and interpret visual images. Not being optometrists ourselves, we sought the assistance of an expert. Cecilia C. Heiges, O.D., with Vision Fitness, answered questions that we had about how our eyes really function and, more importantly, how this knowledge can enhance our pool games. Dr. Heiges has long been fascinated with vision as it applies to sports performance. Heiges claims that sports vision represents an area of medical science yet to be fully explored, but one that is quickly coming to the forefront of research in both the medical profession and sports performance arenas.

Many myths promulgated by players throughout the years can quickly be dispelled after a little explanation. And, if you have the foundation of knowledge about your own vision, troubleshooting for many visual problems is possible and will help your game.

The Dominant Eye Theory

Spend more than a month or two at your local pool room and this is a subject that's bound to surface. Do you have a dominant eye? How do you find it? Can it hurt your game? According to Dr. Heiges, everyone does indeed have a dominant eye, with obvious variations to the extent of dominance. "We're asymmetrical beings and not everything is in perfect balance," explained Heiges: "at age 7 and beyond, most everyone has established a dominant eye."

How do you find your dominant eye? As it turns out, the test is quite simple:

1. Pick a spot in the distance on which to focus, such as a picture on a wall.

2. Hold your hands up to this spot, keeping them in the center of your body. You will be using your hands as a "viewfinder," as shown in figure 2.10. View this spot through your hands with *both* eyes.

Figure 2.10   Use your hands as a viewfinder
to find your dominant eye.

3. Close one eye first, and then the other. What you will discover is that only one eye is fixating on the target seen by both eyes. The other eye, your nondominant eye, will not see the intended target at all!

Dr. Heiges negates the common misconception among pool players that eye dominance will affect one's aim or focus on a target, at least to the point that any conscious decision regarding your aim need be made. She explained that this may occur only in the very early stages of childhood play.

There are so many activities that force us to make a choice about how we use our eyes. You don't realize it because we're not aware of each subtle movement we make, what eye we may use, right or left. We just do the job, whatever that might be. A classic example is taking photos. You're at a family party and you automatically put that viewfinder up to your dominant eye. You're not thinking about that body decision. It will just happen. Your body figures it out for you and makes the necessary adjustment.

This can explain why some players with otherwise perfect form may have their head tilted to one side or the other, yet nearly never miss a ball. Their own bodies have made subtle adjustments to making aiming techniques work for them. The next time this conversation comes up at your club, impress your peers with the official story!

Vision Particular to Pool Players

The vision demands in our sport turn out to be very particular. According to Dr. Heiges:

With pool you don't have the challenges of equilibrium and dynamic vision because the table is not moving and the player is not moving during the shot. However, pool players are utilizing a very unusual head posture (as compared to other sports) and resulting eye posture. Volleyball is one of the few other sports that I can think of where the eyes are turned up so often, and yet, unlike pool, their head position is up so that the eyes do not have to move so much. In pool the eye and head position are very unusual—you are working in a visual field that is very unusual—a superior hemi-field.

The "superior hemi-field" refers to the use of the upper half of your visual field. Picture yourself at the table for a moment. Your head is down, but your eyes must focus through this upper half to see the shot. Because we are an information society, most of what we do, explained Heiges, involves the use of the lower portions of our visual field—in reading, writing, working on computers, and so on. When forced to look up, our heads move to accommodate that.

What does that mean to your own game? First, if you don't play often, and then expect to play an all-night session, your eyes may tire before the rest of you. This portion of your eyes hasn't been used or exercised as often, and therefore can be prone to earlier fatigue. Second, if you are too low on your shots, you could be putting undue stress on your eye muscles, resulting in poor or slow focus. Indeed, you may be causing yourself other physical maladies, as your neck and head will have a tendency to "crane" in order to compensate. Position your body to keep it comfortable for your back, neck, arms, and legs, and to allow the easiest use of your eyes.

What Gets the Vision Nod?

Here's another popular pool room topic: What do you, or should you, look at when you shoot? Answers range from the cue ball, to the object ball, to the pocket. Peripherally you may see the other end of the table, the waitress walking by beyond the table, the wall beyond that. But what's most important? Can you look at everything at once? Should you?

According to Dr. Heiges, you're best off sticking to your focus on the object ball.

If you're trying to see anything else, or worse, everything at once, you're getting too central. You need to get global. Your peripheral retina is what tells you features of an object's location and its relative position in space with other objects. When you're looking at that ball (the object ball), you really want to be just feeling everything else. You don't even need to be looking at your cue stick or the cue ball; everything else falls into place.

Heiges says that this can be illustrated through a classic vision therapy exercise:

1. Hold your thumbs out in front of you, with one arm fully extended, and the other arm only halfway extended between your eyes and the farther thumb, as shown in figure 2.11.

2. Now, focus first on the thumb closest to you. While keeping your focus on this thumb, your distant thumb should appear (in your peripheral vision) to be blurry (not focused) and doubled. In other words, there will appear to be two blurry thumbs in the distance. You should simply be aware of this.

Figure 2.11   Check your focus with this simple exercise.

3. Shift your attention to the background thumb. It will appear clear and single. Now, you should be aware that your near thumb is blurry and doubled.

This simple exercise is called physiological diplopia. This is the normal vision process when the target that you're not looking at falls off center. This is a technique that gives you biofeedback and lets you know your eyes are working. The ramifications to the pool player are obvious. Try to focus on everything at once and you will quickly wear out your eyes. Instead, as Dr. Heiges advises, look at the various parts of the shot before you settle into your stance, but once down and ready to pull the trigger, allow your body and mind to feel, rather than "see" all these spatial relationships, keeping your focus on the object ball.

TROUBLESHOOTING

There are a number of things that can alter your optimal vision skills, many of which can be improved and/or corrected with knowledge, and in many cases, professional vision therapy. The following cause and effect topics will help you gauge whether you want to seek professional advice, and help you achieve your own optimal vision at the pool table.

Stress and Anxiety

One of the questions that we posed to Dr. Heiges was how stress might affect vision, and if exercise and relaxation exercises could improve vision as much as other areas of the body. "When people are under stress they tighten up, and this really does affect your processing of visual information," explained Heiges. "The flight/fight syndrome kicks in, and the functional field of vision actually becomes tunneled."

As a result, focus may be heightened for execution of a shot, but the player could lose sight of the big picture. The remedy—relaxation and breathing exercises that relax the entire body, and thus the amount of adrenaline produced, and eye-specific exercises that will both relax and strengthen the eyes.

Range of Motion

If your head and neck have a limited range of motion due to inflexibility, injury, arthritis, or even a great deal of tension in your neck and shoulders, the ability to keep your head up and eyes focused can also be limited. Correcting or minimizing the problem will depend on the physical source or cause of your limitations. Tension, stress, and inflexibility due to lack of exercise and relaxation can be easily corrected through stretching and relaxation exercises. Prior physical injury or arthritis in this area requires professional counseling and therapy.

Nearsighted/Farsightedness

Dr. Heiges has her own theories about the correlation between nearsightedness and farsightedness as these conditions relate to the pool player.

There are two "types" of vision: what is called your central vision, composed of roughly the central five percent, and the rest, which is called your peripheral or what I refer to as "global" vision. I've found that nearsighted people tend to focus on the central vision, and have a more difficult time integrating central vision with the global. They may be more perceptually central and thus can have more difficulty seeing "the big picture." Farsighted people may be less detail oriented, seeing the big picture, but having less of a propensity for central focus.

While Heiges stresses that there is no hard data on this, the theory can be of value in identifying and/or monitoring problem areas in your own game.

Weak Eye Muscles

Known to eye professionals as strabismus, weak eye muscles or eye muscles that work independently of each other, whatever the reason, can and will affect your game. If your eyes are not working together, you will experience double vision and a lack of depth perception, critical in the cue sports. Dr. Heiges explains that often a person will compensate for this lack of depth perception, completing an incomplete spatial relationship in their minds through discerning other factors such as light differentiation, shadow, color, tonality, and so on.

If your eyes do not work together, there are a variety of corrective measures you can take—from exercise (reading is a great way to make your eyes work together), to vision therapy, to surgery on the eye muscles themselves.

The Effects of Aging

Can age affect vision and perception? Can hand/eye coordination be improved at any age? Great news! While advanced age certainly can affect function, both vision and hand/eye coordination can be enhanced through vision therapy, which is just

Enhance Your Vision

Before starting any exercise program to enhance your vision, a couple of techniques for relaxing the eyes are recommended to achieve maximum benefit. When a person feels tension in his or her body or is placed in a tense situation, the eyes are the first part of the body to be affected. Not surprisingly, tension is the main culprit for the deterioration of one's vision. If you have any eye problems at all, seek the advice of an optometrist or ophthalmologist. Many now prescribe various forms of vision therapy, including exercise regimens, to optimize your visual performance in sports activities. The medical community has realized in recent years that the eye muscles, like other muscles in the body, tend to deteriorate, not from age, but from lack of exercise and proper care. Your vision and hand/eye coordination can be improved at any age, if you're willing to take a few minutes a day "for your eyes only."

For relaxation, first take a few quick, deep breaths, then massage your eyebrows in a circular motion. You can also try placing your thumbs on your temples, and with your index and middle fingers placed between your eyebrows, pull them toward your thumbs and gently rub your eyebrow line from the center out to the sides of your head. These motions will relax the eyes enough to start an exercise routine. In all cases, caution should be used not to rub your eyes directly.

Another way to prepare your eyes for exercise is to release tension in your neck. Simply massage the base of your neck, or try stretching your neck back, and then forward, chin to chest. Do this slowly, as sharp, jerky movements tend to increase tightness and tension. By relieving tension from your neck, you also relax your eyes.

In the first exercise, you'll need a pencil. Straighten out your arm while holding the pencil straight up in the air. While keeping your eyes focused on the eraser, slowly pull the pencil toward your nose until it touches. Reverse the process by slowly moving the pencil away from your face until your arm is fully extended. The key point is to not lose focus on the eraser. Try doing 10 to 20 repetitions, once or twice a day. This accomplishes two things: strengthening your eye muscles, and forcing your eyes to work together.

This next exercise helps strengthen your muscular control. You'll need about a yard of string. Hold one end of a string against the end of your nose. Stretch out the string before you about 36 inches and attach the other end to a door knob. At first you will see only one string, but continue looking at the far end of the string and suddenly you will see two strings. As long as you are actually seeing with both eyes, you will see the two strings coming to a V point, regardless of where you look along the one string. At the V point, two strings appear to cross, forming an X. By closing either eye, you will find that the illusory string you thought you were seeing with your left eye is actually seen by the right eye, and vice versa. Place your fingers on the string at a point closer to the nose. See the two strings.

See how close to your nose you can move your fingers along the string and still see two strings—optimally three or four inches. Resist the temptation to close one eye during any part of this exercise; this defeats the purpose of the drill. Continued daily practice strengthens eye muscles and rests the eyes.

Another activity that really helps your hand and eye coordination is juggling. There are several books available on the subject. We do suggest that you start with small plastic balls rather than sharp knives or chain saws.

Regular relaxation techniques and eye exercises will help you to stay focused and prepare you for those times when you play for long periods. Aside from the obvious benefits to your pool game, these techniques will bring you a lifetime of healthier eyes.

starting to catch on with the general public. So much of what was once thought of as naturally deteriorating function due to age can in fact be slowed through proper care, knowledge, and exercise. What medical doctors in all specialties are discovering is that so much of what were once considered symptoms of age are in fact indicators of a sedentary lifestyle and physical inactivity. Unfortunately, much of medicine is still very closely tied to the pharmaceutical/surgical industry. Functional therapies are often considered "suspect" or "unscientific" by many M.D.s.

For pool players, exercise is recommended for every body part involved in the sport, including your eyes. Again, refer to our special section on eye exercises to enhance your vision. And don't be afraid to ask your doctors for specific advice about maintenance and preventive measures you can take in caring for your eyes, rather than waiting until drugs or surgery are your only alternative!

Smoking Is Worse Than You Think

Smoking is very bad for the eyes, especially for contact lens wearers. Particles can get trapped between the lenses and the eye surface, thereby damaging this very sensitive area. Smoke can cause excess tearing, rubbing, and early eye fatigue. Worse still, smoking results in constriction of the blood vessels, and many of these tiny vessels at the back of the eye contribute to optimum vision. If you're a smoker who puts off quitting because you imagine the damage may be long term and something to worry about later in life, think about the damaging effect it is having on your vision right now.

Color "Blindness"

Perhaps you miss the same color ball all the time, such as the 7-ball or 3-ball in variations of red, or the 6-ball (green) on green cloth. This could suggest a color perception deficit or lack of color discrimination.

There is a remedy. Color discrimination can be checked easily at the eye doctor's office. Today, there are contact lenses that can improve the discrimination of color, which is really the way to go. Though color discrimination lenses for glasses have been and still are available, they've not been highly sought after items, simply for reasons of vanity. (If one of your glasses lenses were tinted red, you might feel odd.) The contact lens also has the advantage of being close enough to the eye so as not to interfere with light transmission. These colored contact lenses don't cure color vision problems, but they do help people better discriminate between colors.

Glare Caused by Lighting

Light reflects off round, shiny surfaces such as object and cue balls. The glare caused by the reflection can be misleading, bothersome, and quickly tire the eyes. Players who wear glasses have it even worse. Dr. Heiges informed us that there is a coating available for your glasses that reduces this glare, and again, that contacts are better, since they are too close to the lens of the eye to produce this distortion.

As we discussed in chapter 1, proper lighting will ensure the maximum use of your equipment by preventing troublesome shadows and painful eyestrain. Fluorescent lighting is easier on your eyes, and to prevent shadows on the balls, lights should extend the length of the table. One long fluorescent light is better than three small bulbs, as additional glare and light spots will reflect off the surface of the balls. Daylight-balanced fluorescent bulbs are best, as they are much less fatiguing to the eyes than standard fluorescents. (Dura-Test Corp. in Fairfield, New Jersey, is one source for these.)

Use Your Common Sense

Finally, as you practice your aiming techniques and work to enhance your vision for optimal aiming, don't overdo it. Becoming fixated on an object and staring for long periods of time can produce unnecessary eyestrain, and it won't help your game anyway. Glance at your shot, your cue ball, your cue stick, and the object ball rather than take a long, hard stare. As you've probably already discovered, staring at anything too long will actually disturb your focus, and the object of your scrutiny will even seem to move or waver in your vision. Perhaps you've seen professional players stay down on the shot for a very long time before pulling the trigger, and wish to emulate this technique. We'd advise against that. They may have particular vision demands that require this kind of lengthy focus, and have the advantage over you in years of practice and discipline to make this work for them.

Above all, if you notice that your eyes are beginning to tire, take a break from your practice session, or come back another day. Just like other muscles in your body, your eye muscles need time to train for specific tasks and to build up their strength to maximize efficiency. Overtraining can result in poor or lackluster performance due to redness, burning, and even transient blurring in your vision due to cornea swelling. Although these are temporary conditions, there's no point in continuing your practice session if your vision is blurred or if you're uncomfortable!

A sound program of vision exercises, relaxation techniques, and common sense will allow your most valuable aiming tool, your own two eyes, to function at their optimal level for as long as you play pool!

Cue Ball Control

If you've been taking your lessons in order, you've now developed great physical fundamentals, along with learning the principles behind aiming and knowing how your eyes work. You're well on your way to pocketing plenty of balls! And for millions of players, that often seems to be enough. In reality, pocket billiards is so much more. Just pocketing balls is like playing Monopoly without ever actually buying any property or putting up any houses and hotels!

The next logical step is getting control of your cue ball. Chances are you've been noticing, at least a little, where the cue ball goes after you make a shot. If not, start paying attention! What you may not have noticed are the myriad of options you have, on each and every shot, to make the cue ball head in a direction that will give you an easier attempt on your next shot. It's often been said that the pros make it look so easy. Indeed, it seems as if they never have to shoot a tough shot! That's no accident—that's position play—and you can't achieve it without the necessary knowledge and developed skills in cue ball control.

The elements of cue ball control include speed control, mastering center ball, and the use of follow, draw, and english. The combinations of all these elements, and how each of these affects speed control, themselves, are endless. No matter how many years you play the game, you will always be learning a new combination that works for a new position on a new shot. What few people realize is that, despite the desire we all have to take the easiest path between point A and point B, on the pool table, there are dozens of ways to get there, and hundreds of places you can make your cue ball go after each and every shot!

In the exercises provided for stroke development using various forms of english, we've included position drills using one rail, and where applicable, two and three rails. With these variations, you'll not only work on your use of english, but you'll have an excellent opportunity to learn a very important part of position play that many players never reach—using the rails for effective position. (And you thought they were there just to keep the balls from falling off the table!)

Finally, you'll get the chance to try out a few shot inventions of your own. While we cannot possibly illustrate all the results of using combinations of english on every different shot, we can let you know what to expect as you begin to experiment.

BUT FIRST, A WORD ABOUT CHALK

Chalking the tip of your cue is a simple and vital part of the game of pool that most people take for granted. Your tip should be chalked before every shot, especially on the draw shot. Chalk isn't just a decoration, it maintains friction between the cue tip and the cue ball, preventing the cue tip from sliding off, which is called miscueing. Frankly, it would be difficult to effectively perform many of the exercises in this chapter without a little basic chalk knowledge!

To effectively chalk the tip of your cue, actually place the chalk on the tip with a feathering motion, making sure the tip is completely covered. Avoid caking on the chalk too thickly. If you do, chalk will transfer to the cue ball, and this could cause problems if the chalk happens to be transferred to the same spot that the cue ball contacts the object ball. This causes a clinging effect, and your object ball will have a tendency to skid or slide.

The most common material used today for cue tips is leather, which suffers continual abuse from constantly hitting the cue ball! The leather will become smoother and shinier with use, which doesn't help you a bit. To combat this, there are dozens of tip tappers and scuffers on the market to scuff, shape, and maintain your tip. Use these products with a light hand. You don't want to tear up your cue tip, just scuff it up a little so the chalk will hold better.

Create a good habit in your game by putting chalk on your tip before every shot. Eventually it will happen automatically without even thinking about it. This habit will also actually help prolong the life of your cue tip. Without regular chalk use, your tip will flatten out faster and need more care and scuffing, resulting in quicker wear and more frequent replacements.

SPEED CONTROL

Once you've mastered the basics, everything, and we mean *everything,* in pool comes down to speed control. Pool has often been referred to as a game of inches, and for good reason. You can send your cue ball three rails and 15 feet around the table, be an inch off, and get **snookered** (hidden) behind another ball, losing control of the table. You can be a few inches on the right side of your shot and look forward to a simple runout, but get a few inches on the wrong side and you're spending the rest of the rack trying to get back in position. Speed control in a well-played safety can guarantee you **ball in hand** on your next shot, but bad speed control can force you to give up the table for your opponent to run instead. Getting the picture? Watch any tournament match, on television, on tape, or in your local club. Most often the deciding factor in each match is speed control. The cue ball went too far, it didn't go far enough—you'll hear these tales of woe as long as you wield a cue.

There are things that affect cue ball speed that you cannot control, but what you need to learn and study are all the fascinating ways that you can control the speed and position of your cue ball. The possibilities of controlling the cue ball are virtually endless, and you could spend the rest of your life working on various techniques for speed control. Knowing the basic elements you can control will (pardon the expression) speed you on your way!

Thin Versus Thick Hits

The angle at which the cue ball hits the object ball is the first and most obvious physical element that makes a tremendous difference in the resulting speed of the cue ball after contact. A full hit on an object ball by the cue ball will leave little energy left on the cue ball (as the energy has been transferred to the object ball). That means a full hit will result in the cue ball traveling a short distance. Conversely, a thin hit (greater angle) will leave most of the energy on the cue ball. Even with the same force of hit, the cue ball will travel a much greater distance after contact with the object ball.

Cue Stick Speed

Different forces of shots also come into play. Cue stick speed alone offers an unlimited amount of variations: the faster the cue's speed (greater force imparted), the farther the cue ball will roll. Slower speed translates to less distance. In fact, most of the game can be played with follow, draw, and middle-ball shots with a proper stroke, and it's definitely to your advantage to master these techniques that allow you more control of your speed. It's much more difficult to control speed with spin.

Most players, especially beginner and intermediate players, have a tendency to hit the balls too hard. They assume that they have to overpower everything. But it's a smooth and level swing that provides for the most action on the cue ball. Never forget one simple fact—pool balls are round and they will roll!

Using the Cushions

The cushions on the pool table itself are often used to control the speed of the cue ball. The softer the hit into the rail, the more speed will be taken off the cue ball as it leaves the rail. The harder the hit, the less speed will be taken off, as the rubber cushion will have a greater tendency to spring the cue ball back out onto the table after impact. Additionally, you can use the cushions to take speed off a shot. Say you have a very thin cut on an object ball, but you don't want to lose control of the cue ball traveling up and down the table. Every cushion you contact will take more speed off the cue ball. There are theories of how much speed is taken off with each subsequent cushion, such as 60 percent diminished off the first rail, 30 percent off the second, and 10 percent off the third. This will vary, however, since much depends on the speed at which the cue ball entered the cushion in the first place. You'll learn much more about speed control off the cushions in chapter 6 on pattern play.

Bridge and Grip Hands

Here's a little speed control gem that lots of players never learn. The closer the bridge hand is to the cue ball, the easier it is to take speed off the cue ball. The

Equipment Affects Your Speed Control

When it comes to controlling speed on the table and controlling your cue ball for optimal position play, many variables will come into play that you cannot control. Types of equipment, wear and tear of the equipment you're playing on, and even weather conditions can affect your speed control.

Speed of the billiard fabric covering the table is the most obvious item. Your speed of stroke will first be dictated by how new the cloth is. A very new cloth will be quite quick. Balls have a tendency to skid more easily, as the cloth has less chalk, dust, and dirt in its fibers to increase friction. As time goes on, the cloth will become worn and will actually slow down. Nonworsted wools will have a tendency to pill, as fibers loosen from the strands and make the playing surface less consistent. Conversely, once the cloth becomes very old and worn (you'll note the dull shine on such tables) the balls tend to speed up again, due to a return to less friction provided between the ball and the playing surface.

If you're playing in a billiard club that properly maintains its equipment, dirt and dust should be less of a factor. But a dirty table that hasn't been vacuumed will play slower. If you have a home table, try to vacuum it weekly. Billiard fabrics also come in directional versus nondirectional varieties. A directional cloth is in the direction of the nap, and must be brushed or vacuumed with the nap (from head spot to foot spot) and never against it. Most clubs today are leaning towards the napless variety.

The next big variable you'll run into is humidity, which can wreak havoc with any player's game. It has such a tremendous effect on playing conditions that manufacturers have invented tables with heated slates to keep tables warm and dry. These haven't really hit much of the mainstream American public yet, but are popular, especially in Europe, in tournament play. Humidity will slow down the cloth but actually speed up the rails. This becomes even more noticeable in older tables where the rubber rails have aged and become more porous, thus allowing in more moisture. This will also affect the angle at which the cue ball rebounds off the rail, producing further difficulties in your position play.

New rubber versus old rubber can also affect speed control. New rubber has a tendency to cause the cue ball to rebound off the cushion farther. Another important fact: the rubber cushions on your pool table are actually glued to the rails of the table. If, for instance, someone sits on the edge of the table, the glue seal can be broken, and you'll end up with a dead spot on the rail. What this means is that you can shoot the ball into that part of the cushion, and you'll hear a thud and the ball will not carom off the rail as far as it should, or in the direction that it should. Add to that the variables of different textures of rubber and different heights of rubber cushions. The higher the cushion, the less chance of the ball contacting the cushion at its center, resulting in the ball coming off the cushion at a lesser angle.

Naturally, the balls themselves will also come into play. Newer balls have more elasticity and will go farther. After years of being beaten on, older balls will not be completely round and will just not roll as far. Dirty balls will not roll as far as clean balls. Balls that have been waxed will be very slippery and have more of a tendency to skid.

Do remember this: if you are playing an opponent, he or she is playing under the same conditions. Simply direct your attention to pocketing balls and getting as close to your next target ball as possible. By doing this, your subconscious mind can automatically adjust to your surroundings.

farther the bridge hand is from the cue ball, the easier it can be for the player to follow through farther for power shots. For example, there are the little "nip shots"—short bridge shots with an inch or less of follow-through. You'll see pros be able to kill the cue ball on these short shots despite extreme angles. They're using a short bridge and more grip pressure to "kill" the cue ball. Your length-of-the-table position shots will require more follow-through, and often a longer bridge.

Grip pressure will also dictate the speed at which the cue ball leaves the cue stick. The lighter and looser the pressure, the farther it will go. The tighter the grip, the slower the reaction. As mentioned in the preceding paragraph, if a player wants to kill the cue ball, they'll tighten up their grip to take the spin off the cue ball and produce a stunning effect on the cue ball. You'll see that same player produce a beautiful long draw shot with a wrist that's loose as can be.

The Use of English

Finally, english can be used to control speed. **Inside english** (right sidespin if you are cutting a ball to the right, and left if you are cutting a ball to the left), for example, can be used to "stun" the cue ball so it doesn't roll as far, though extreme angle shots require a great deal of experience and feel to accomplish this. The opposite takes place with **outside english** (often called **running english**). Outside english can lengthen out the shot, and the cue ball will "run" or roll a lot farther. In other words, with everything else being equal (same force, same stroke) the speed on the cue ball will definitely change depending on your use of english.

CENTER BALL

Before you can begin learning and experimenting with different forms of english, you need a reference point. At this stage of development in your pool game, it's time to find the center of the cue ball. And the easiest way is the "tried and true," a simple drill.

Begin by facing the width of the table to keep the shot very short and easy to execute. This will help you gauge your initial progress. Place two balls no more than 3 inches apart and 6 inches from the long rail, as shown in figure 3.1a. You'll be shooting the cue ball between the two balls, and, since standard pool balls are $2\frac{1}{4}$ inches in diameter, this will be more than enough space for the cue ball to pass through. Place your cue ball 12 inches from the long rail directly opposite the middle of the two balls. Finally, to give yourself a reference point at which to aim, place a piece of chalk on the opposite long rail closest to the two balls, and midway between them.

Using the piece of chalk as your target, step into your stance, aim the ball at the chalk, and shoot. Be careful to contact the cue ball directly at what you believe to be its center. If everything is lined up correctly, and you execute the shot with slow speed, a proper swing, and a smooth follow-through, the cue ball should hit the long rail and bounce back without disturbing the two balls. Ideally, the cue ball will pass between the two balls and directly back into the tip of your cue stick.

If you don't accomplish this ideal, make one of the following adjustments:

- If, on the rebound off the long rail the cue ball hits the left ball, reposition that ball and shoot again, this time aiming a touch to the right of what you see as the center of the cue ball.

- If your cue ball hits the right ball on the rebound, aim a touch to the left.

In other words, what looks like center ball to you may not result in a center-ball hit. Why? Usually there's one of three explanations. You either have a slight natural crossover in your stroke; your head may have a slight tilt and not be directly in line over your cue stick; or your dominant eye (as discussed in the previous chapter) may be giving you an illusion. If it doesn't *look* right, but you're achieving center-ball effect—trust it!

Practice this exercise until you can create the same results at least 10 times in a row. Once the first exercise is mastered, set the same shot up, this time down the length of the table as illustrated by figure 3.1b. Use short distances at first until you feel comfortable. Gradually increase the distance between the two balls and the cue ball until you can achieve a true center-ball hit over the length of the table.

Finally, perform the same exercise, but add an object ball as illustrated in figure 3.2. The chalk on the rail will be your target. Keep the cue ball about 12 to 18 inches from the object ball. In this exercise, you want the cue ball to stop, and the object ball to rebound off the cushion and directly back to hit the cue ball. This will also give you a bit of feel for the speed of the object ball and the cue ball. Move the cue ball and the object ball farther apart, in increments of 6 inches at a time, to increase the difficulty of the exercise.

Another helpful hint when trying to find center ball: determine your dominant eye (refer to our section in chapter 2 on how to find your dominant eye), then close your nondominant eye to see if you are correctly looking at center ball.

After you're sure that you've found center ball, you need to play a few racks using the center-ball hit on every shot. While you are doing this, concentrate on one thing and one thing only—how the cue ball reacts off the object ball. Which way does the cue ball go after contact with the object ball?

The direction the cue ball travels after contact with the object ball is called the tangent line. Examples of the tangent line are shown in figure 3.3. The tangent line is the 90-degree line (from the target line) at which your cue ball will normally glance off a ball with a middle-ball hit. Another way of looking at it is to add up the angles. For instance, with a 25-degree cut shot, the cue ball comes off the object ball from the approach line at about 65 degrees. 25 + 65 = 90 degrees. Knowing the tangent line is the first critical step to knowing where your cue ball is headed. Only by knowing the reaction with center ball will you know what paths can result when altering that line with follow, draw, or different stroke forces.

The other important thing to note is where the cue ball goes after contacting the object ball and then the rail. Optimally, the cue ball should travel from the cushion out onto the table at roughly the same angle it traveled into the cushion, as illustrated in figure 3.4. And of course, this line too can be altered with speed, left or right english, or a combination of these.

Confused yet? Don't be. It gets more interesting from here!

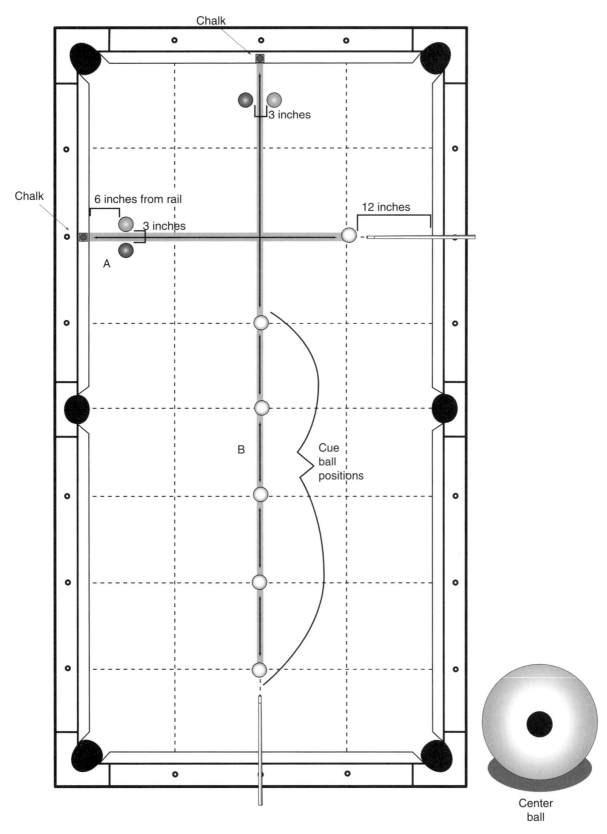

Figure 3.1   Find the center of the cue ball with the simple drill, A;
then see if you still achieve a center-ball hit with shot B.

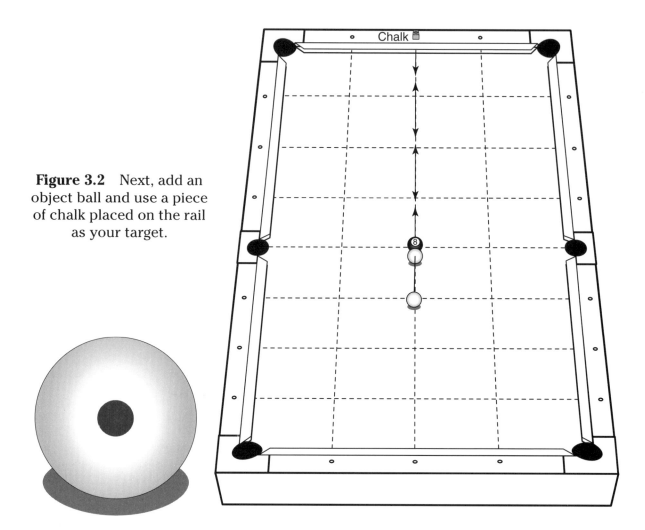

Figure 3.2 Next, add an object ball and use a piece of chalk placed on the rail as your target.

FOLLOW

Because it is easier to learn initially, we'll begin our study in cue ball path alterations with the follow stroke. As the name implies, your cue ball, when hit above center, will follow the object ball after it makes contact. You are putting topspin on the cue ball, which will cause it to continue rolling forward.

To execute a follow stroke, you will, in most cases, need to shoot a one-half to full cue tip above center, as shown by figure 3.5. Frankly, for maximum results you should never need much more than a full cue tip. Shooting too high on the cue ball will result in miscues, and it's really not necessary. The most important things to remember while executing your follow stroke are to keep your cue stick level (simply elevate your bridge hand slightly to raise the cue tip) and to follow through completely.

If you are shooting a ball straight in the pocket, a follow stroke will send the cue ball directly into the pocket after it. But, since few of your shots will be straight in, you must also understand how follow affects your other shots. Follow can be effectively used to minimize the angle at which your cue ball travels after contact with the object ball, because it in fact alters the tangent line—that is, the 90-de-

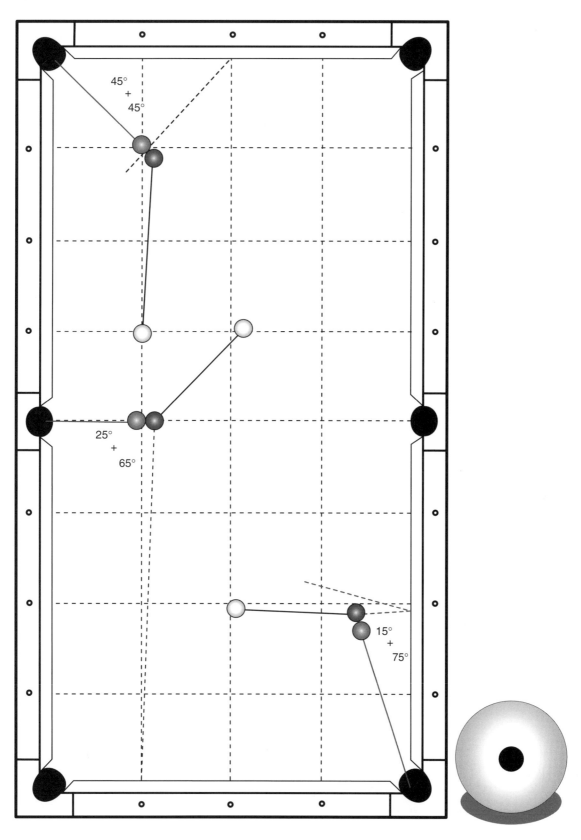

Figure 3.3   The natural direction at which the cue ball glances off
the object ball after contact is called the tangent line.

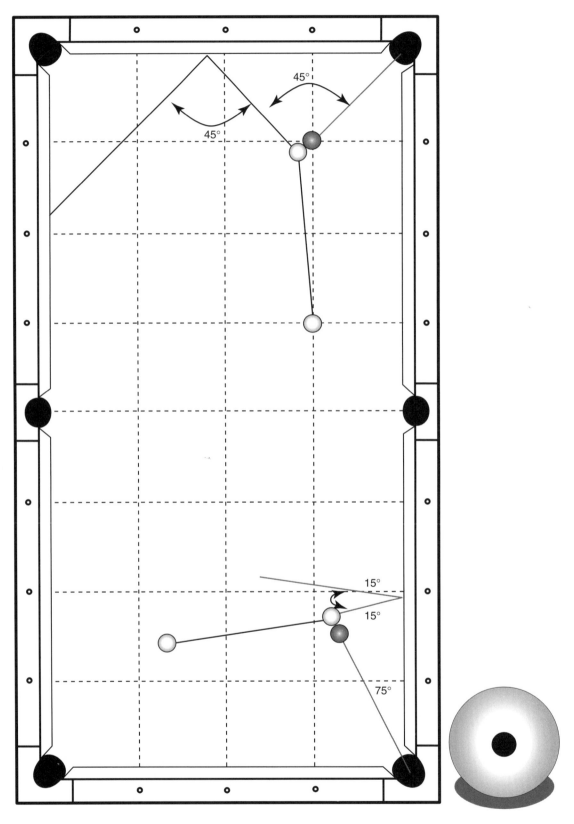

Figure 3.4 "Angle in equals angle out." But remember that this line
can be altered drastically with speed, english,
or a combination of both.

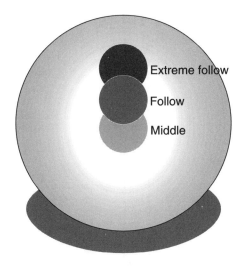

Figure 3.5 Cue tip position for a follow stroke on the cue ball.

gree line at which your cue ball will normally glance off a ball with a middle-ball hit, as shown in figure 3.3.

The softer and smoother the hit, the more you can minimize your angle coming off the object ball. This becomes an important tool in your arsenal, especially when you want to avoid a scratch or avoid hitting other balls on your way around the table, as in our example in figure 3.6. And, of course, it is a simple way to get from one end of the table to the other. In a game of Nine Ball, for instance, the follow shot may prove invaluable if every other numbered ball is on the opposite end of the table!

An excellent way to develop your follow stroke is to set up a simple follow shot as illustrated in figure 3.7 and play position for the balls labeled A through D, by arriving at the corresponding labeled areas. As you will note, to arrive at area D, you'll need to hit your shot harder than you did for area A. Also note that this changes where the cue ball contacts the cushion. The greater the force of your hit, the more the cue ball will skid or slide sideways off the object ball before starting its forward roll.

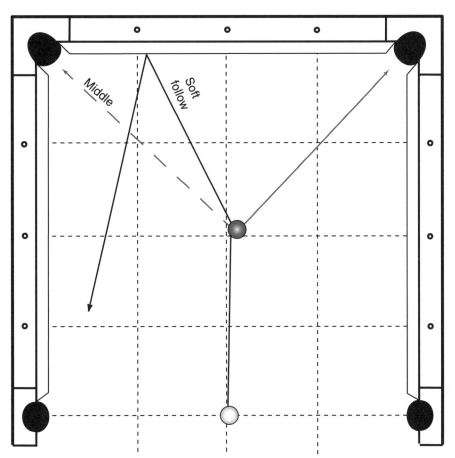

Figure 3.6 Using follow to minimize your angle after contact with an object ball.

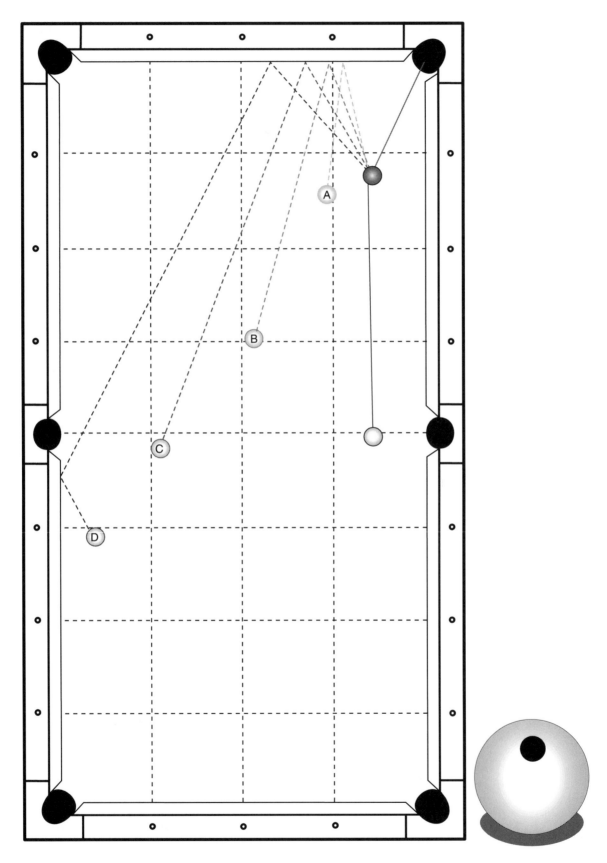

Figure 3.7 Set up this simple drill to improve your follow stroke.

While learning position play and cue ball control, it is simpler to picture your pool table divided up into small quadrants and to visualize having your cue ball arrive in that desired quadrant when shooting. This is called "area" position. (As your stroke and speed-control skills develop, you will play more and more for "pinpoint" position.) Once you can successfully position your cue ball in each of these areas, you will have a very good idea of the difference in the hit needed to get to position A or B as opposed to position C or D.

Now try the shot illustrated in figure 3.8. This shot is a thinner cut on the object ball. You'll notice that to get to the position indicated by the illustration, you need only hit the ball as hard as you did in speed A of figure 3.7, but your cue ball will travel much farther. Remember, the speed of the cue ball is not only dictated by follow-through of the cue stick, but also by the angle the cue ball is deflected off the object ball. In shot A of figure 3.7 you were required to hit the ball very full, transferring most of the energy to the object ball. But in this shot, a thin hit allows most of the energy to stay with the cue ball, causing it to travel much farther with less effort.

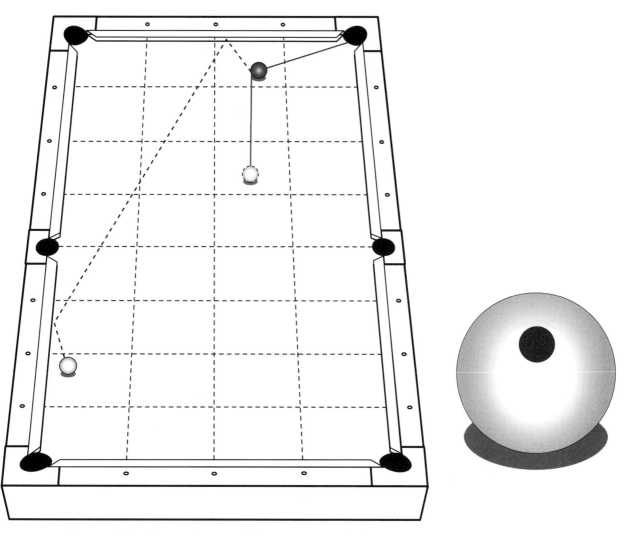

Figure 3.8   Expand your follow position skills with this drill, noting that the cue ball will travel farther with less force on the thinly cut shot.

THE DREADED DRAW

The draw stroke isn't as tough as people make it out to be, but you'll always see amateurs who think that because someone can draw their ball, they must play good pool. True, it looks impressive, and there's nothing that gives you quite the same feeling of power as a well-struck draw shot that commands the cue ball to come whizzing back toward you. But, if you remember a few simple rules of pool and physics, you too can quickly experience that feeling and look like a champ!

As in the follow stroke, rule #1 is that your cue must remain as level as possible. You will be using a below-center hit, which, after contact with the object ball, will allow the cue ball to hesitate, and then "magically" reverse its path and head backward. Figure 3.9 illustrates draw position on the cue ball.

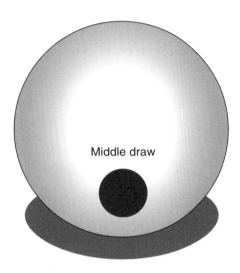

Middle draw

Figure 3.9 Cue tip position for a draw stroke on the cue ball.

Rule #2—Keep that grip loose! A loose grip keeps the wrist loose and a loose wrist creates more draw. A death grip on the cue will kill your follow-through, and thus kill the cue ball.

Rule #3—Don't jump out of the way of the shot. The cue ball will not roll back and hit your cue! Trying to get your cue out of the way too quickly, or pulling your cue stick back as if a string is attached to the cue ball and your cue, are the biggest mistakes people make. Only follow-through brings the cue ball back toward you! The practice exercises we've illustrated in this section will allow you to follow through completely without fear of the cue ball hitting your cue, and this will help you develop a feel for the draw shot and its timing for those short, straight-in shots where you will need to get your cue out of the way a little more quickly.

Begin with a shorter shot, as illustrated in figure 3.10. The slight angle (as shown) will allow you to draw the cue ball without fear of bringing it straight back into the opposite pocket! As you execute this shot, visualize trying to move a heavy ball with your cue stick. This will allow you to use a softer stroke and develop a feel for the shot.

The farther the object ball is from the cue ball, the more chance the cue ball has to run out of backspin as friction from the table slowly removes the draw effect. Because of this little law of physics, you will need a very well-developed stroke and follow-through to really get any draw on a long shot. Shooting too hard will not produce the desired effect, as the force of the hit will also give the cue ball more forward momentum! Once you've accomplished the first shot a few times, gradually increase the difficulty of the shot by progressively adding six inches distance between the cue ball and the object ball. Notice that it may take slightly more force to get the same results each time. Concentrate less on force and more on follow-through. Also experiment with moving your cue stick lower, but only if you're keeping it level. Too low without a level stroke and you'll be miscueing more often than shooting the ball.

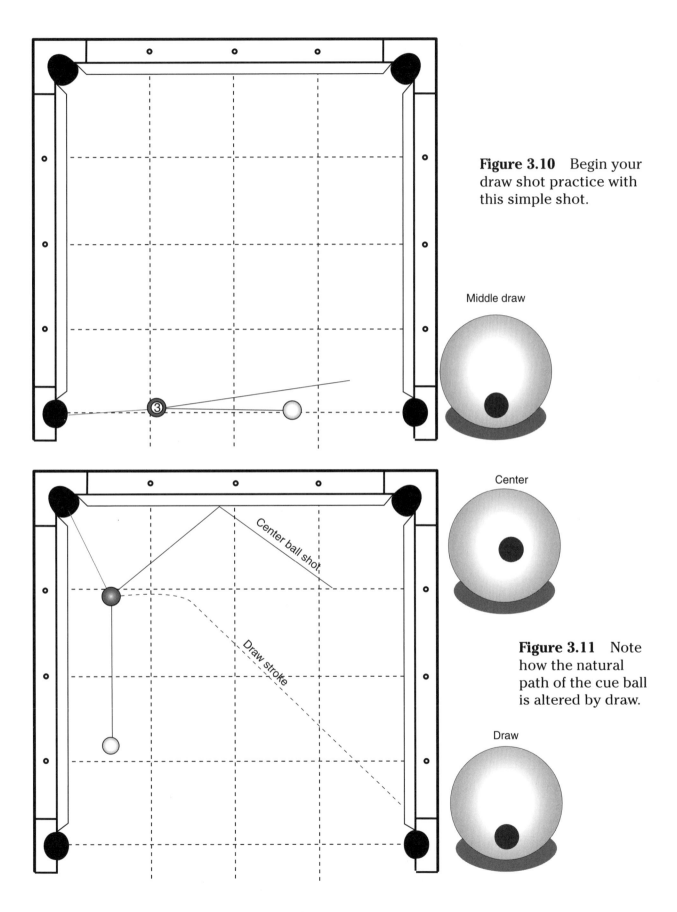

Figure 3.10 Begin your draw shot practice with this simple shot.

Middle draw

Center

Figure 3.11 Note how the natural path of the cue ball is altered by draw.

Draw

Center ball shot

Draw stroke

Keep in mind that if your cue ball is too close to the rail, the draw shot will be impossible, since you cannot keep your cue level. You'll simply be digging your cue stick into the table, and probably irritating the owner of your local establishment.

Once you feel comfortable with your draw stroke, try to imitate the results in figure 3.11. Note the path taken by a center-ball shot, and how that path is altered with the use of a draw stroke. As you perform these exercises, you'll begin to realize just how much difference the draw shot can make in your position play.

COMPLICATING MATTERS WITH ENGLISH

Now you're ready to get fancy. A word of caution—fancy doesn't always equal great. If you haven't really gotten a feel for cue ball control with center ball, draw, and follow, you're not ready to use english. If you have, you've already been using a form of english. For example, if you're using center ball and cutting the object ball to the left, your cue ball will naturally pick up right spin, and vice versa. The amount of english picked up by the cue ball will be determined by the angle of contact, unless of course you are executing a straight-in shot. The greater the angle, the less sidespin, if any, will be transferred to the cue ball. As you can see, english, as it is used in pool, can be a whole other language! Even the pros try to limit their use of english, or sidespin, to situations where it is absolutely necessary.

English refers to putting left or right spin on the cue ball to change the path of the cue ball after contacting a rail. Since you will be approaching shot exercises using english from both sides of the table, it is more easily referred to as inside english (cueing inside the angle of the shot) and outside english (cueing outside the angle of the shot). Figure 3.12 shows you two examples of inside english. Shot A uses left english, and you'll note that english is to the inside angle of the shot. Shot B uses right english. Both are *inside* english, because, simply put, you are cueing to the inside of the angle.

Now look at figure 3.13. In this case you're using outside english to lengthen the angle of the cue ball coming off the object ball. In shot A this is now right english. In shot B it's left english. This can be a bit confusing at first, so just remember to think inside and outside the angle of your shot.

Note also from figure 3.13 that outside english, sometimes also called running english, will alter the path of the cue ball by widening the angle it comes off the rail. Inside english will shorten or "close" the angle.

To execute a shot using english, you will be using the same principles you learned in follow and draw: a level cue stick and smooth follow-through are paramount. Begin by using no more than one-half to a full cue tip of english on either side, especially when you are still learning to execute these skills. Figure 3.14 illustrates left and right english tip positions on the cue ball.

Now things get a little more complicated. You see, there's not just center ball, follow, draw, left and right english. You have to contend with all the combinations that will make possible nearly any position on the table. In the next six diagrams (figures 3.15–3.20), you'll see three different examples of shot situa-

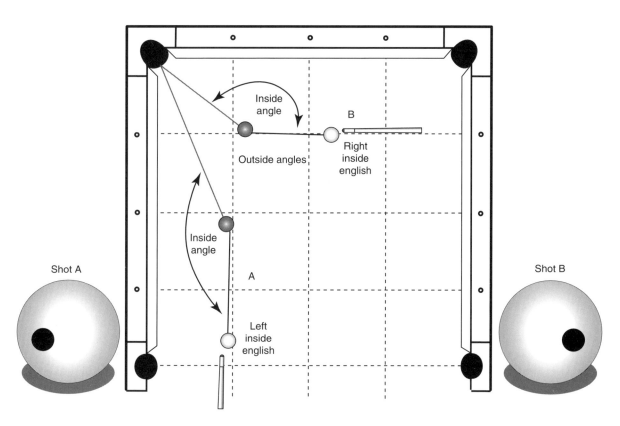

Figure 3.12 Examples of the effects of inside english.

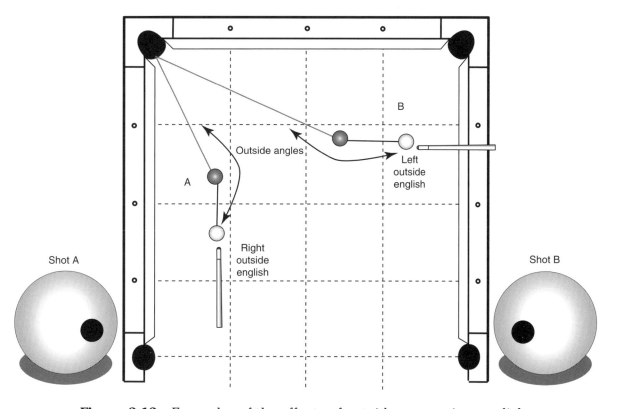

Figure 3.13 Examples of the effects of outside, or running, english.

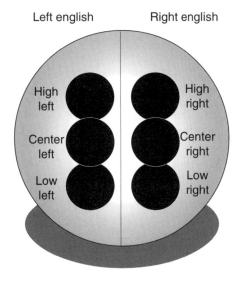

Left english   Right english

High
left

High
right

Center
left

Center
right

Low
left

Low
right

Figure 3.14   Cue tip positions for left and right english on the cue ball.

tions, representing a 15-degree cut, a 45-degree cut, and a 75-degree cut shot. In figure 3.15, you have shot results for the 15-degree cut using center right, high right, and low right english. In figure 3.16, the same shot shows results using center left, high left, and low left english. The same is then diagrammed for the 45-degree (figures 3.17 and 3.18) and 75-degree (figures 3.19 and 3.20) cut shots. The resulting path of the cue ball for each shot is illustrated using both inside and outside english, along with combining this english with high ball (follow) and low ball (draw). You'll note that all of the shots illustrated are cut shots to the left, with the cue ball coming off at an angle to the right. To get a real feel for the use of english, you should also set up each shot the other way to cut the ball to the right.

Here are some important items to note while trying each of the shots illustrated:

- Execute the shots with a medium speed, not too hard or too soft. Here is one good way to gauge what medium speed is: shoot the cue ball up and down the table once with a center-ball hit (as you would do in a **lag**). (See figure 3.21.) This is medium speed and will produce results most like the illustrations.

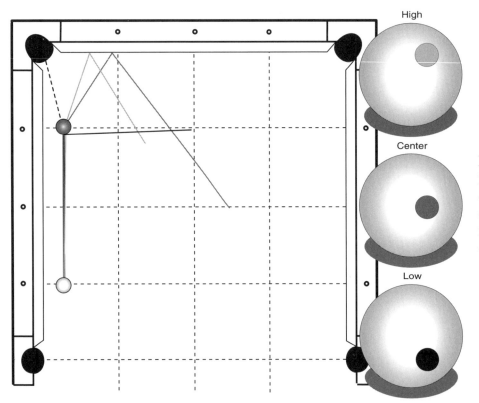

High

Center

Low

Figure 3.15   Resulting positions for a 15-degree cut shot using center right, high right, and low right english.

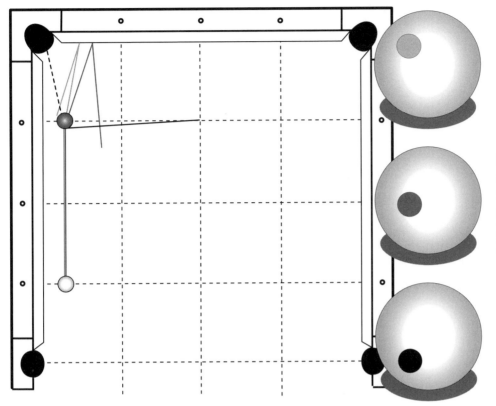

Figure 3.16 Resulting positions for a 15-degree cut shot using center left, high left, and low left english.

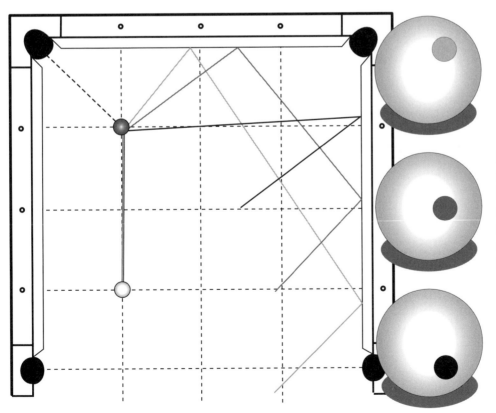

Figure 3.17 Resulting positions for a 45-degree cut shot using center right, high right, and low right english.

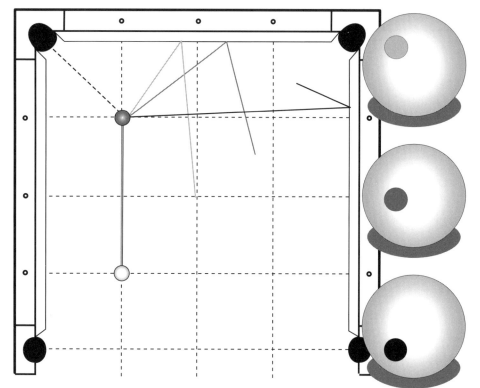

Figure 3.18 Resulting positions for a 45-degree cut shot using center left, high left, and low left english.

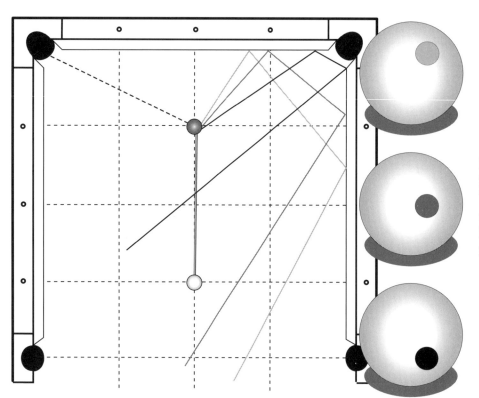

Figure 3.19 Resulting positions for a 75-degree cut shot using center right, high right, and low right english.

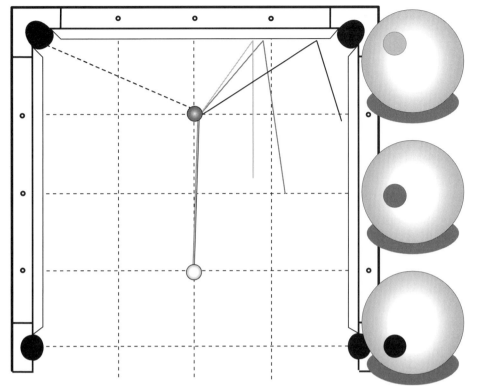

Figure 3.20 Resulting positions for a 75-degree cut shot using center left, high left, and low left english.

Figure 3.21 Jim Rempe and Buddy Hall lag for the break.

- Look at the shots using inside english (in these illustrations, left english) versus the shots illustrated using outside (right english). With all things being equal, and using a medium stroke as advised above, the shots using outside english will travel much farther. Inside english, as mentioned before, can be used in your speed control to take speed off of the cue ball, while outside english can lengthen the shot without using additional force.

- Now look at the difference in how far the cue ball travels between the fuller 15-degree cut and the thin 75-degree cut. Again, because less energy is transferred to the object ball in the thinner cut shots, the cue ball will travel farther.

Therefore, which combination of elements will cause the cue ball to travel the least amount of distance? The farthest?

Now think about all the options you can exercise simply by changing the force of your shot. Set up the same three shots that we illustrated for you in the previous diagrams, beginning with the 15-degree cut shot. Experiment with different speeds of the cue ball for this shot. What happens to the cue ball when you shoot very softly? What happens when you shoot very hard? Play each shot not only with the range of area hits on the cue ball, but also the range of speeds.

Without getting too technical (and changing this from a sports book to a study in physics and geometry), the force of your hit can and will alter the path of the cue ball. The harder the hit, the more you can "force" the cue ball to slide. Force-follow and force-draw shots can be great assets in your game, but only if you've first mastered your swing. Too many players attempt to force everything, or, worse, develop a poor swing that results in too many force shots. You'll never learn the true reaction of the cue ball this way, and will be less able to predict your cue ball position after even the simplest of shots.

DEFLECTION AND THROW

These are terms you're bound to come upon as you progress in your game, whether from other instructional materials or from other players. Let's define these terms, and then explain how they'll really affect your game.

Deflection, sometimes called squirt, is the altering of the path of the cue ball when english is used. Simply put, a cue ball struck on the right side will shift slightly left, and a cue ball struck on the left will veer slightly right. According to the experts, a soft stroke at a short distance will produce the least amount of deflection. A harder stroke at the longer distance will produce the most amount of deflection. Also, the more english that is put on the cue ball, the greater will be the deflection of the cue ball's path.

Whereas deflection refers to the altering of the cue ball's path, throw refers to the altering of the path of the object ball. Right english will "throw" the object ball to the left; left english will throw the object ball to the right. Because the cue ball hits less of the object ball on sharper cuts, the sharper the angle of the cut, the less throw will result. And, opposite of deflection, a softer shot will actually produce more throw. Again, the more english used, the greater the result.

These are scientific facts of the game. Nobody disputes the existence of deflection and throw, and how could they? Dozens of experts have tested these theories in laboratory conditions. Many have even come up with lovely charts depicting how much you need to adjust your aim for different shots with deflection and throw. Their laborious efforts have often been applauded by students of the game. Unfortunately, they've also convinced otherwise talented players that their aim should constantly be in question if they plan to impart anything but center ball on the cue ball.

Just try to apply this knowledge and put yourself into a game situation. You're shooting at the 8-ball to get to the 9-ball. To aim at it correctly, you're going to need to predict the amount of throw you'll get, because you have a pretty good angle, which will minimize most of the throw, but you're going to hit the ball softer, which will give you more throw, but with the right english you want to put on the shot, your cue ball is going to head slightly to the left of where you want to hit it, though since you're not hitting it hard it shouldn't matter as much, but—*stop!* If everyone thought about all this on every shot, it would take a long, long time to finish a game, and the tremendous popularity of the cue sports would plummet. Ask pros how they compensate for squirt. Chances are good that their answers will range from "What?" to "I just do" to "Squirt and throw cancel each other out anyway." Now the third statement isn't always true, but you get the idea. Every sport has interesting and unique physical properties. Just think of the football traveling through the air, spinning as it heads towards the receiver. Does the football player calculate the spin on its approach, combined with the day's wind velocity, to determine exactly where his hands should be to grasp the ball? Of course not.

The lessons you can take from this are much simpler. First, the less english you use, the better off you are. This is another reason why only one-half to a full cue tip of english is recommended. Second, shooting too soft or too hard can be dangerous tactics unless you have a very specific reason for doing so.

Finally, while it is true that these physical properties exist, you don't need (or want) to take them into consideration on every shot. Try a few experiments of your own, if you wish, to observe the results with extreme english and speeds. Then move on—play pool. Your mind and body learn to compensate for minor adjustments without you having to consciously calculate them.

Once a player has established the basics, learned center ball, tangent lines, and how balls react coming off the object ball and the cushions with the use of follow, draw, and english, the game of pool becomes one of feel and confidence. And, while each individual's ability varies, every student can create his own feel for the game and all its beautiful and mystifying shots, whether it be a length-of-a-table draw shot or a three-rail high-ball shot. Develop good habits of experimenting with shots you are unfamiliar with and allow yourself to try variations of shots as they occur. This will be the beginning of a lifelong pursuit of the ultimate in cue ball control, and allow you to move on to another of pool's most interesting features—game breaks.

Chapter ④

Game Breaks

When your ability on the pool table reaches a certain level of competence, the break shot becomes one of the most important shots, if not *the* most important shot in your arsenal. Games and matches are won and lost all the time on the break, especially in the professional arena. All too often, players treat the break like a pregame shot, not giving it the attention it deserves. Armed with the knowledge included in this chapter, you will come to understand the importance of a solid break, and never take it for granted in your own game.

There are two distinct methods of breaking: the power, or offensive, break, and the finesse, or defensive, break. The power break is used in the games where it is to your advantage to scatter the balls on the table as much as possible, such as Eight Ball and Nine Ball. The lesser-known games requiring a power break are Six Ball, Seven Ball, Rotation, and Banks. (Breaking the balls wide open for a Banks game means you want to play a very offensive strategy.) Games where a finesse break will come into play include Straight Pool (14.1), One Pocket, and very defensive games of Banks.

At this point we should also stress that the balls should be tightly racked. Older balls, imperfect racks, and worn or damaged foot spots and cloth are among the many variables that will cause gaps in the rack, but your goal should be to freeze as many balls to each other as possible. It is reasonable (and a professional courtesy) to expect a tight rack from your opponent and to give the same in return. Also make sure the rack is straight, with the center balls lining up down the center of the table, and not twisted to either side.

POWER BREAKS

In all the games where the balls must be pocketed in numerical order, the power break takes on more significance. The reason is obvious: not only do you have to scatter the balls, but, to continue control of the table, at least one ball must be made while the cue ball should have an unobstructed path to the lowest numbered ball.

One of the most popular games played today is Nine Ball. It is also the one played in the majority of professional tournaments. And, with the structure of virtually all pro events, players compete in a race. Whoever wins the set number of games first (e.g., race to 11) wins the match. Formats are "winner breaks,"

The Right Way to Rack

The following answers one of pool's most common questions: *What is the correct way to set up the break shot?* There is more than one correct arrangement for the balls in Eight Ball, Nine Ball, Straight Pool, and One Pocket racks; however, there is only one correct *way* to set up these arrangements. In other words, there are specific rules governing the way in which you rack the balls. You can find these and other rules in *Billiards—The Official Rules & Records Book* put out by the Billiard Congress of America. Here's what you need to know.

Eight Ball

All fifteen balls are racked in a triangle with the 8-ball in the center of the triangle, the apex ball on the footspot, a stripe ball in one corner of the rack and a solid ball in the other corner. The figure to the right is one example of a correct Eight Ball rack.

Nine Ball

The balls in this game are racked in a diamond shape with the one ball on the foot spot, the nine ball in the center of the diamond, and the other balls placed randomly. Shown here is one correct 9-ball setup.

Straight Pool

Straight Pool (14.1 Continuous) follows a triangular rack as in eight ball with the apex ball on the foot spot, the 1-ball on the racker's right corner, and the 5-ball on the left corner. The other balls are placed randomly. Use the figure to the right as a guide to setting up your Straight Pool rack.

One Pocket

In One Pocket you'll use a standard triangle rack with the balls placed entirely at random. This is just one of many correct combinations.

Rotation

Rotation also uses a standard triangle rack with the 1-ball on the foot spot, the 2-ball on the right rear corner, the 3-ball on the left rear corner, and the 15-ball in the center. All other balls are placed at random. The figure to the right will help you set up your rotation rack.

Banks

Banks, like One Pocket, uses a standard triangle rack with all the balls placed at random.

Six Ball

In Six Ball, the 1-ball is placed on the foot spot, and the 6-ball is placed in the center of the rear row. The other four balls are placed randomly. Shown to the right is one correct way to set up a Six Ball rack.

This information should put an end to any confusion, as well as ward off potential pre-game battles on the correct way to set up the balls. To learn the right way to rack in other games see the official rules of the Billiard Congress of America.

meaning that the winner of each game breaks the next rack. It is not at all uncommon to see a player, in a race to 11, get control of the table to break and run out the last three, four, or five games to win the set, never letting his opponent back in the match. Or, think of the mental anguish in playing someone a race to 11, and having her break and run the first four racks. Naturally, it's difficult to start out this far behind and chase a match. This shows you how important a good power break can be. With just nine balls on the table, a strong player will break in two or three balls, scatter the remaining six or seven, and have a simple runout for the game.

In the professional arena, the Nine Ball break has become a contest of who can propel the cue ball into the rack with the most power. However, it is more important to hit the 1-ball solidly than it is to hit it with great velocity.

There have been tests conducted with electronic devices to see just how fast the cue ball travels during the power break of some top pros. At your local pool room, ask your fellow pool players to guess the speed of the cue ball. You'll probably get answers ranging from 50 to 200 miles per hour. In fact, the top speed reached by the cue ball in such tests has been only a little over 31 miles an hour! Interesting to note, though: more often than not the cue ball didn't contact the 1-ball solidly on most of the higher-speed tries, and also had a tendency to jump off the bed of the table. If you could hit the 1-ball solidly at 31 miles an hour, the sound would echo throughout the room like a cannon shot! Impressive maybe, but hitting the 1-ball with more accuracy at a lesser speed will result in a better outcome.

Your foundation is critical for a power break, and your fundamentals used on most other shots on the pool table will need to shift slightly to accommodate your power break. To achieve more power and spring in your upper body, you need to spread your legs a little farther apart than you would on your normal swing. Place at least 60 percent of your body weight on your front leg. In doing so, you can rock your body forward on the break to increase cue stick speed. Also, stand up a little higher on the shot. This keeps your body from getting in the way of your arm and will enhance your follow-through.

Your grip will need adjustment, too. A good place to hold the cue stick is roughly three to six inches behind where you grip the cue under normal shot circumstances. This allows you to have more cue stick with which to follow through toward the rack when you break the balls.

Finally, you may need to change your bridge. There has been much discussion among top players regarding use of an open bridge versus a closed bridge in the power break. The advantage of the open bridge is that it is easier to follow through, driving your cue stick toward the rack. With a closed bridge, you'll discover that you need to open up your bridge hand anyway to follow through toward the back rail within a second after impact. Begin with what feels comfortable and keeps you in control, but work up to the open bridge.

As we mentioned in chapter 1, when you are breaking the balls, you will probably find that looking at the cue ball last, rather than the object ball as with your other shots, will produce better results initially. The reason for this is that when you look at the cue ball last you will create more of a stunning stroke. Looking at the 1-ball will produce more of a follow-through reaction on the cue ball, which creates more spin. When you create more spin in your power break, you're going to have a harder time controlling your cue ball.

However, having said this, once you have worked for a time on your break and developed a feel for the power stroke necessary to execute the break, you will probably want to return to looking at the object ball. In Nine Ball, it is often helpful to look at the base of the 1-ball when you break—the spot where the 1-ball and the table are in contact. This can help keep you grounded on the shot and give you a more definite target on your break shot. Many players who have had problems with their break have had great success with this particular visual reference on the break shot.

Setting Up the Power Break

In each of your power break games, placement of the cue ball on the table is important. That placement will depend a lot on you. Most players find that it is easier when starting out to break the balls with the cue ball at or near the center of the table behind the head string. As you will soon see, however, there are many variables in the games and in your own swing and personal preferences that may quickly alter your choice of cue ball placement.

Nine Ball Break

Let's first talk about the break in Nine Ball. If you are right-handed, a good place to set the cue ball would be on the right side of the table. If you're left-handed, the best place will probably be on the left side of the table. See figure 4.1.

However, this little rule of thumb is also influenced by your stroke, whether you more often put left english or right english on the cue ball. Without getting too complicated with our explanation, a right-handed person who has a tendency to

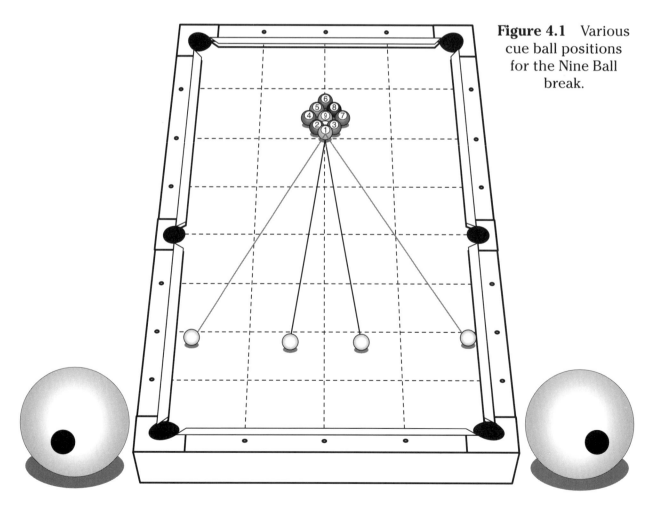

Figure 4.1 Various cue ball positions for the Nine Ball break.

put left english on the ball, especially when the ball is hit hard, is actually better off putting the cue ball on the left side of the table or moving the cue ball in toward the center. Anywhere in this area at all and the left english will automatically come into play on the 1-ball. This will result in a better stunning effect to "kill," or stop, the cue ball after it hits the rail. If, on the other hand, you have a tendency to put right english on the ball, the right side of the table is the better place to break from—again, anywhere from the side rail to the middle of the table.

Players used to break from the center of the table until they found out that it was easier to make the corner ball from the rail. There are still different schools of thought on this. Some players still prefer breaking from closer to the center of the table to achieve what they feel will be the fullest hit on the 1-ball. Remember, the most important part of the Nine Ball break is a solid—and we do mean *solid*—hit on the 1-ball! Shooting the ball from either side means you are hitting the 1-ball from an angle, instead of head-on. Because of this, you sometimes will have a tendency to glance off the 1-ball, more so than with the head-on hit from the center of the table. With the cue ball on the foot spot it's much easier to get a solid hit on the 1-ball because you're shooting at the whole ball, as with a straight-in shot. If you move the cue ball to either rail, it becomes more difficult to get the solid hit on the 1-ball.

A good way to practice getting a more solid hit is to visualize your cue ball driving right through the 1-ball into the rows of balls behind it. This will also help you to focus on your follow-through as you execute your break shot.

Let's get back to those tendencies in your normal stroke. Suppose you naturally put right english on the cue ball, whether by accident or design. (Very few players in fact hit absolutely dead center on the cue ball, due to variances in crossing-over in their stroke, having a dominant eye, etc.) In this case you would use just a bit of low left english for your break shot. This is because your natural tendency is to cross over the cue ball with your cue stick. Without the compensating english, your timing would have to be perfect to hit dead center on the cue ball in order to have a stunning effect (to hit the 1-ball solidly, with virtually no spin). In other words, you are trying to prevent spin on the cue ball; you want the cue ball completely dead, with no sidespin whatsoever. This allows the greatest transfer of power and the most control.

Years ago you could see the top players dig the cue stick into the bed of the cloth after they broke. This is not recommended! Figures 4.2 and 4.3 illustrate the differences. Max Eberle, shown in figure 4.2, employed the method of digging the cue stick into the table. We believe this actually slows down the cue stick rather than speeding it up. You also risk breaking the spine of your cue shaft, making it susceptible to warping. A better move is to raise the cue stick, bringing it up on your follow-through, as employed by contemporary players like Roger Griffis, Johnny Archer, and Tony Ellin. What you then accomplish is to put just a touch of forward spin on the cue ball. You want to hit that 1-ball as solidly as possible, and when the cue ball "grabs," making contact with the cloth and the 1-ball, it will more or less just die in the center of the table, which is the optimal place to have the cue ball after the Nine Ball break. It stands to reason that if the cue ball is in the center of the table, your chances of having a shot at the lowest numbered ball are much greater.

Most top pros today break from the side rail, with the goal of pocketing the corner ball (shown in figure 4.4) so that they may continue shooting. You'll hear color commentators say that the professional player's intention is to try to make the 1-ball in the side. That's ludicrous. What they're actually trying to do is control

Figure 4.2 Max Eberle's break. Note how his cue bends
into the table.

Figure 4.3 Earl Strickland's break. Note how he brings the cue up
in his power break follow-through.

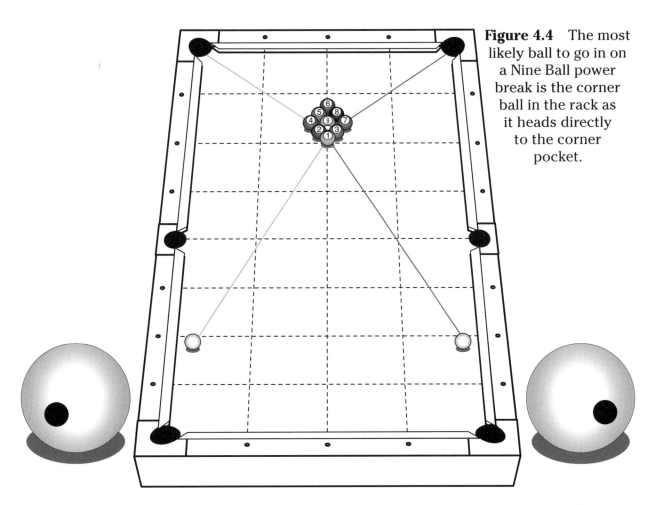

Figure 4.4 The most likely ball to go in on a Nine Ball power break is the corner ball in the rack as it heads directly to the corner pocket.

the 1-ball, keeping it near the cue ball for their first shot after the break. They don't necessarily want to make the 1-ball, because they have no control over the 2-ball! The 2-ball could be anywhere in the rack except in front where the 1-ball is or the center where the 9-ball is. So it makes sense that if you make the 1-ball, there's no guarantee of a shot at the 2-ball.

Can you predict where the balls will land on the break? Not all of them. But let's say that you hit below center on the cue ball. What happens most often is that the 1-ball will go above the **head spot,** and the cue ball will go to the bottom of the table as shown in figure 4.5. Now let's say you use high ball instead. The high ball will have the effect of sending the cue ball forward and the 1-ball to the bottom of the table. Neither option will produce an optimal shot on the 1-ball! What you do want to do is to hit the cue ball as close to the center as possible into the 1-ball. You will be attempting to send the 1-ball either to the right or left rail, close to the side pocket. (Old-time players would refer to this as trying to "trap" the 1-ball near the side pocket.)

You'll soon discover that weaker players do not hit the balls as hard on the break, and yet the balls still seem to gravitate toward a pocket. And yet, you can see a very powerful player hit the balls 30 miles an hour and it seems as if the balls stun themselves. It can be explained in this way: if you hit the balls too hard, the balls will explode, then implode, then explode again. So even people with powerful swings would never want to hit the balls with 100 percent of their strength. Just remember that accuracy is the key. The more solidly you hit the 1-ball, the better your chances of making a ball.

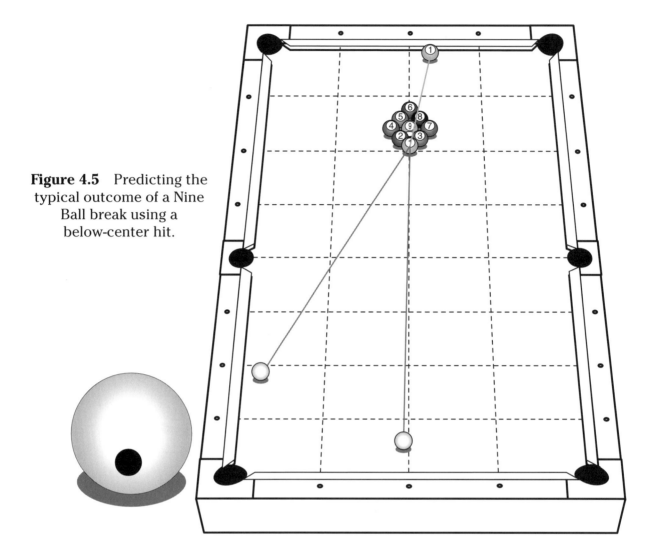

Figure 4.5 Predicting the typical outcome of a Nine Ball break using a below-center hit.

Eight Ball Break

Today's most popular game played in amateur tournament and league competition is Eight Ball. Breaking in Eight Ball offers a few advantages. First, as in Nine Ball, with a well-scattered rack better players will run the table. Second, if a runout opportunity does not exist, pocketing any ball on the break still gives the player the first option of which group of balls to shoot at, leaving the opponent with the less desirable group, where balls may be tied up or clustered on the rail. The Eight Ball break, while also a power break, is totally different from the Nine Ball break. You don't try to hit the head ball in the rack, but rather aim for a hit on the second ball. Refer to figure 4.6.

To achieve this break, move the cue ball toward one rail or the other, as close to the cushion as possible. Try to hit the ball *behind* the head ball as solid as possible, with below-center spin. If you contact the cue ball with center or high ball, chances are very good that you will scratch in the corner pocket. Hitting that second ball very solid and below center gives you a much better spread of the balls on the table. This is especially crucial in bar league play because the table is smaller, typically 3¹/₂ by 7, as opposed to the 4¹/₂ by 9 professional-size table. And, because the table is smaller, you have a tendency to end up with more clusters or

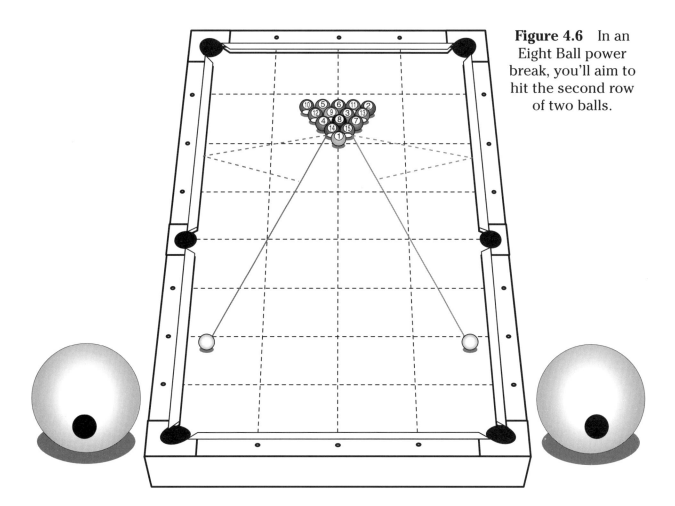

Figure 4.6 In an Eight Ball power break, you'll aim to hit the second row of two balls.

groups of balls in different places on the table, so you'll need to spread the balls around as much as possible. On a 4½ by 9 table, it's a little different. Some people believe you should hit the second ball, and/or row, and some believe you should actually aim for the third row in order to get a better spread of the balls on the bigger table. At this time, we don't think it makes any difference. You can hit the second or third row, but the crucial point, again, is to hit the ball solid and below center to avoid the scratch. The bonus of the below-center hit is that it has a tendency to bring the cue ball back to the long rail just on the side of the rack and then closer to the center of the table. And, just as we discussed in the Nine Ball break, you're more likely to have a shot with your cue ball in the center of the table.

Alternative Game Breaks

The break in Rotation is similar to the Nine Ball break. Once again, the 1-ball sits at the head of the rack, while the 2-ball is in one corner of the rack and the 3-ball in the other corner of the rack, as illustrated in figure 4.7. Your goal, naturally, is to spread the balls as much as possible, make a ball, and also get a shot at the 1-ball. You must hit the 1-ball first, for the shot to be considered a legal break.

Breaking in the game of Banks straddles the line between offensive and defensive breaks. If you have a very tough opponent and your games are quite similar, the majority of players may opt for the safety break or Straight-Pool-style break. If you intend to play an offensive game of Banks, then you would opt for a power break,

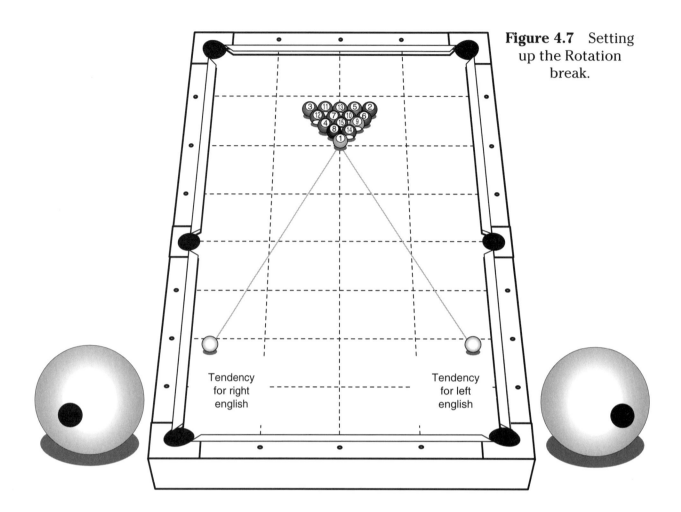

Figure 4.7 Setting up the Rotation break.

Tendency for right english

Tendency for left english

similar to the Eight Ball break. Again, you want to spread the balls as much as possible and pocket a ball. Chances are then very good, if you keep your cue ball near the center of the table, that you will have a very makable bank on your first shot after the break, especially considering that you can shoot at any ball on the table.

For a Six Ball break you will need a little different break technique because of the configuration of the balls. Break from one side of the table or the other, but with the intention of having your cue ball land near one of the long rails. The reason: if you get a solid hit on the 1-ball from one side or the other, you will have a tendency to make one of the back two corner balls four rails in the corner. To execute this break, you hit on the cue ball well below center, with the intention of drawing back from the rack of balls. If your cue ball stops in the center of the table, it could interfere with the four-rail shot outcome, as shown in figure 4.8.

All of these games are great exercises in developing your power break while enjoying play. Even if you lean toward one game or another, take a bit of time to learn the other games and their related breaks. It's often a great way to break the monotony of a tired practice routine or weekly outing with your friends!

Practicing Your Power Break

Developing a solid break takes a little time, work, and effort. But, hey, doesn't everything? The most important thing to learn while practicing your power break is that you don't need to accomplish everything at once. Nobody will naturally perform a

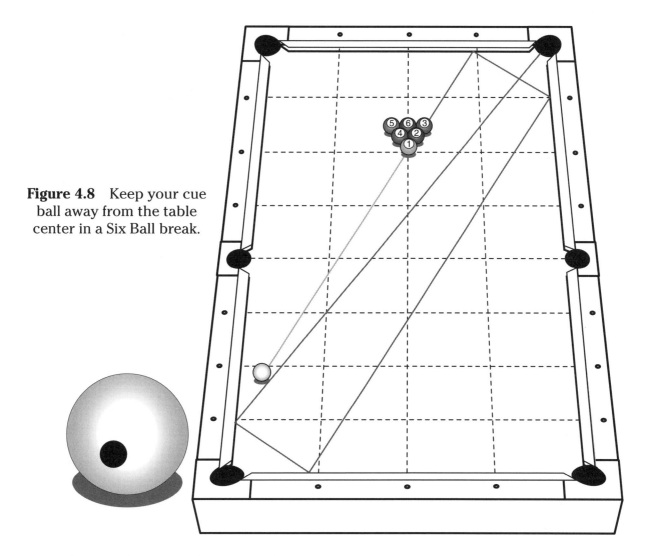

Figure 4.8 Keep your cue ball away from the table center in a Six Ball break.

perfect break shot the first time. You have to slowly build up your speed with the cue stick. This may seem like a tedious process, but it's well worth the time. Keep in mind, a solid hit on the target ball is first and foremost. Building speed comes next.

Start your break development by exerting just 20 percent of your hit strength, similar to a slow or medium hit on the cue ball. Your objectives in this exercise will be simply to control the cue ball, control your speed, and get a solid hit on the target ball.

Slowly build up the speed of your stroke. Once you can perform five to six good solid breaks in a row, you can step up to 40 percent, then to 60 percent, then to 80 percent. If you still have total control of the cue ball at that point and you are able to hit 100 percent of your stroke, go for it. Very few people can exert 100 percent of their force and still get a solid hit on the 1-ball. You will probably settle in at 70-80 percent, which is just fine.

There are a couple of ways to determine how you are progressing on your break shot, or if you have physical adjustments to make. Have your partner either stand in front of you by the rack to watch where the cue ball hits the pack, or get behind you to see where you contact the cue ball with the tip of your cue. This can help show you the kind of english you tend to put on the cue ball—dead center, a touch left, or a touch right.

Another method of checking where your cue tip is contacting the ball is to use the 8-ball in a single-ball test. Without racking the balls, put the 8-ball on the head spot with the number 8 dead center and facing you, so that if you were shooting exactly in the center of the ball, you would hit directly in the center of the number. Scuff your tip to rough it up quite a bit, and apply plenty of chalk. Shoot the ball straight down table with plenty of force, as if you were breaking, then have your partner catch the 8-ball immediately after it hits the bottom rail. Now, check the chalk mark. Is it actually in the center? If it's to the right or left, too high or too low, you need to adjust! This exercise can also be done using a bit of double-sided tape, or the tape that golfers use on clubfaces to check their own hits. The tape will pick up the chalk mark left by your cue without the need for so much chalk or a partner to catch the ball before the chalk is rubbed off by the cloth. One company has even invented practice balls that allow the chalk to stick to the ball, for just such hit checks.

On the power break (and many harder-hit shots in your regular game), the cue ball actually travels above the table surface, in some cases skipping along the way. On the power break, it will skip anywhere from one to three feet in front of the rack. This is easier to see on a table covered with new billiard fabric. Here's a fun exercise to determine when your cue ball is coming back into contact with the bed of the table. Lay out a line of dimes along your path from the cue ball to the object ball to see how far your cue ball goes on the fly before once again coming into contact with the table. Most people are amazed at how far the cue ball travels across the table without being in contact with the table bed. After the amazement, though, keep in mind the point of the exercise—to create consistency. When you know that your cue ball is going to skip over the cloth, you then want to gauge with what power you have to hit the cue ball and to what point on the table the ball skips, given that power. You're literally hitting the 1-ball on a bounce. This is very good to know because you really would like to hit the 1-ball on the fly, so that the cue ball actually comes down and into the 1-ball. This is a rare shot indeed, but you can strive for it by adjusting your power so your cue ball landing is timed just perfectly. You can also learn to avoid the speed at which your cue ball jumps the table, resulting in a foul and possible injury to onlookers! Be sure to keep your stroke as level as possible, as too much of a downward hit can send the cue ball airborne.

THE FINESSE, OR DEFENSIVE, BREAK

Games where a defensive break will come into play include Straight Pool (14.1), One Pocket, and very defensive games of Banks. The finesse break requires a soft to medium hit. You are breaking the balls only hard enough to drive the required number of balls to the rail for a legal break, or, as in One Pocket, to drive balls toward your pocket. In both cases, you want to leave your opponent with no shot, or at least a difficult shot. While not offensive in its execution, a solid defensive break is necessary for winning strategy in these games. Your opponent is left with the tough shot, and this can translate into one of pool's greatest strategies—forcing your opponent to take the tough shot and capitalizing on what is left to you.

Setting Up the Finesse Break

Finesse breaks, like power breaks, will benefit from different setups and points of aim, depending on the game you play and what you need to accomplish. The following sections discuss a bit of the technique necessary for your finesse break.

Selecting a Break Cue

The game has changed over the last few years with the introduction of specialty cues in the billiard marketplace. Specialty cues include those models designed for power breaking, jumping over impeding balls, and the hybrid break/jump cue combinations that allow removal of part of the butt of the cue to jump balls when not using the cue to break. Newer models of break/jump cues feature quick-release screws to turn your break cue into a jump cue in record time. Best of all, newer models of cases accommodate increasing numbers of cues, in addition to space for extra shafts and accessories, making the inclusion of a break cue in your arsenal more practical than ever.

The break cue has become increasingly important in the power break. Because you hit the balls so hard, this particular shot has a tendency to flatten out the tip of your normal cue. As many professional players will tell you, the break cue (while initially difficult for some pros to get used to) has resulted in better break performance, along with increasing the longevity of their regular playing cue. Power breaks put stress on your normal cue shaft, along with the aggravation of having to change your tip more often.

What you'll want in a break cue is a flatter and relatively thinner tip, along with some form of phenolic (plastic) ferrule (preferably a slip-on as opposed to screw-in type of ferrule). For shaft size, a good rule of thumb is to purchase a break cue anywhere from $1/4$ millimeter to $1/2$ millimeter larger than the cue stick you normally play with.

The reason for this is twofold. First, you get a sense of security, because the cue feels a little more stable in your bridge hand, you have a little more control over the cue tip, and even your miscues will be a little closer to center. Second, the larger the millimeter of the tip, the more surface area the tip will contact the cue ball with, offering you more control. A thicker shaft may also prove more durable over the long haul.

As for break cue weights, some professionals and experts believe that the heavier stick will create more force, while most subscribe to the theory that the lighter stick will allow more speed, thus creating more velocity. Professional players are leaning more and more toward the lighter break cues, which they claim provide more "whip," which translates to more action out of the cue.

We agree with the latter theory: the best cue to use would be the lighter cue, to create more velocity. It's comparable to a golf swing, where greater clubhead speed generates more distance, only in this case you're creating more tip speed or cue stick speed.

Also gaining in popularity are the graphite and other composite material cues. Even those professionals who lean toward the traditional in their regular playing cue have made the move to graphite in their break cues, explaining that these models can offer more action and power in the break shot. We advise speaking to a reputable dealer or owner of a billiard club pro shop before making your selection.

Straight Pool Break

When playing Straight Pool, it is to your disadvantage to break the balls (the loser of the lag or coin toss will be the one breaking). In the rules of Straight Pool, you must drive two balls, plus the cue ball, to a rail. The optimal place to put the cue ball on the break shot is three to six inches from the side rail. You will aim to hit one quarter to one third of the corner ball in the back row with outside english. In other words, if you're on the right side of the table, you're going to hit the right back ball with a touch of high right english. The desired result is that you drive the ball you've contacted to the bottom rail. The object ball on the other side of that row of five balls will move toward the long rail and hopefully back into the stack of balls. The cue ball will bounce off the short rail, back into the long rail, and then travel down toward the lower left corner pocket. This break is illustrated in figure 4.9.

There are also a couple of fancy breaks in Straight Pool, where you actually attempt to pocket a ball off the break, but these aren't breaks we'd suggest in competition because of the optimum conditions they require. Nevertheless, they can be fun and worth learning to impress yourself and your friends. In the first of these (see figure 4.10), line up the cue ball between the head spot and the side rail and shoot the cue ball with almost 80 percent of your power into the short rail, banking it back to hit the last ball in the back stack very solid. This will send the front ball two rails into the side. It's a very fun shot when it goes, but a lot depends on the rack—that is, if all the balls are frozen, if the rack is straight or twisted, and so on. The conditions have to be perfect.

The other shot is to make the side ball in the row of five at the back of the Straight Pool rack, as shown in figure 4.11. This is a straight high-ball shot with no left or right english to bank the object ball back. It will pick up right spin off the hit from the cue ball. Then, as it caroms off the ball next to it, the spin will send the ball straight back into the corner. We've actually seen this shot played in competition by European champion Oliver Ortmann (Germany), during his win at the 1989 U.S. Open in Chicago, Illinois. Risky? Probably. Impressive? Most definitely.

One Pocket Break

The One Pocket break offers different types of breaks—from the ultraconservative to the more aggressive, and every variation in between. We've included a few of the favorites, beginning with a more aggressive break. Suppose that you have the upper-right corner as your pocket. You place the cue ball near or along the long left side rail, and try to split the front two balls with your cue ball. In other words, shoot the cue ball between the head ball and the row of two balls behind it, as illustrated in figure 4.12. Use high inside english (in this case, right english) with a nice, smooth stroke. Your objective is to send as many balls as possible to your side of the table. Even if the left corner ball pops up by accident, the cue ball will have a tendency to also send that ball toward your side of the table. This is a very good break when executed correctly. Optimally, you want your cue ball to end up three to six inches above the side pocket, and frozen on the side rail. When playing One Pocket, the best places to leave the cue ball for defensive purposes are frozen on the rail or frozen on an object ball. This reduces the options your opponent will have in maneuvering the cue ball and executing shots with ease.

Another One Pocket break is to kick rail first into the balls. To execute this break, you take the cue ball to the right side of the table, and shoot toward the first diamond past the side pocket on the left side of the table, using a below-

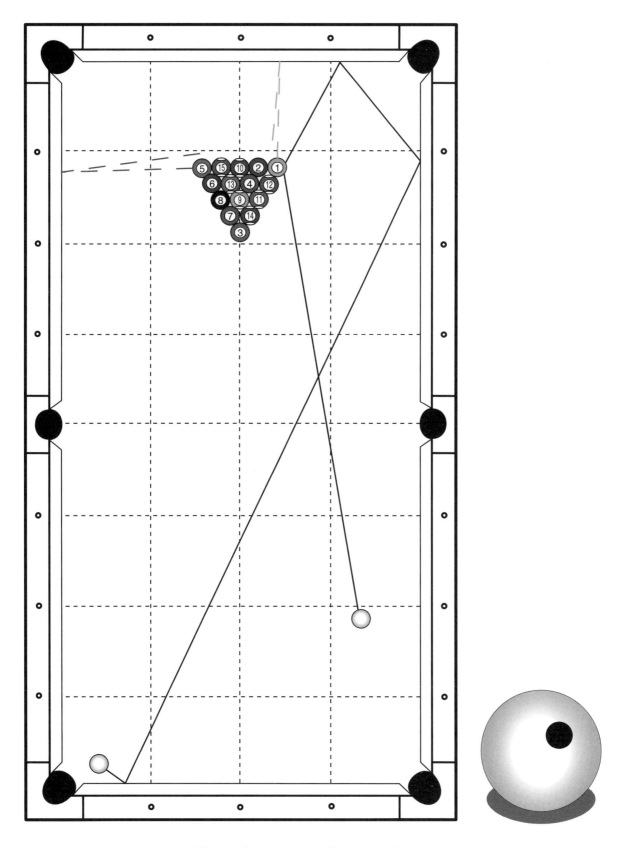

Figure 4.9 A typical opening break
in Straight Pool.

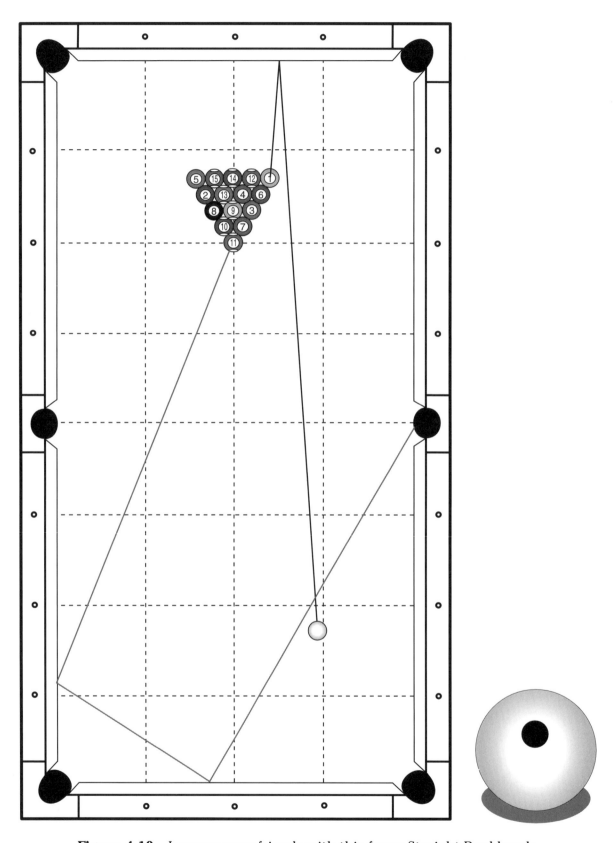

Figure 4.10 Impress your friends with this fancy Straight Pool break.

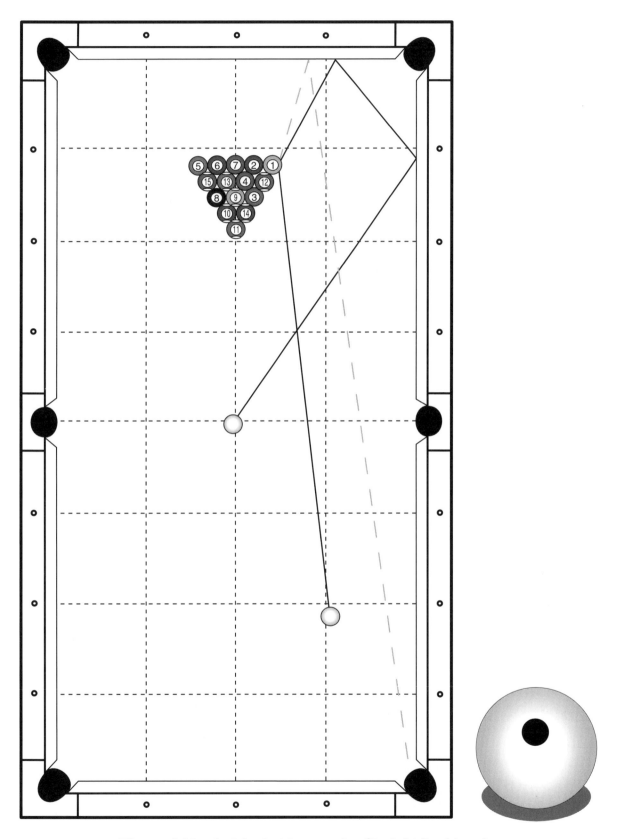

Figure 4.11 A risky but impressive Straight Pool break.

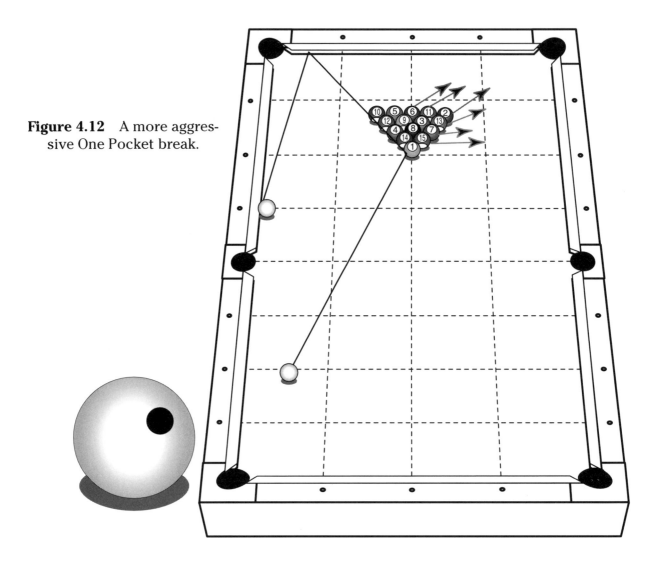

Figure 4.12 A more aggressive One Pocket break.

center stroke, as shown in figure 4.13. The cue ball will then actually be traveling with a high-ball effect after it contacts the rail. When it hits the rack, it will stick, pushing balls toward your pocket. You are trying to freeze the cue ball on the stack, while sending balls toward your side of the table.

For a more defensive break, line up the cue ball with the row of balls going toward your pocket and in line to hit the front ball solid. What you're attempting is to freeze the cue ball to the head ball, and move just one ball toward your pocket (see figure 4.14). This is a weaker, defensive brand of break, and you must remember that in the game of One Pocket, one ball must hit a rail for a legal break.

We've also seen people playing One Pocket who use a Straight Pool break, but this is a very weak shot unless all you want to do is bunt balls around the table for the next three hours. This shot is just too defensive for most players' tastes.

Banks Break

The safety break in Banks is really very much like the Straight Pool break, with the object being to send the cue ball down to the other end of the table and leave your opponent with the rack pretty much intact, and with a very long shot. This, like the very defensive One Pocket break, simply prolongs the game and immediately sends it into a safety battle. Nevertheless, if this is your preference, go ahead and have fun.

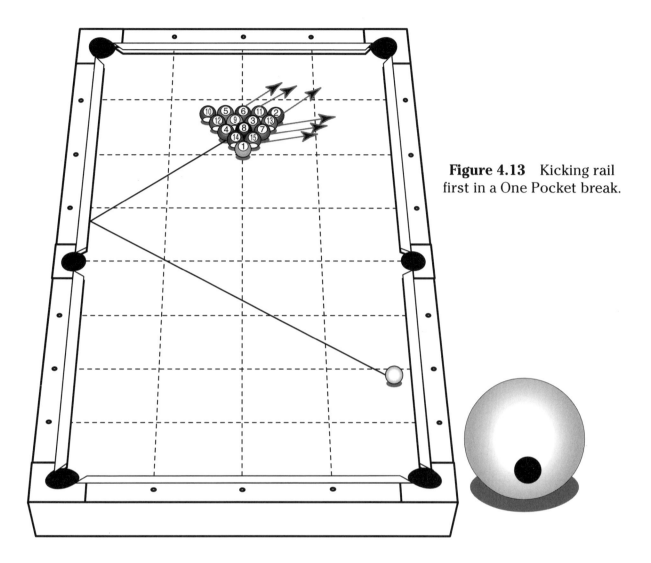

Figure 4.13 Kicking rail first in a One Pocket break.

Practicing Your Finesse Break

Developing a finesse break also takes a little time and a bit of work. While you do not have to work on building up speed, you do need to develop a feel for the finesse break shot. Too hard, and you're certain to leave your opponent a shot. Too soft, and you risk not making a legal break, again giving your opponent control of the table. You won't need to change your stance or bridge for these shots as you would in the power break; instead, execute them as you would a normal shot. This eliminates part of the work, but only if you've invested the time to feel the shot and know what you need to accomplish.

Set up the various breaks we've outlined here and practice them with special attention to the amount of force you are giving to the shot. If you have the opportunity to play on different size pool tables, you will notice that it will take less force to perform the same shot on a small table that it does on the bigger table. As you learned in chapter 3, speed of the equipment will also come into play. If you're preparing for a match involving a defensive break strategy, take a couple of practice break shots before you play, to gauge the speed of the cloth and the cushions.

It is especially important in the finesse break to achieve a smooth swing and follow-through. Anticipating the hit on this break can force you to hesitate and

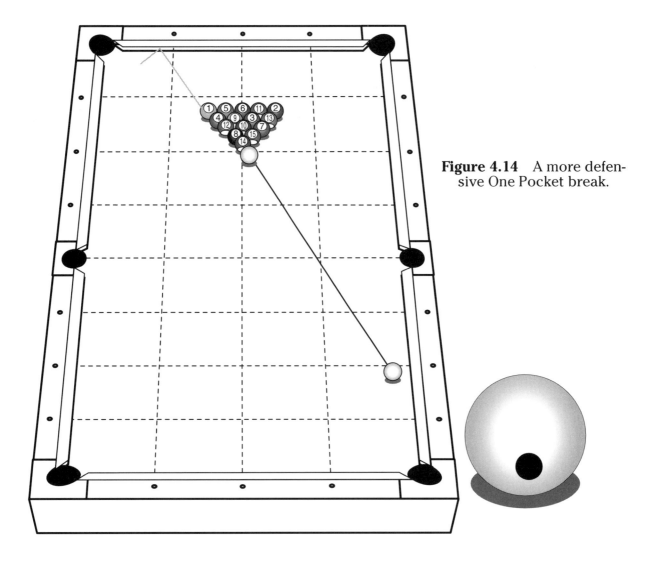

Figure 4.14   A more defensive One Pocket break.

either undershoot the shot, or force your arm through it, resulting in a choppy stroke that won't allow control over your resulting cue ball position. Visualize a gentle, relaxed, and controlled swing through each shot.

Finally, in the finesse break, knowledge is power. Have an exact idea of where you want your object balls and cue ball to arrive. Decide this before you get down in your stance. Once you have made your decision, step into your stance, let your body take over, and perform the break shot as you would any other shot.

No matter your choice of game in the cue sports, it will pay to practice break suggestions for each of the games we've described. Different breaks, whether power or finesse, allow you the opportunity to witness different focus points on the rack and different reactions of the cue ball off the rack. Once you've honed your breaking abilities, you're ready to tackle some critical shots—shots, like the break, that could make or "break" your game!

Chapter ⟨5⟩

Critical Shots

Critical shots are those shots seldom fully discussed or taught, namely, the stop shot, stun shot, and drag shot, along with rail shots, banks, combinations, caroms, **massé** shots, and **jump shots**. Mastery of these skills can mean the difference between winning and losing. In discussing each of the critical shots, we offer you information on the technique used for the shot, along with suggested application in typical game situations. It is very important to understand that some critical shots also translate into low-percentage shots. That means you may want to opt for a safer alternative. However, if no such alternative exists, a well-played critical shot could win you the game!

THE STOP SHOT

Many assume the stop shot is the easiest shot to master. Perhaps. But until you do master it, sliding or rolling your cue ball one way or the other will cost you position play and, consequently, games. Stop shots, by design, decrease the distance the cue ball travels after contact with the object ball. What's the advantage of less distance traveled? Simply put, predictability. You may have heard a player comment on a game or match, "Ah, well, the guy had nothing but stopouts." That means the player didn't have to move the cue ball around the table as much, resulting in less margin for error in his or her resulting cue ball positions. Whenever possible, a stop shot is a great position play. Not only will the cue ball not have to travel after contact with the object ball, but you also know exactly where your cue ball will be for the next shot. The stop shot is therefore a vital part of the cue sports that must be mastered for you to play your best game.

Keep in mind that when you execute a stop shot, the cue ball does not replace the space where the contacted object ball was, as many players mistakenly believe. Rather, since it stops on contact, that means it occupies the space $2^1/_4$ inches *behind* where the object ball was prior to contact. This common misconception can result in bad position plays, especially when executing pattern plays that demand pinpoint position.

Here's how to perfect your skill in performing a stop shot. Take one of the striped balls from your rack and place the ball down on the table (around the head spot) with the stripe placed horizontally (parallel to the bed of the table). Then, hit the ball toward the other end of the table with a below-center stroke and observe the stripe on the ball. Watch how the ball, while moving forward, will reverse for a period of time, then slide, then begin rolling.

Once you've seen this initial physical reaction, you can experiment with different types of strokes and different aiming points, as shown in figure 5.1. Attempt the shot in three different positions, with a just-below-center hit (one-half cue tip), a full cue tip below center hit, and even farther below center (but only if you can maintain a level stroke). Use the same force on your stroke in each of the different positions. You'll recognize very quickly that the farther below center you go, the farther the cue ball will skid forward before it actually grabs and starts rolling forward. This action, when the ball begins the forward rolling motion, is sometimes referred to as a "perfect roll." A perfect roll describes the cue ball rolling forward with absolutely no sidespin or english on the cue ball.

Now you're ready to transfer this knowledge to proper execution of the stop shot. What you are trying to achieve with the stop shot is to have the cue ball hit the object ball at the point when there's still a touch of backward spin on the cue ball, just before the cue ball ends its slide and starts its perfect roll. First practice the simple shots shown in figure 5.1 to see how the cue ball reacts with the different strokes, before entering any object balls into the equation. This will give you a good idea of the distance the cue ball is traveling before it grabs in each of your cue tip positions. Once you get the technique down, you're ready to move on to the next exercise.

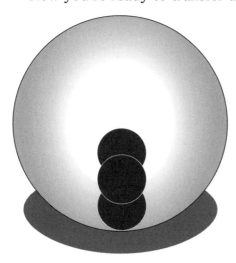

Figure 5.1 Practicing the stop shot with different strokes and hits.

The other exercise we've set up for you (in figure 5.2) will do two things for quick development of your stop shot skills. First, you'll learn to quickly recognize a "stopout pattern" when you see one. As you'll note in the diagram, no balls are tied up or clustered together, and nothing is too close to a rail. Without these conditions, a stopout will be nearly impossible. The point of the exercise is to run the balls in rotation, as indicated, executing a stop shot with each shot. It's easy to set up variations of this exercise on your own, again, keeping in mind that no balls should be too close together or too close to a rail.

Second, you'll be practicing stop shots at short and long distances. While in normal play it may be more practical to draw the cue ball back for better position, the exercise is designed for you to get a feel for executing the stop shot from varying distances. You'll discover that lower cue ball position (slight draw), combined with a slightly harder hit, will be necessary to stop the cue ball on the longer shots. Again, this is because in a stop shot the cue ball will slide to the object ball, ideally with no forward or backward momentum left. That's why it stops! All the remaining energy is thus transferred from the cue ball to the object ball. With a longer shot, the cue ball will need extra force and a lower hit to maintain the slide, before the natural forward roll takes place and causes the cue ball to drift after contact with the object ball.

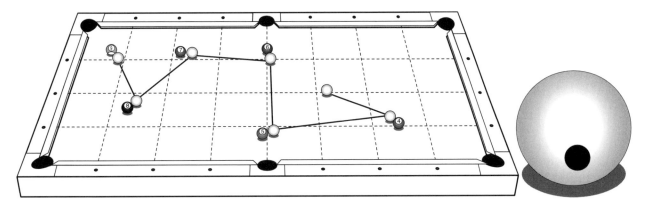

Figure 5.2 Can you run the rack, using a stop shot with each shot?

THE STUN SHOT

What happens to the stop shot if the shot isn't exactly straight in? Let's add some shots with a slight angle and see what occurs. Note the shots in figure 5.3 and the resulting cue ball positions. Knowing how to perform the stun shot can help you to minimize drift of the cue ball, allowing you to play position and avoid impeding balls.

The stun shot is a variation of a stop shot that happens when you're not quite straight in on the object ball. As you've learned already, your cue ball will come off at a 90-degree angle from the angle to the pocket (the tangent line). In other words, if you have a 10-degree-angle shot, executing the stun shot is just like a stop shot, only the cue ball will react sideways off the object ball, not forward or backward. The stun shot then becomes an equally good way to control the cue ball off the object ball without sending the cue ball very far at all or having to go back and forth across the table for position. Set up several off-angle shots to develop your stun shot skills, noting in each how the cue ball reacts and how little distance you can make it travel.

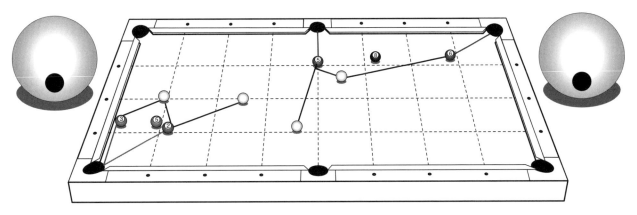

Figure 5.3 Slight-angle stop shots, called stun shots,
can minimize cue ball movement.

THE DRAG SHOT

The drag shot, like the stun shot, is useful when you want to move the cue ball a short distance. This shot will allow you to roll the cue ball forward just a little, anywhere between 3 and 12 inches. Skill development in this shot requires a bit more feel. You will continue to use a below-center hit. However, upon contact with the object ball, you will have forward spin left on the cue ball. This is another reason why it's crucial to know when that forward spin will take over, and very difficult to see without the striped-ball (used as a cue ball) exercise.

In the drag shot, most of the energy you put on the cue ball is gone. Take a look at the shots illustrated in figure 5.4. In both cases, you want the cue ball to drift forward a bit for ideal position on the next shot, but at the same time you're trying not to lose control of the cue ball. A follow stroke will allow the cue ball to travel too far; a stop shot will bring you up short. A soft, slightly below center hit will get you where you need to be. Again, experimentation with several different drag shots will be necessary to develop a feel for allowing the cue ball to drift forward.

FROZEN SHOTS

Very often in your playing career, you will come upon shots where the object ball is frozen on (touching) the cushion. Actually, these shots are very easy to make, but fall into the category of the critical shot since so many people need to develop their skills in this area. There are three options on how to pocket a ball frozen on the cushion. You can contact the object ball and cushion at the same time; you can hit the cushion first; or you can hit the object ball first.

There are a few players who swear by one method or another. What actually should dictate the method used is the force of the shot and where your cue ball needs to go. If, for example, you need to hit the shot hard to achieve position on the next shot, we recommend hitting the object ball first. If you hit the object ball first, you are also able to keep more english on the cue ball, whereas if you hit rail first the hit will take the english or any spin whatsoever off the cue ball.

In figure 5.5, we've shown an example of an object ball frozen on the long rail, with three rail positions indicated for the cue ball after execution of the shot. Using inside english (in this case, right english), if you hit the object ball first, or the ball and cushion simultaneously, your cue ball will "grab," meaning it will pick up the necessary english, and thus you will be able to go around the table three rails. If you hit the rail first in this shot, you'll almost always come off sideways, no matter what spin you've put on the cue ball. In other words, as we've also shown you in figure 5.5, your cue ball will never get to the short rail to go three rails. Instead, it will shoot straight across the table to the other long rail, no matter what sidespin you have on the ball, even with draw.

In executing the frozen ball shot, don't get caught up in so-called optical illusions, of seeing too much of the rail and losing focus on the ball. Aim as you would any other shot and shoot the ball. Again, the shot is much easier than people think, and is actually easier than a ball just off the rail, which can be over- or undercut. Fear of the shot translates into a poor follow-through, which often reinforces the miss. A little secret, then: when practicing frozen-to-the-cushion shots,

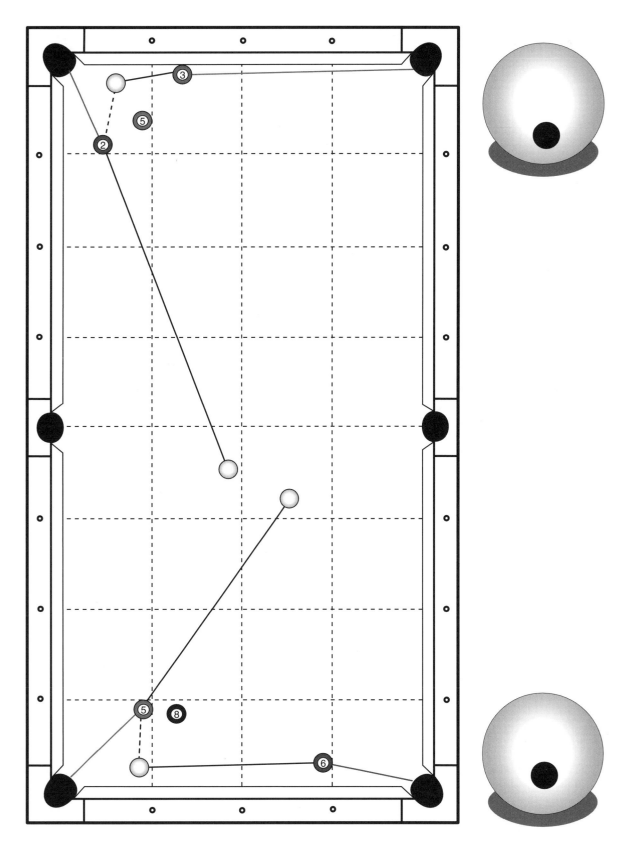

Figure 5.4 Letting the cue ball drift forward just slightly with a drag shot.

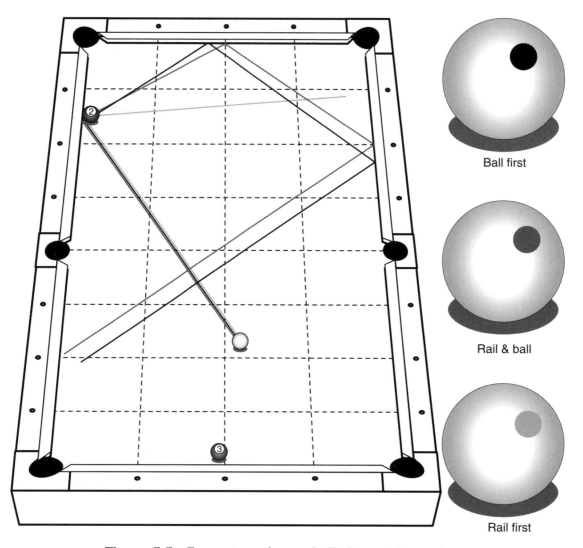

Figure 5.5 Executing a frozen ball shot, with resulting
cue ball positions.

attempt to execute them with an exaggerated follow-through. This will force you
to stay down on the shot, and allow you the best opportunity for full, firm contact
with the object ball. A little practice and you'll have plenty of confidence in making any ball that's frozen to the cushion!

BANKS

The **bank shot** may be the most misunderstood shot there is in the cue sports.
There's been so much written about the bank shot, and there are so many variables to take into account to pull off a bank shot, that players get just plain confused. Here then are the basics of the bank shot, and a couple of different systems
for banking.

Speed

The main variable to concern yourself with in bank shots is speed—how fast (or how hard) you hit the object ball. In figure 5.6, you can see a graphic illustration of this. Each shot has been hit with center ball. But shot A has been hit too hard, shot B too soft, and shot C is just right! As you will quickly see, the harder you hit the ball, the shorter the angle coming off the cushion. The angle into the cushion will therefore not equal the angle coming out.

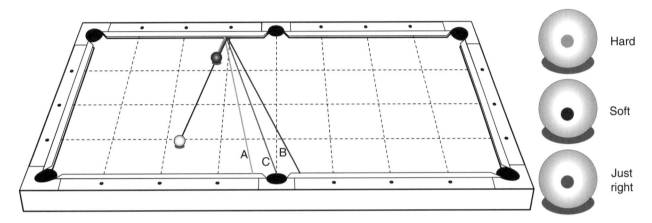

Figure 5.6 Using speed to increase or decrease the bank shot angle.

Simple so far, right? What many players do not understand is why this is so. There are two reasons. First, with the hard hit, the object ball is not rolling, but skidding off the rubber cushion. Second, because the cushion is rubber, a ball hit into it with force will compress the rubber, causing the object ball to bounce back off the rail at a shorter, or more shallow, angle. A ball hit too softly into the rail, then, will roll long in comparison to the angle of attack, or angle into the cushion. This is why speed is the most crucial part of banks.

Figure 5.7 shows you how this knowledge can translate into a game-winning opportunity. You are presented with a bank shot on the 8-ball that, if hit with medium

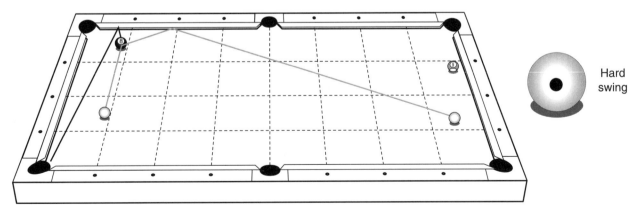

Figure 5.7 Translating your knowledge of bank speed for position play.

speed, would send the cue ball to poor resulting position for the 9-ball. But, with a harder hit, you can open up the angle coming off the 8-ball because you have to cut the 8-ball more to pocket the ball. This will allow you to send the cue ball down table for the 9-ball, using a middle-ball hit (no english required). This is just one example of how speed affects the angle at which you aim to make a bank and get position at the same time.

So far, so good. Let's add another variable. In figure 5.8 we've shown you the same shot, hit with medium speed, but have changed how we've hit the cue ball. Shot A shows you the shot hit with follow. Shot B has been hit with draw. And again, shot C, hit with middle ball, is just right. High ball on shot A will transfer low ball to the object ball. As the object ball picks up the draw off the cue ball, it will spring off the cushion with low-ball effect, thus cutting down the angle at which it bounces off the rail. If, on the other hand, you put draw on the cue ball, you will be putting follow on the object ball, and the high-ball effect will result in the object ball coming off a little longer, depending on your angle of attack into the cushion.

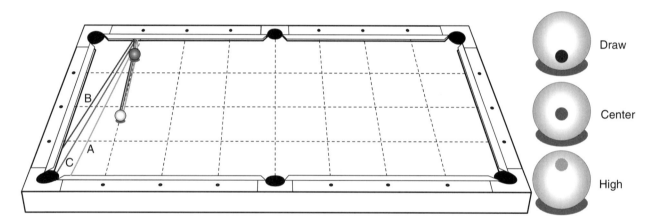

Figure 5.8   Using follow and draw to change the bank shot angle.

The best way, then, to initially practice your bank shots and to get a feel for each individual bank is to begin with a medium hit using center ball on the cue ball.

English

The next variable that will affect your bank shot execution is the use of english. Like the use of follow and draw, the resulting spin on the object ball will be the opposite of that which you imparted to the cue ball. In other words, left english on the cue ball will transfer to right english on the object ball; right english on the cue ball will end up as left english on the object ball. Again, the results will differ depending on the angle of attack. And, if you wish to impart english, you can transfer more spin to the object ball with the use of low ball—that is, low right or low left as opposed to high right or high left. The speed of the swing will also determine how much spin is transferred to the object ball. The slower the swing speed, the more spin is transferred. Illustrations of the altered paths using right english and left english versus center ball are shown in figure 5.9.

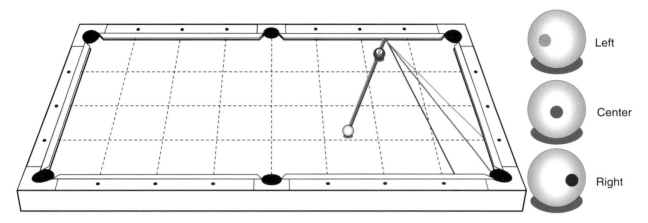

Figure 5.9   Using left and right english to change
the bank shot angle.

Angles of Attack

The final variables that influence bank shots are the angles of attack. These include the angle from A, the cue ball to the object ball, and B, from the object ball to the cushion. Let's first discuss A. Figure 5.10 indicates a crossover bank, so named because you are crossing over the angle of the bank shot with your cue ball. A glancing blow on the left side of the object ball will put left spin on the object ball, even with a center-ball hit. This will cause the ball to go long (sending it to the

Figure 5.10   Crossing over the
angle on a bank shot.

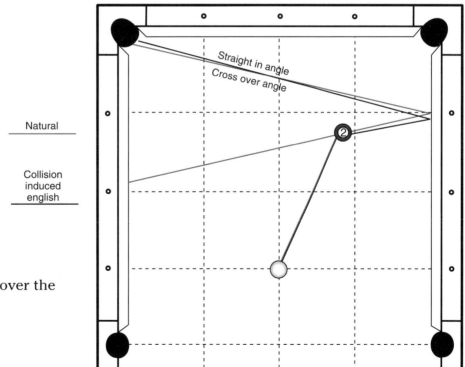

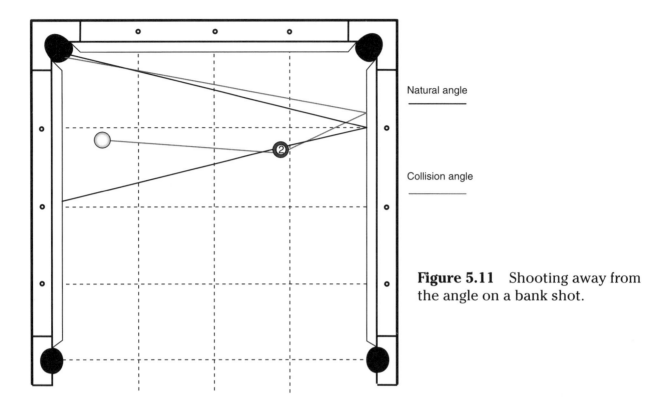

Natural angle

Collision angle

Figure 5.11 Shooting away from the angle on a bank shot.

right of the corner pocket). You must also remember that the fuller the hit, the more sidespin that will be transferred. Figure 5.11 illustrates the opposite situation. Here, you're not crossing over the ball; you are in fact shooting away from the bank angle of the object ball. On this shot, you'll come up short on the bank (to the left of the pocket) because english is put automatically on the object ball from the glancing blow away from the angle of attack. In other words, the angle will change from the natural angle (which we've already learned is approximately the same angle out from the cushion as the angle at which it approached the cushion).

Which brings us to B. The angles between 20 and 60 degrees pick up the most collision-induced sidespin. After about 60 degrees, the more severe the angle, the less sidespin is picked up on the object ball. A cross-side bank with very little angle (5-10 degrees) will not pick up much sidespin coming off the cushion. With a center-ball hit, then, the only variable that will affect the shallow angle bank is the speed at which you hit the ball. The shallower the angle coming into the cushion off the bank, the less distortion you're going to get off the cushion.

A steep angle coming into the cushion will allow the object ball to pick up a great deal of sidespin or running english. Figure 5.12 illustrates a steep-angled, two-rail bank shot and its resulting altered path from the cushion. "Angle in" does not equal "angle out" in this case; you're going to pick up sidespin, and that will force the object ball to go longer. This will occur on the first rail of a bank shot, and also on the second rail in shots using multiple rails. By the third rail the spin will be gone. This will also hold true in **kick shots**. This factor must be taken into account when hitting multi-rail banks; aim that shot shorter than you actually would on the shallow-angle shot.

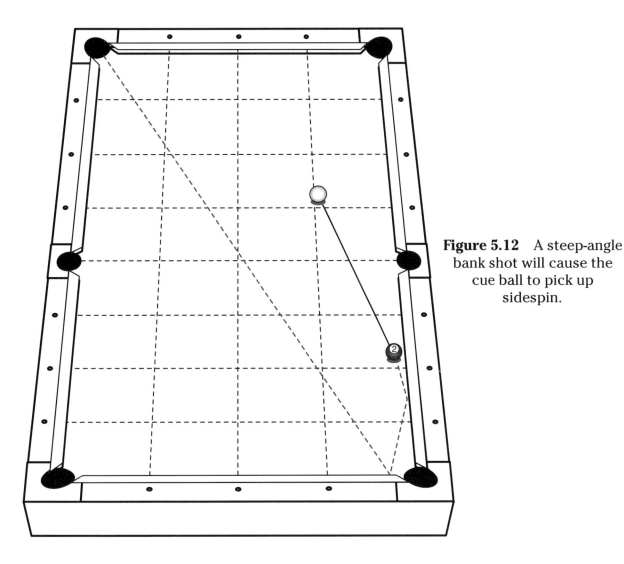

Figure 5.12 A steep-angle bank shot will cause the cue ball to pick up sidespin.

Banking Systems

Chances are, the above information has either made you take up tennis or really whetted your appetite to try a few banks on your own. We hope the latter is true. If you've experimented at all, and studied the diagrams already provided, you'll have noticed that everything starts from the point of "angle in equals angle out," and then adjusts based on the aforementioned variables. Now it's time to take that knowledge one step further with a few fun systems built just for banks.

Creating a Mirror Image

The first system involves aiming the bank shot with the use of a mirror image table. The theory can be explained and illustrated in a few different ways. If you practice with a partner and have access to a mirror large enough for that person to hold up directly next to the table, this could be the best visual you'll ever get of a bank. Assuming you don't have this luxury, you can recreate the mirror image using your imagination. In figure 5.13, a simple cross-side bank shot is illustrated on the primary table. Adjacent to the primary table is your imaginary table—your

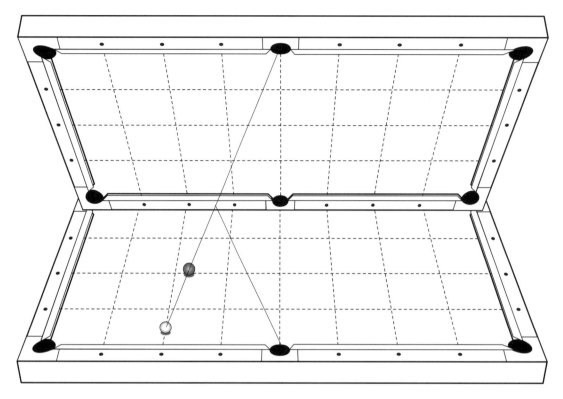

Figure 5.13 The mirror image system for aiming a bank shot.

mirror image. To bank the ball cross side, you simply aim to make it in the side pocket of the mirror image table. Pretty cool, eh?

As you experiment with this system, you'll probably come up with variations of your own. In some clubs the tables have everything mapped out. There are actually tape marks on the walls, furniture, other tables, and so on. Some people swear by that, and if it amuses you, you can decorate your home rec room with tape of your own. At that point, speed, english, and angle of attack will be the remaining variables that dictate how you actually execute the bank.

Spinning the Bank

Here's a method to pocketing banks that we've seldom seen taught—using english to spin the bank into the pocket. After you have ascertained the angle of the bank itself, continue the imaginary line through the object ball from the rail so that you can visualize the point at which you need to make contact with the object ball. Line up the cue ball and the object ball head on, and then adjust the cue tip to that contact point. This will impart english on the object ball, which will send it straight to the rail and then throw it back to the pocket.

Now we'll add an illustration to simplify this explanation. In figure 5.14, we have an object ball on the foot spot, and the cue ball is dead in the middle of the table. We want to bank this ball straight back to the right. The angle at which the object ball must hit the bottom short rail in order to bank it back (the angle of attack) is shown by the broken line. But, rather than shooting straight center ball into that angle, you line up for a fuller hit on the object ball. Then, looking at where you have to hit the object ball at that angle, you instead put that much english on the

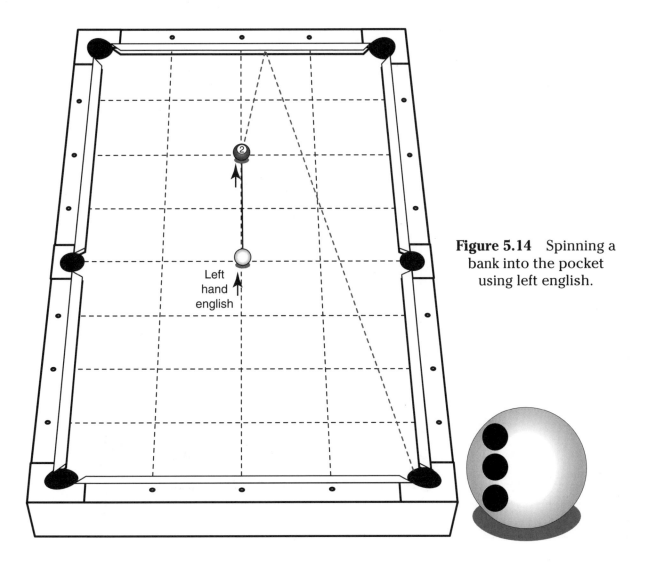

Figure 5.14   Spinning a bank into the pocket using left english.

cue ball. In other words, you know that you will have to hit the object ball to the right, so you put left english on the cue ball to throw that bank into the short rail in order to bring it back into the pocket.

This becomes a very easy banking system once you have learned where the object ball must contact the cushion. You'll hear it referred to as "throwing the bank," "englishing the bank," or "spinning the bank." And it works with inside or outside english, depending on where you want the cue ball to go after the bank. In figure 5.15, we've illustrated the same bank, back to the right, only now we want to use right english. Line up the cue tip with right english, and you'll observe that you have to cross over just about the entire cue ball to make the bank. Try a couple of these to expand your banking versatility, and at the same time learn the myriad of options you have to place your cue ball after a bank shot.

Now let's take the theory of spinning the banks one step further. Some of the best bank players who ever lived would rather bank the balls with inside english. Why? They execute banks this way in order to transfer the english to the object ball; thus the bank bounces off the rail at a more shallow angle, increasing the size of the pocket! Take a look at figure 5.16. A center-ball hit is shown for a simple

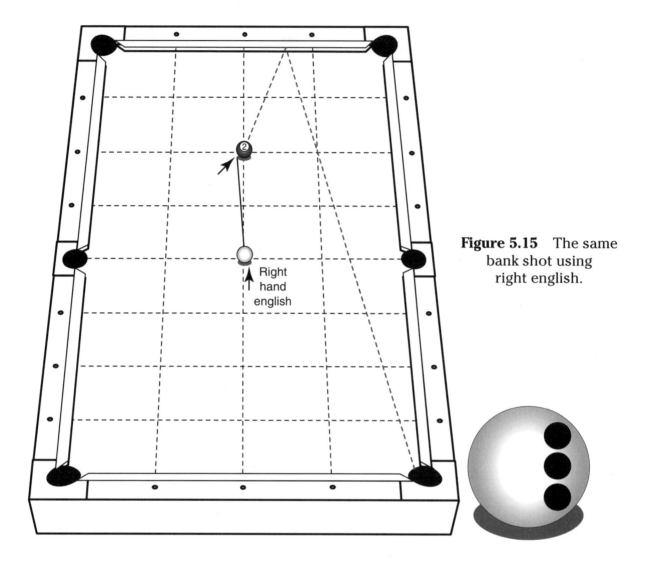

Figure 5.15 The same bank shot using right english.

bank, along with a hit using inside english (in this case, left english) to pocket the ball. Notice how the inside english will allow a more shallow angle, actually increasing the size of the target pocket. This method also takes the spin off the object ball that you would naturally get from hitting it at an angle. In other words, if you are cutting a ball to the right, you've already learned that you will naturally put left english on the object ball. But, if you intentionally put left english on the cue ball, you'll take the english off the object ball. Taking this sidespin off the object ball gives you a truer roll and allows you greater margin for error.

When spinning in a bank, it's important to realize that how much english is transferred to the object ball will be dictated by the amount of english you put on the cue ball. Once the object ball hits the cushion, a lot will depend on your equipment. How tightly stretched the cloth is will dictate how much english is kept on the object ball. Loose cloth will decrease the spin; worn cloth, which allows more contact with the rubber than thicker, new cloth, will increase spin. New cushion rubber will hold more spin, but if the rubber is detached from the rail, it will be virtually impossible to hold the spin coming off the cushion.

Nevertheless, with all the variables that you now know can affect your banking, you should also realize it's better to observe where the object ball must be hit in simple banks and apply this knowledge to learn more banks. Just as we've pointed out to you throughout other areas in this book, simple keys to shots and situations lead to more keys and more knowledge. You will progress farther and faster by experimenting on your own.

Virtually every professional player will tell you that they've learned much of the game of pool, and especially critical shots like banking and kicking, strictly by rote and by memory. After shooting so many of these during practice and experimentation, their subconscious automatically knows what to do! Sure, it takes a little time for the subconscious to adapt to different conditions on different tables, but then banking will become automatic. You'll very quickly find that it's not so difficult to memorize different angles and then let your subconscious adjust to game and table conditions. This will allow you to make subtle changes necessary to continue pocketing balls.

KICK SHOTS

Kicking at balls, which means having the cue ball first contact a cushion and then come into an object ball, is really just a form of banks without the object ball. Instead of figuring placement of the object ball to the pocket, you're trying to figure placement of the cue ball to the object ball. The object ball could be one diamond from the side pocket or one diamond from the corner pocket, and all you do is make an adjustment from your banking to kick at the ball.

The mirror image system of banking can therefore be used in kicking balls anywhere on the table. Here again, "angle in equals angle out" will work on a one-rail

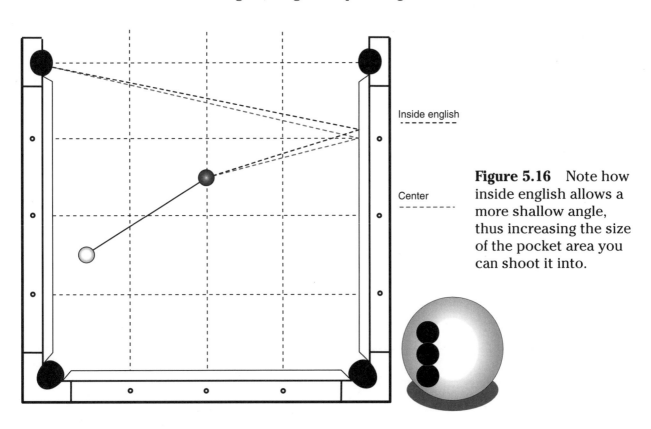

Inside english
- - - - - - - -

Center
- - - - - - - -

Figure 5.16 Note how inside english allows a more shallow angle, thus increasing the size of the pocket area you can shoot it into.

kick shot the same way it will on the bank shot, provided you're working with medium speed and a center-ball hit. You'll need to experiment here, too, learning exactly how the cue ball reacts as it bounces off the cushion.

Practicing the Kick Shot

To begin your practice of kick shots, eliminate the object ball. Just try shooting the cue ball into the rail, with the intention of making it cross side and cross corner until you get a little bit of feel for the shot. Once you can regularly scratch (pocket the cue ball) using just the cue ball, place a ball in front of the pocket. Try the two shots illustrated in figure 5.17. These utilize angles under 45 degrees, to enable you to practice learning the "angle in equals angle out" theory. Once the angle becomes wider than 45 degrees, the cue ball will pick up sidespin (just like the effect on the object ball in banking). Your cue ball will seldom scratch on this shot, unless it is hit in exactly the right spot to follow the object ball into the pocket. The chances increase the closer the object ball is to the pocket.

As you become proficient at the first exercise, start moving your cue tip off center, in increments of a quarter cue tip, to see how the reaction of the cue ball

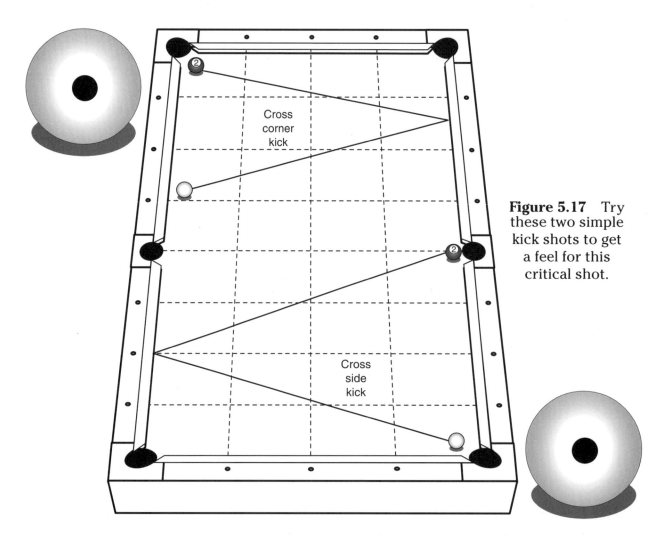

Cross corner kick

Cross side kick

Figure 5.17　Try these two simple kick shots to get a feel for this critical shot.

changes coming off the rail. Note how much you have to adjust your aim on the cue ball to the cushion to still bounce off and pocket the object ball. English used to one side or the other will change the angle of the cue ball on the first rail, but will not make any difference coming off the second rail. If you paid attention to your lessons in banking balls, you will very quickly develop a feel for the kick shot using all the variables that can occur in banks, without the additional element of the object ball to confuse you!

Sometimes you won't be able to achieve a hit on your designated object ball using just one rail. In this case, a two-rail kick is usually available to you, and here's a great system that will have you making impressive two-rail kicks in no time at all. Refer to figure 5.18. You'll note that this is a Nine Ball rack, and you must hit the 2-ball to make a legal shot, but you have no one-rail kick available to you due to impeding object balls. Find the point on the table that is midway between the 2-ball and the cue ball, and aim an imaginary line from that point to the corner pocket (as indicated by the broken line in the diagram). That angle represents a line parallel to the line at which you must shoot the cue ball into the first

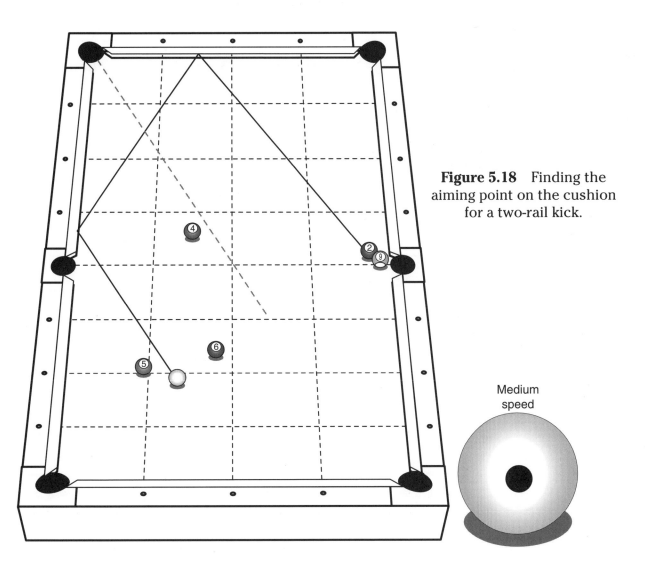

Figure 5.18 Finding the aiming point on the cushion for a two-rail kick.

Medium speed

rail. The path of the cue ball is indicated by the solid line. As you can see, the cue ball will naturally bounce off the first rail, into the second, and out again at the line parallel to the angle of attack, to contact the object ball!

Three-Rail Kicks

Now you're ready for the real challenge: three-rail kicks! Frankly, we think you'll be surprised to learn how easy they can be! To line up a three-rail kick, begin by placing the cue ball near one of the corner pockets, as shown in figure 5.19, with the intention of sending it three rails around the table, resulting in a scratch in the other corner. You've heard about using the diamonds to calculate shots; here's your big chance. To aim at your first rail, you will shoot roughly five and a half diamonds up from the corner in which you are trying to pocket the cue ball. Simply count the diamonds up from the corner, using the side pocket as the fourth diamond. Again, you must extend your visual field out beyond the table to a point on an imaginary table or the wall beyond your shot. Now go ahead and execute the shot, using your center-ball hit and medium swing.

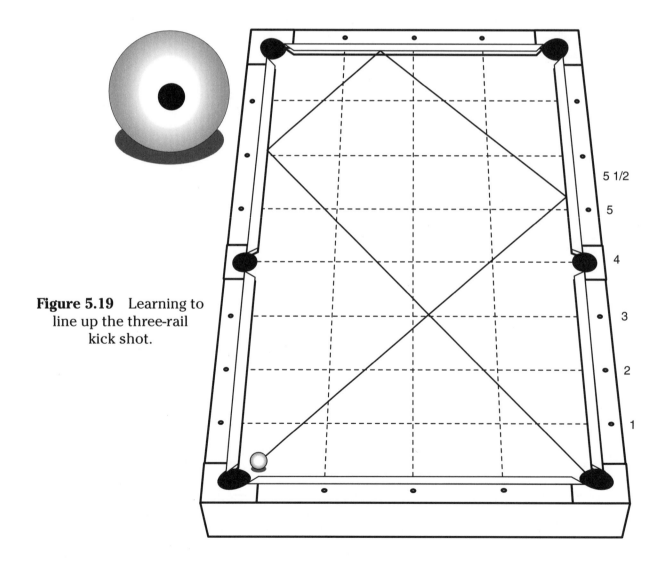

Figure 5.19 Learning to line up the three-rail kick shot.

How did the cue ball react? Did it come up long (hitting the short rail adjacent to your intended pocket), or did it come up short and hit the long rail first? Depending on where it landed, make an adjustment to the point you are aiming at beyond the pool table and try the shot again. Once you've found your spot, you know where the "track" is for this table at this time. What this tells you is that anywhere on the table, so long as you can see the point past the long rail that you shoot into first, you can make that three-rail kick shot! When attempting to execute a three-rail kick, you first make sure your cue ball can be shot toward that starting point. If it can, you can make it!

This exercise will work as a very good starting point to practice your three-rail kicks. With a little practice and careful observing, you can become proficient in no time, noticing how the ball stays on that track to go three rails. By learning this, you'll also know that if you're trying to go three rails but cannot see your starting point off the first long rail, you can't make the three-rail kick with a medium-speed, center-ball hit. You might try a little massé or extreme english to make the shot, but it's not highly advisable except in the most dire of circumstances. Do your best in this case to look for another option!

The Offensive Kick Shot

The offensive kick shot is a critical shot that is often overlooked. Players seldom recognize the opportunities that await them with these game-winning shot selections. In figure 5.20 you cannot see the 1-ball to make it directly. But, a well-placed offensive kick shot will allow you to pocket the 1-ball and end up with perfect shape on the 2-ball. Best of all, there's even a clever system for measuring this shot. Use your cue stick as a measuring device (eventually you will be able to visualize these without such an aid) and run a perpendicular line with the cue stick from the spot you wish to hit on the object ball to the rail. Say this distance is about four inches. Extend the line four inches out past the edge of the cushion. That point off the bed of the table (labeled in the diagram) will be your aiming point for the cue ball. Use middle-ball hit or a touch of follow with a smooth stroke. Your cue ball should kick into the cushion, contact the 1-ball to pocket it in the corner, and deflect at roughly a 90-degree angle (the tangent line), arriving in perfect position to make the 2-ball in the corner pocket! This aiming method can be used anywhere on the table by just remembering that you figure the distance from the object ball to the cushion, and then match that distance from the cushion out beyond the table surface to find your aiming point.

Figure 5.21 illustrates another offensive kick, this time using a billiard off the 2-ball. Again, once you decide where to hit the 2-ball, measure that distance to the cushion and extend it for your aiming point on the cue ball. This is a soft shot requiring a light touch. You'll come into the cushion, glance gently off the 2-ball, and pocket the 9-ball. Because the 9-ball is close to the pocket, you have some margin for error here. The cue ball can go straight into the 9-ball, or if you contact the low side of the 2-ball, your cue ball will contact the long rail adjacent to the 9-ball first, which will still pocket the 9-ball. Nevertheless, players often assume this is too fancy a shot and opt for a safety when the win is well within their grasp.

If you've had the opportunity to see professional players in action, whether live or on the tube, you know that they have the ability to kick extremely well, especially

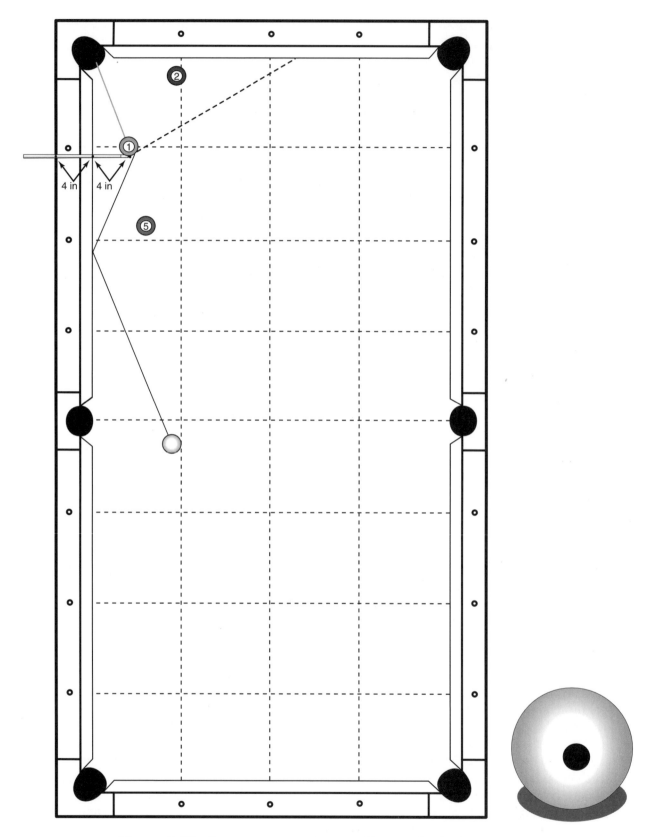

Figure 5.20 Learn to recognize an offensive kick shot opportunity.

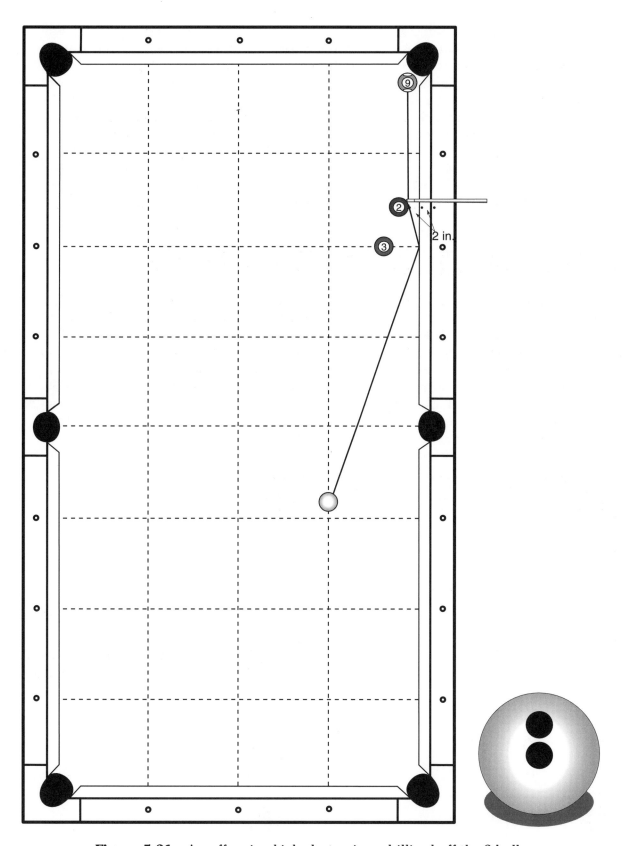

2 in.

Figure 5.21 An offensive kick shot using a billiard off the 2-ball.

in the game of Nine Ball. Ninety-nine percent of the time, if you hit the correct side of the ball when you are kicking at the object ball, your opponent won't have a decent shot, which is discussed further in chapter 7 on safety play. The point we want to make here is that once you have some ability to kick at balls, experiment even further by trying to contact one side of the object ball or the other. Don't just aim to hit the object ball, aim to send your cue ball to an advantageous position for you, but not for your opponent. The biggest secret to kicking on the correct side of the object ball is to not try too hard. Do not begin calculating new aiming systems, and so on. Rather, let your subconscious do the work by visualizing the cue ball coming off the object ball on one side or the other. You'll be surprised how your body will make the minor adjustments for you if you let it do the work!

COMBINATIONS AND CAROMS

Combinations and caroms are critical shots that use object balls to make other object balls. Combination shots require shooting one object ball into another to pocket the ball, while in a **carom shot**, you will shoot your intended object ball off a "helper" ball, allowing it to carom off that ball and into the pocket. You'll also learn how make a successful billiard shot, caroming the cue ball off a helper object ball to pocket your intended object ball. Knowledge of how to make these shots can prolong a run that otherwise looks dismal, allow an excellent safety opportunity, or shorten the game with a crowd-pleasing winning shot! Bottom line—practicing their proper execution will win many games for you.

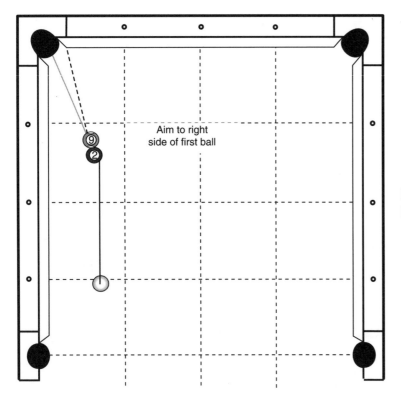

Aim to right side of first ball

Figure 5.22   Throwing the object ball in a frozen ball combination.

Types of Combination Shots

We'll talk about combinations first, since they seem to be easier for most players to understand. Let's begin with the execution of the frozen ball combination. In figure 5.22, you have two balls that are frozen together, and they do not line up exactly to the pocket. The broken line shows that if hit full, the shot will play to the right of the pocket. This is one of those times you'll realize that pool is often a game of opposites! Most people would assume that you would want to cut the first object ball to the left to make the second object ball go to the left. Wrong! Instead, contact the 2-ball on the right side to "throw" the second ball to the left, as shown. The farther the shot is from the pocket, the more you can alter the final destination of the object ball. In figure 5.23, you have such a shot. At a short distance, the shot would not get thrown enough before reaching the pocket. But with this shot you have plenty of distance for the path of the object ball to be altered enough before it reaches the pocket. The more you cut the shot to the right, the more throw will be induced.

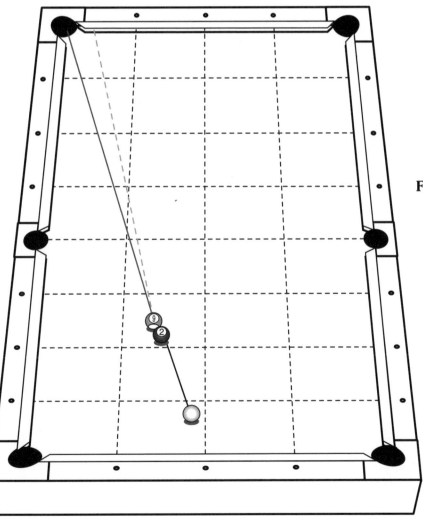

Figure 5.23   The greater the distance to the pocket, the more room to alter the frozen ball combination shot that isn't in line for the pocket.

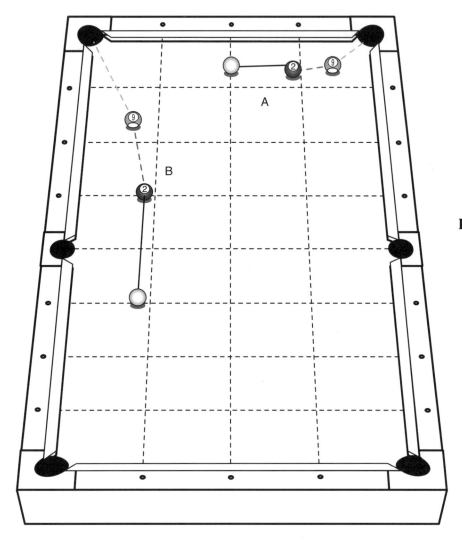

Figure 5.24　A high-percentage versus low-percentage combination shot.

　　In combinations where the balls are not frozen, two rules of thumb are worth mentioning. First, the farther the object balls are apart, the more difficult the shot. Second, the farther the ball that you intend to pocket is away from that pocket, the more difficult the shot becomes. Take a look at the two shots illustrated in figure 5.24. Shot A is a good bet for a solid combination shot. Shot B is a lower-percentage shot, since the balls are farther apart and the 9-ball is a bit of a distance from the pocket. And, as you may or may not have already learned, in pool, it's best to stick with the high-percentage shots and let your opponent make the mistakes!

　　In order to consistently make combination shots, you have to keep your focus, as you're adding a ball to the execution equation. If you're not ready to make the shot, your eyes just won't have decided where to focus and you'll be in trouble. The mistake most people make is trying to watch the entire shot at the same time. This can throw you off. If you take your eye off the first object ball to anticipate the hit on the second object ball, you are cheating yourself out of the possibility of making the combination. Instead, stay focused on the first ball for much better results. One trick players find helpful is to use parts of the rail to aim at. Once you line up toward the hit on the object ball, aim right through the ball to the point

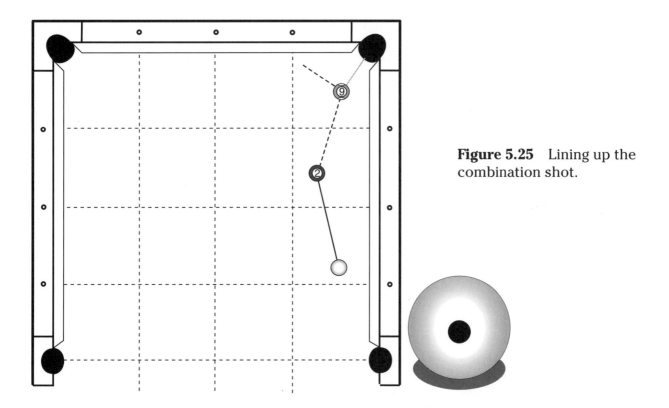

Figure 5.25 Lining up the combination shot.

beyond it on the cushion. This will help you to stay down on the shot and visualize the whole shot without trying to look at each ball during your execution.

Figure 5.25 illustrates a makable combination shot. The target 9-ball is 6 inches from the pocket (a reasonable distance at which to try the shot under normal game conditions), and the 2-ball is 12 inches from your target ball, not allowing too much room for error. Ignore the cue ball for a minute. Instead, line up the 2-ball as your cue ball to make the 9-ball. When you have chosen the spot where you would hit the 2-ball to pocket the 9-ball, then go back to the cue ball and line up to contact the 2-ball.

Now, here's a little hint. If you are cutting the first ball to the right to make the combination, you will put left english on your first object ball. This has to be put into your equation. But, if you hit the ball firmer, the shot will incur less spin, and you're more apt to make it. Thus, when shooting a combination shot, you're always better off trying to keep the hit on your cue ball as close to center as possible. The use of english magnifies the variables. There are players and teachers who believe you should use outside english to "straighten out," or take the spin off, your first object ball. There's a lot to be said for this, but less-experienced players often have a tendency to overdo it. If you would like to experiment with this method, we strongly advise that you use no more than a one-quarter to one-half tip of english. (Using english means you'll have to hit the combination a bit fuller than with a center-ball hit.) Your goal is only to take the sidespin off the first object ball before it hits the second object ball. Abundant use of english won't accomplish that goal.

Players often find themselves in trouble on combinations if they do not properly plan where the first object ball and the cue ball will travel to after pocketing the second object ball. They end up hooking themselves on the combination and are forced to kick at the ball they could see just fine on the last shot! Be sure to have a destination for the cue ball and the first object ball. Sometimes, if your second object ball is hanging in the pocket you may want to make both balls (the ball in the pocket and the ball you are shooting into it). This works especially well when you know you can pocket both of these balls and that your cue ball, after contact, will be in perfect position for the next ball in your run. The only way to force your first object ball to consistently follow the hanging ball into the pocket is to use draw on the cue ball. This will allow the first object ball to pick up follow spin.

Caroms and Billiards

Like the combination shot, a carom shot also involves more than one object ball, but the ball you intend to pocket will glance off the "helper" object ball, rather than being driven into the pocket by it. Caroms can be simple. The biggest problem is that few players know how to line up a carom shot correctly. We can solve this mystery for you.

First, take a look at figure 5.26, an illustration of a simple carom shot. As you can see, the object ball must be shot into the "helper" ball. As you learned earlier in this book, the object ball you intend to pocket will glance off the ball on the tangent line. If you want to find what spot on the "helper" object ball you must contact with your intended object ball, just line up the outside of the pocket (as shown in the diagram) with the edge of the "helper" ball. This is the point at which you must aim your object ball because the outside of the pocket compensates for aim versus the actual contact point. Now, go back to the cue ball and simply line

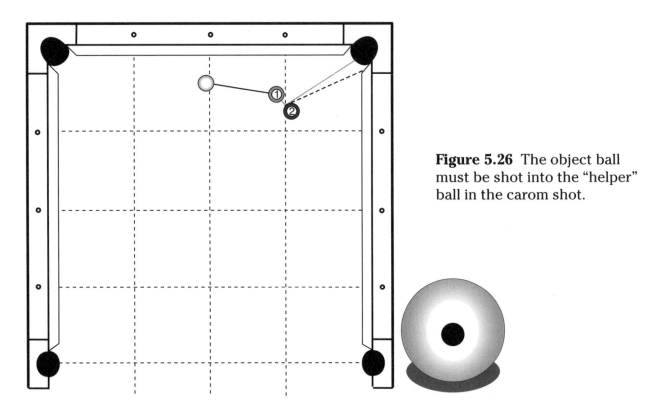

Figure 5.26 The object ball must be shot into the "helper" ball in the carom shot.

up middle ball to shoot your intended object ball at that point on the "helper" ball. Try to visualize shooting straight through the "helper" ball. This will help your stroke and targeting. Use center ball with a medium hit in your swing.

Depending on what force you use and where you put the cue tip on the cue ball (high, low, or center), you can slowly increase and decrease the speed and learn to carom off object balls at many different angles. The speed of the object ball will determine the angle coming off the carom ball. Experiment by using different speeds and cue tip placements on the cue ball to learn at what angles the object ball will glance off the helper ball.

To avoid complicating matters with spin, let's first look at speed only. If the object ball is sliding (it will from a hard hit), the angle coming off the helper ball is shorter than if the ball were rolling, as with a slower speed of the object ball. Therefore use a fuller hit for a slow-speed shot, and a thinner hit for a faster-speed shot.

Using high ball (follow) will send the cue ball forward off the tangent line, while draw will bring it back. You'll want to experiment a bit with this since the force and

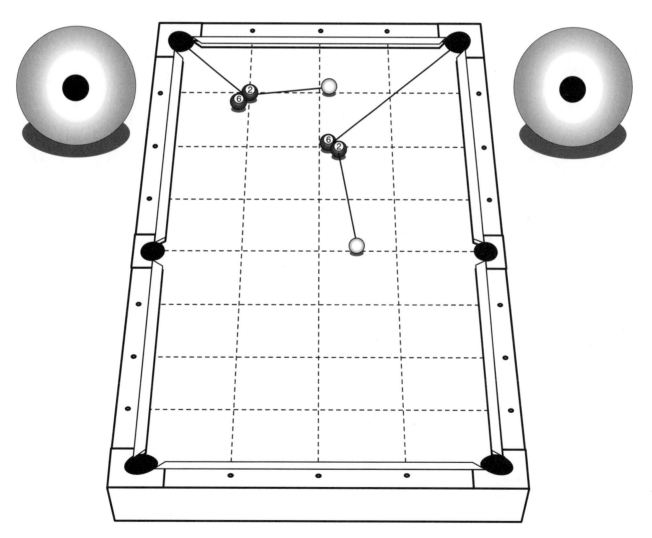

Figure 5.27   Examples of "dead" caroms with a center-ball hit.

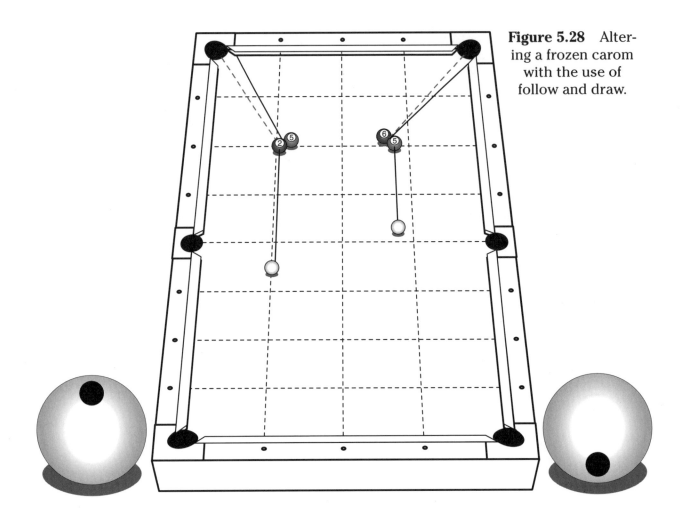

Figure 5.28 Altering a frozen carom with the use of follow and draw.

swing used on your hit will affect the resulting path and position of your cue ball, as mentioned earlier.

Now take a look at figure 5.27. If the balls end up like either of the examples here, consider yourself fortunate. With a medium, center-ball hit, these are considered to be dead caroms, and the 2-ball in both examples can travel to the pocket as if pulled by a string. Now, set up either of the same shots and use draw. As you'll see, the shot is no longer dead. On the other hand, a frozen carom that isn't quite dead can be altered in your favor with the use of draw or follow, as shown in figure 5.28. Draw or low ball on the cue ball will actually push the 5-ball forward and make it in the corner. High ball or follow on the other will bring the ball back off the carom line to make the 2-ball in the corner pocket. Set up these shots a few times and see how far you can move them off the carom line.

Now, say you want to pocket an object ball using the cue ball to carom off the "helper" ball. This is called a **billiard**, but it incorporates the carom theory. Take a look at figure 5.29.

You are presented with a potential situation where you can carom your cue ball off the 1-ball and pocket the 9-ball. You know that your cue ball (with medium speed and a center-ball hit) will come off the object ball at a 90-degree angle (the tangent line). And you also know that this cut shot would normally produce a

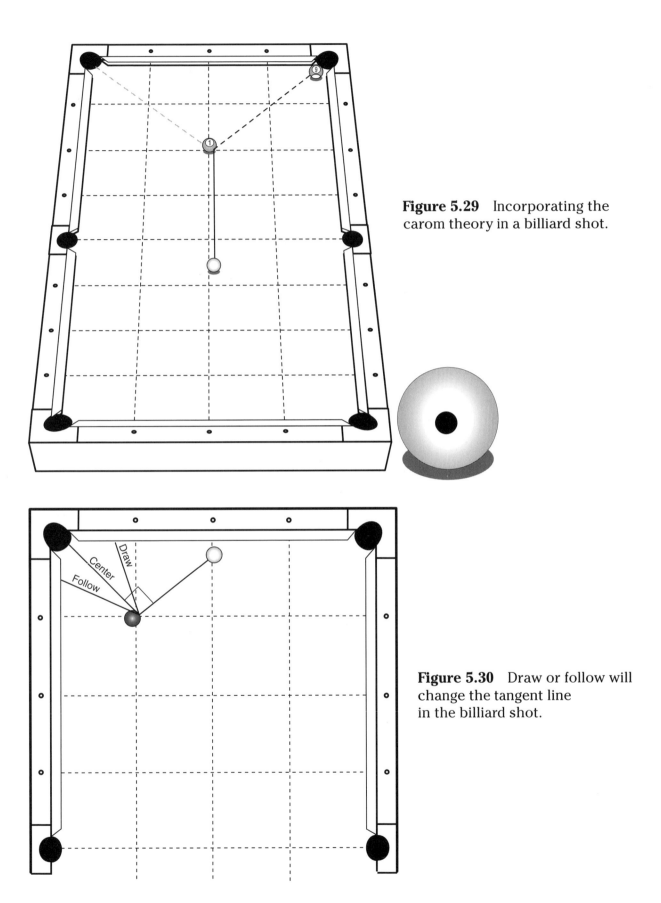

Figure 5.29 Incorporating the carom theory in a billiard shot.

Figure 5.30 Draw or follow will change the tangent line in the billiard shot.

scratch. You've probably experienced avoiding this scratch with the use of follow. But now, you can use this knowledge to try and scratch, knowing that your cue ball will knock the 9-ball into the pocket and win the game!

Let's take a look at how follow or draw on the cue ball will alter its natural path off the object ball. This is illustrated in figure 5.30. As you can see, the use of draw or follow will change the tangent line of the ball coming off the helper ball. In other words, the cue ball will not come off the helper ball at a 90-degree angle.

Billiards are most often used in Nine Ball for game-ball (pocketing the 9-ball) situations. This is because if you are continuing your run, it becomes much more difficult to control the speed of the object ball you carom off when you are already controlling the cue ball and pocketing the caromed object ball! In rare instances, however, it can produce a runout earlier in the game. For example, in figure 5.31, your object ball (the 6-ball) is blocked to the corner pocket by the 7-ball, but lies near the 8-ball in the side. A simple carom will pocket the 8-ball, and you know that the 6-ball (hit with soft to medium speed) will travel down toward the short rail

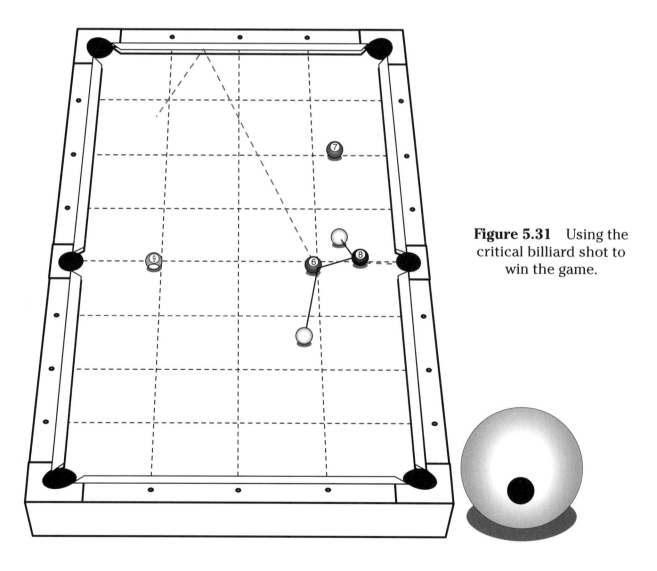

Figure 5.31 Using the critical billiard shot to win the game.

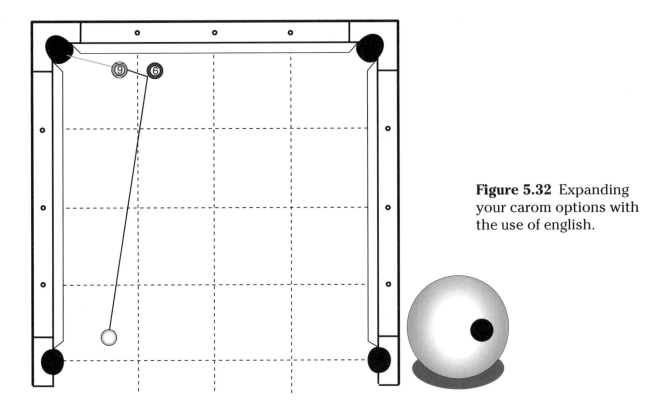

Figure 5.32 Expanding your carom options with the use of english.

and back out. Your cue ball will travel very little, offering you a shot on the 6-ball with position on the 7-ball.

Now let's explore how the use of english can alter the path of a carom shot and expand your options. In figure 5.32, you cannot pocket the 6-9 combination because you can't hit the 6-ball thin enough to contact the 9-ball at the proper spot. Instead, line up the carom. On this particular shot you'll want to use inside, or right, english in order to throw the 9-ball to the left, taking the spin off the carom with your cue ball and literally throwing the 9-ball into the corner. Little variations of this shot come up quite frequently and few players are aware of the possibilities!

Remember, caroms can be game winners, like the 9-ball shots we've illustrated, but they can also extend your run earlier in the game. In the game of Nine Ball, the difficulty will be in making sure you control the lowest numbered ball on the table that you've used to carom off and into another ball. It won't help to carom off the 2-ball, pocket the 5-ball, and send the 2-ball sailing into another disadvantaged point on the table.

If you're seeking a fun and interesting way to bone up on your carom skills, try the game of Philadelphia. Rack all 15 balls, but replace the front ball with the cue ball. Break the balls with the object ball you removed from the rack and attempt to pocket balls by caroming each of them off of the cue ball. (Helpful hint: continuing a run in this game becomes much easier if you keep the cue ball close to a pocket, resulting in less distance the object balls must travel to the pocket after contact with the cue ball.) Philadelphia is an excellent game for learning reactions and angles off balls, and also for learning to control the speed of the object ball.

JUMP SHOTS

With today's rules of one foul, ball in hand (where the incoming player gets cue ball in hand anywhere on the table if their opponent does not hit the intended object ball), the jump shot, like kicking, has become a vital part of the player's game. Years ago, before the advent of the jump cue, only a few players could jump a full ball with any kind of accuracy, and did so with their regular playing cue. Today, there are all sorts of jump cues produced by cue stick manufacturers. If you are interested in purchasing a jump cue for your arsenal, you'll need to check your local league and/or tournament rules for specific regulations dictating their use. While most models are effective, not all are legal in competitive play, and are often restricted based on materials or size.

A legal jump shot must be executed by sending the cue ball into the bed of table, causing it to bounce from the table bed and over an impeding ball to contact your object ball. You may not use the cue stick to dig under the cue ball and lift it from the table. Not only is this particular shot illegal, it can do irreparable damage to the billiard fabric covering the table and you will be the likely candidate to incur the costs of that folly!

The jump shot requires a different type of physical approach, inasmuch as you must move your body sideways in order to elevate the cue to the proper

Figure 5.33   You must alter your stance for a jump shot so that you can elevate the butt of your cue stick.

height. Figure 5.33 shows a typical stance used to jump the ball, but this will take a bit of experimentation on your part to develop a stance that is comfortable, and yet effective, for your particular body type. The mistake most people make is to elevate the cue too high in an attempt for increased chances of success, or to look fancy in their execution. If you do this, chances are you'll end up looking silly since you're approaching the cue ball too high, and thus trapping the cue ball between the bed of the table and the tip of the cue. It's much better to come in at a 30-degree angle than a 45-degree angle (depending of course on the distance of the shot and the force with which it must be hit). A little experimentation will show you that you simply don't need to elevate the cue that high.

Now for a tried-and-true method of quickly developing your jumping skills. Begin with a piece of chalk first. Place the chalk about 12 inches from the cue ball, and keep the cue ball at least a few inches from the rail, but not so far that you need to stretch for the shot. It won't take much effort at all to jump the piece of chalk, and this will give you an immediate feel for the jump shot. The swing required of a jump shot will be more of a throwing action versus your normal smooth follow-through. Though difficult to put into words, you're really sort of whipping the cue down at the ball. At the same time, you don't want to force the cue down; you still need to keep your back hand loose. The first time you successfully jump the piece of chalk, you'll feel the stroke that allowed you to do so, and successive attempts will become easier.

Once you've jumped that piece of chalk a couple of times successfully, move the chalk up and down the table, toward and away from your cue ball. This will help you to see at what distance the cue ball reaches its highest point during its airborne flight down the table.

Okay. Assuming you have accomplished these exercises without damaging any equipment or fellow players, you're ready to replace the chalk with an object ball. You will find that it is more difficult to jump impeding object balls that are very close to the cue ball. Typically, unless you have a great jump cue, are adept at jumping with just the shaft of your own cue, or simply have a rare talent for this shot, you'll need at least 6 to 10 inches before the cue ball can reach the height required to clear an object ball. The optimum distance to have between your cue ball and the impeding ball is 12 to 18 inches, depending on the force of shot. In a real game situation, if the impeding ball is too close, you'll most likely be looking at a kick shot. If it's too far, you'll need more force to keep the cue ball higher in the air for a longer period of time.

When you're practicing your jump shots over impeding balls, aim your cue ball at one of the corner pockets. This will give you a target to shoot at so that you learn to jump balls and still maintain some degree of accuracy in contacting your object ball. It won't help to clear the obstruction and miss your shot! This will also help you get comfortable manipulating your body into its jump stance for maximum effect. One secret to aiming your jump shot is to look at that target, and *not* the ball you intend to jump over. If you look at the impeding ball, your body will naturally aim toward it, not over it!

Now, add a little variation to your exercise. Set up the object ball, as shown in figure 5.34, so that it isn't directly in line with the path of the cue ball to the pocket. You should immediately become aware that this is an easier shot, but you'd be

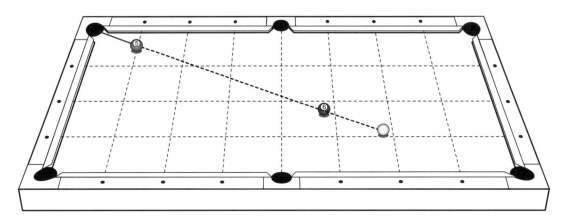

Figure 5.34   Jumping over edges of impeding balls requires
less lift of the cue ball.

surprised how many players don't realize that you can jump over edges of the impeding ball and not have to hit the ball anywhere near as high!

Where you aim on the cue ball dictates how high the cue ball will jump. If you picture the face of a clock imposed on the face of the ball as you are looking down on it (see figure 5.35 for reference), you'll be aiming at roughly 6:00 to get over the

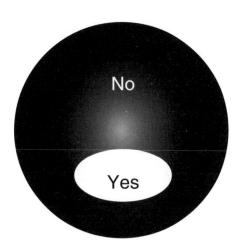

Figure 5.35   Using the face of a clock to determine your cue tip position for the jump shot.

ball. Many players have a tendency to look at the center of that clock face (labeled "No" in the illustration). This is the forbidden zone, where the cue ball will get trapped between the bed of the table and your cue stick. Shooting at 6:00 will allow your cue to go "through" the cue ball, or through the shot, with the least amount of resistance. The lower you can get (below 6:00) without digging under the ball, the better. If you hit a pure enough jump shot, you will actually get draw on the cue ball.

That brings us to your aim on the object ball. You may have already noticed in your preliminary jump shot practice that you're having a harder time hitting your target (the corner pocket) with consistency. No need to despair. This is a common malady, and it may help you to understand why you're having a difficult time, when you can pocket other shots pretty consistently. Because the jump shot doesn't utilize a normal stroke, you're likely to get a bit of an optical illusion. You won't be approaching your line of aim, as you normally do, from behind the shot. Rather, your approach will most often be from the side. This illusion will vary from player to player and will most often correspond to your size and body type. The taller you are, the closer you will be able to get in line behind the shot, as it is easier for you to elevate the cue with minimal stance distortion. But, taller players, or players with longer wing spans (which dictates where you hold the back of your cue), may have a difficult time with the shorter jump cues on the market. If this is you, first give your own cue a try. You may have more success jumping with a full-size model and simply choking up (moving your grip hand closer to the center of the cue).

Besides the optical illusion involved in your aim, you may also experience overcutting many of your shots due to hitting the object ball on the fly. This is one of the reasons it's important to learn just how far the cue ball travels in the air before rolling on the bed of the table again.

Finally, while we're on the subject of hitting the object ball on the fly, here's a tip that even many pros don't recognize—or refuse to believe, as we see them try these shots anyway. Don't attempt a jump shot when the object ball you want to hit is too close to the rail and you are shooting directly at the ball into the rail, especially if your cue ball is within two feet of the object ball. With the force you already know is necessary to get your cue ball over an obstructing ball, you also know that the cue ball will arrive at the object ball on the fly. That means it's most likely also going to hit the adjacent rail on the fly, and leave the bed of the table, resulting in a foul, and possible injury to friends and fans. Frankly, the whole reason you're jumping over a ball in the first place is to avoid a foul, so what's the point of risking another one? Opt instead for a well-played kick.

MASSÉS

For many shots that look otherwise dismal, you won't need to kick or go airborne, even with obstructing balls littering your path to a successful hit. Curve shots and massés are critical shots that will allow you to magically veer, curve, and twist the normally straight path of your cue ball. They are extremely fun shots to execute, and sometimes easier to learn than the jump shot.

Again, let's work with our visualization of the clock face, beginning with a simple curve shot. In figure 5.36, two shots are illustrated that require just a slight curve to get around the 2-ball and successfully pocket the 1-ball. The same shot is shown on either side of the table. With just a slight elevation on the butt of your cue, visualize the cue ball having the face of a clock, and, as you elevate, the clock face will elevate also. In shot A you want to curve the ball just to your left; so you will use left english at 7:00 on the cue ball. In shot B you'll need to curve the ball to your right, which means you'll use right english, aiming at about 5:00.

Time to get a little tougher. Figure 5.37 illustrates two shots requiring more curve. Again, as you elevate the butt of the cue, you get more turning action on the cue ball. The face of the clock will move with the elevation, and now you'll be aiming at about 8:00 for shot A, and about 4:00 for shot B. Experiment with several more shots on your own to find just how much curve you can get on a ball comfortably, continuing to increase the elevation of the back end of your cue until you get up to a 90-degree angle straight down, as in the massé shot.

The photo in figure 5.38 shows a player in a massé stance. As you can see, the cue stick is now perpendicular to the bed of the table. A massé shot will allow you to send the cue ball forward, whereupon it will grab the cloth and come straight back to you. Before we go any further in our discussion of massé shots, a quick

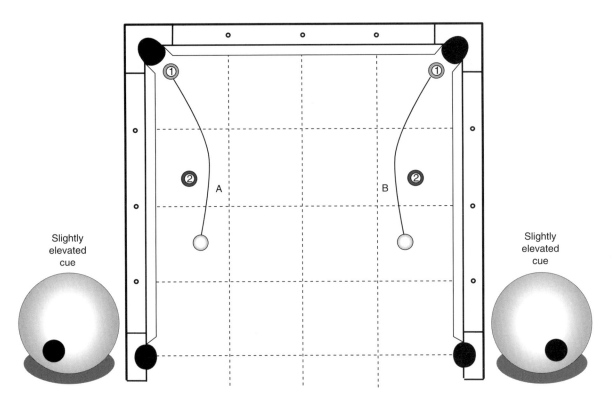

Figure 5.36 Again using the clock face to curve the cue ball around impeding object balls.

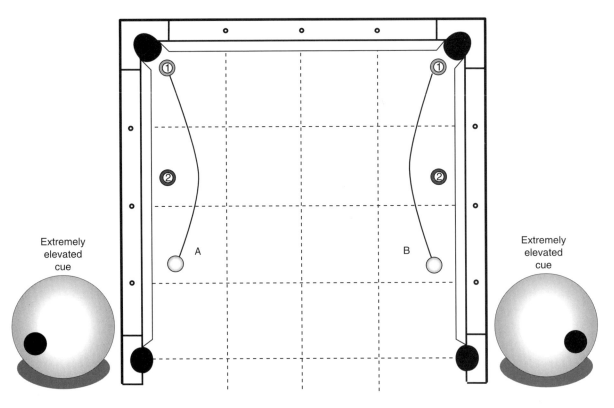

Figure 5.37 Shots using the curve technique.

Figure 5.38 Player is in a massé stance with the cue
perpendicular to the table.

warning is in order on behalf of billiard club proprietors everywhere. When you're
first starting out with massé shots, be very careful of the cloth, because you don't
know yet how the cue tip will react off the ball, and you have no feel for the shot.
It's easier than you might imagine to drive the tip straight down through the cloth
and rip it. Try to obtain a small piece of billiard fabric (many room owners keep
scraps for break and massé practice themselves) or obtain a sample from your
local dealer, and place this on top of the cloth you are playing on to protect it until
you get a little familiar with the shot.

Figure 5.39a shows you a path typical of a massé shot. Your clock face has
elevated so that you are now looking straight down at the clock, and you need a
6:00 hit on the cue ball.

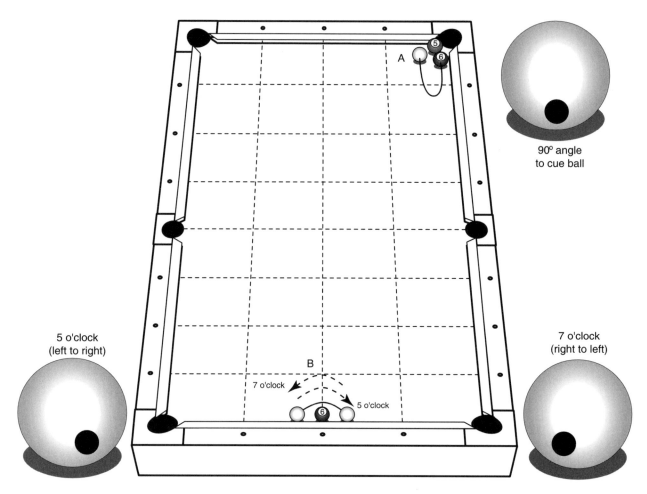

Figure 5.39 (a) The path typical of a massé shot.
(b) Examples of massé shots to the right and left.

Now let's say you want to completely curve the ball around the object ball, and it's just to the left of the cue ball. You would hit it at about 5:00, shooting straight down at the imaginary clock face on the cue ball to massé it to the right. To massé to the left, you would shoot down at about 7:00. Examples of massé shots to the right and left are illustrated in figure 5.39b, along with their corresponding aiming points for the cue ball.

Curve and massé shots are critical shots that are often misunderstood, as players try to overpower the shot. You really don't have to hit them too hard to get a reaction on the cue ball, and a 45-degree turn around the object ball won't take much force at all. Your biggest hurdle, as in the jump shot, will be to get comfortable with your own body and your cue to properly aim and execute these shots. But, once mastered, they are shots that can be used effectively. A majority of players overlook them; therefore, your developed skills in this area will give you the edge.

Crowd Pleasers

If you've been around pool for any length of time, you've seen fellow players, or pros in exhibitions, perform a trick shot or two. Most trick shots are "setup" shots, meaning they take little skill if the balls are placed in a predetermined position. There are shots, however, that do take a bit of talent and practice to pull off, and can be great for practicing certain critical shot skills at the same time. We've offered a little of both. If you enjoy trick shots, there are books on the market solely devoted to this area of the cue sports. Find one for hours of enjoyment!

The following shots must be set up according to the diagrams. Good luck!

Which Ball Goes First?—Set up the 1, 2, and 3 balls as shown in figure 5.40. To perform the shot, your cue must hit exactly in the center of the 2-ball at a medium speed. (Too soft and the shot will dribble, too hard and you'll tend to slide off one ball or another.) The 1-ball will go in one corner pocket, the 2-ball in the opposite corner, and the 3-ball in the side.

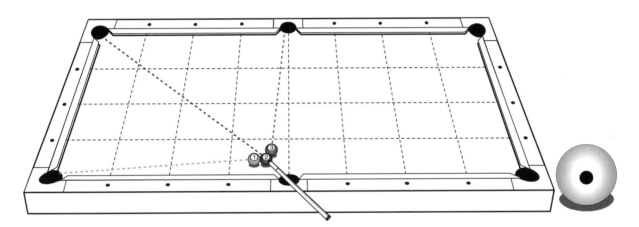

Figure 5.40   Which Ball Goes First?

The Slam Dunk—A firm, steady stroke and a direct hit are all you need to make this shot, but you'll really wow the crowds as the 8-ball pops up from the other three balls and falls into the corner. See figure 5.41. Depending on the table you're playing on, test this shot first. It's easy to fly the ball right off the table if you shoot too hard!

A Simple Proposition Shot—In the old days, gamblers made money off what were called proposition shots. Here's a simple but impressive one. Line up the 2-ball, cue ball, and 3-ball as shown in figure 5.42. The proposition was (before you set up the shot) that you could pocket the 1, 2, and 3 balls in different pockets, in order, and the cue ball would end up in the exact same place it started. The trick? Shooting the shot with the 1-ball instead of the cue ball! This shot requires a medium-hard hit, with a touch of high right english. (Hint: if the 3-ball contacts the long rail before the pocket, move the entire row of balls slightly farther from the pocket.)

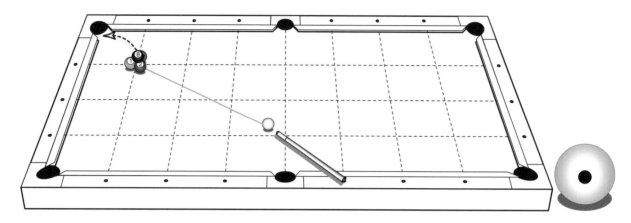

Figure 5.41   The Slam Dunk.

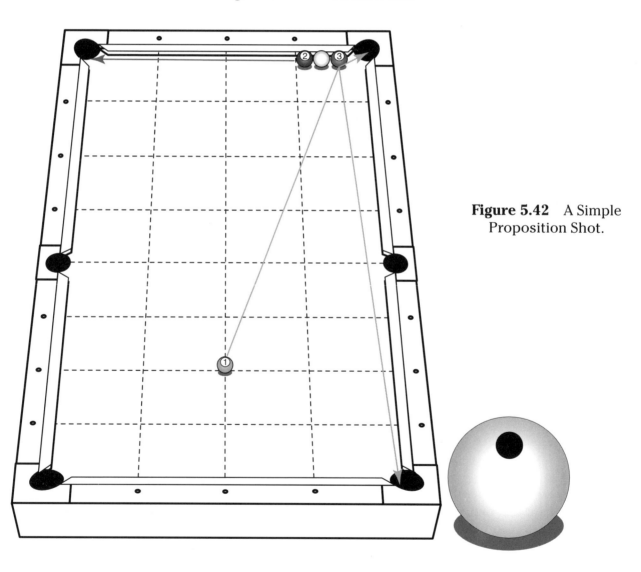

Figure 5.42   A Simple Proposition Shot.

On the Fly—This shot will demonstrate both the frozen ball carom technique and your jumping skills. Set up the 9-ball on the foot spot and the 8-ball frozen to it and aiming into the corner pocket as shown in figure 5.43. Place the cue ball on the other end of the table, and the interfering rack and balls as shown near the head spot. Using your newfound jump skills, you will jump over the interfering balls, through the upright rack, at the 8-ball, and pocket the 8-ball in the left corner pocket and the 9-ball in the right corner. Now that's impressive!

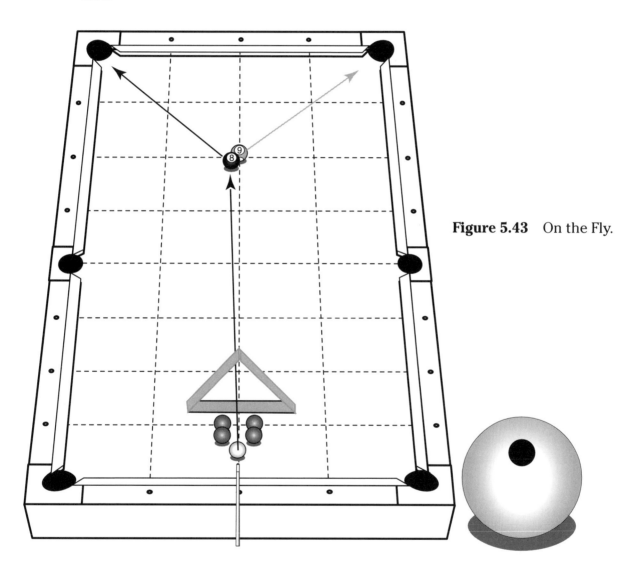

Figure 5.43 On the Fly.

Flying Higher—If you liked that one, you'll love this. Place the cue ball close to the corner pocket, as shown in figure 5.44, and the object ball you will be shooting at on top of two pieces of chalk. Then place several balls (the more you practice this shot, the more balls you will be able to place in the way) in line

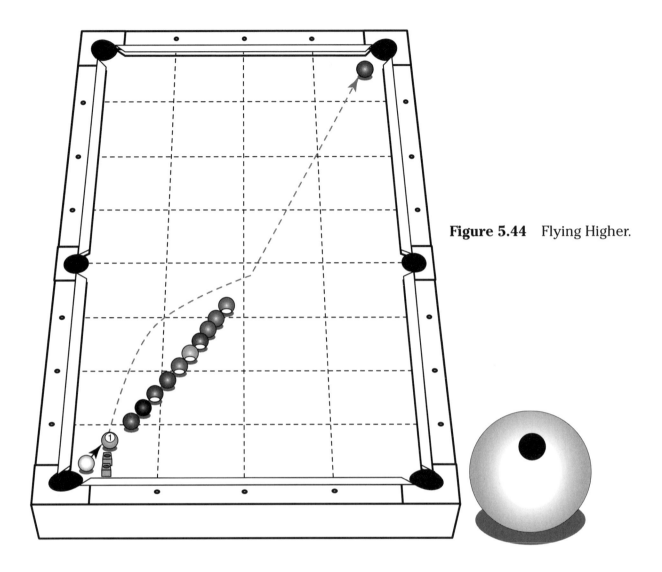

Figure 5.44   Flying Higher.

with the object ball in the corner pocket. Elevate the cue to shoot an above-center jump shot. The object ball will fly over the interfering balls to pocket your target ball in the corner!

Throw It Home—Think you've learned the throw reaction? Well, time to show it off. (Hint: a little chalk on the contact point of the cue ball and the 8-ball makes this shot so much easier!) Aim straight ahead (or toward the right corner if you're having trouble) with low left english and watch the 8-ball head straight into the right corner pocket! See figure 5.45.

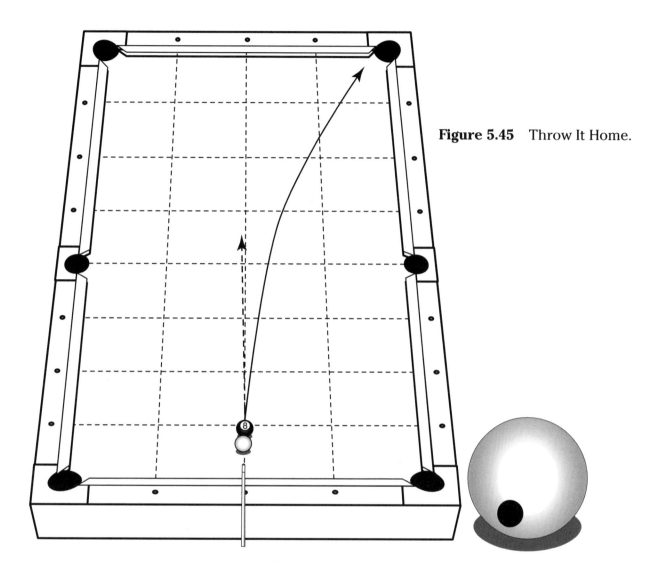

Figure 5.45 Throw It Home.

Out of the Pack and Over the Rack—Tell people you actually had to shoot this shot in a tournament once when someone thought they could interfere with you by throwing the rack up on the table. Freeze the four balls together as shown in figure 5.46 and set the rack upright on the opposite corner, with a target ball (we've used the 9-ball) near the pocket. With a center-ball hit, shoot firmly into the 1-ball. Too hard can jump the 3-ball over the intended object ball and into the pocket (which also makes a nice shot if you announce it ahead of time!). Too soft and the 2-ball won't clear the rack. You may have to move this shot up or down the rail a few inches to hit your target, depending on your equipment.

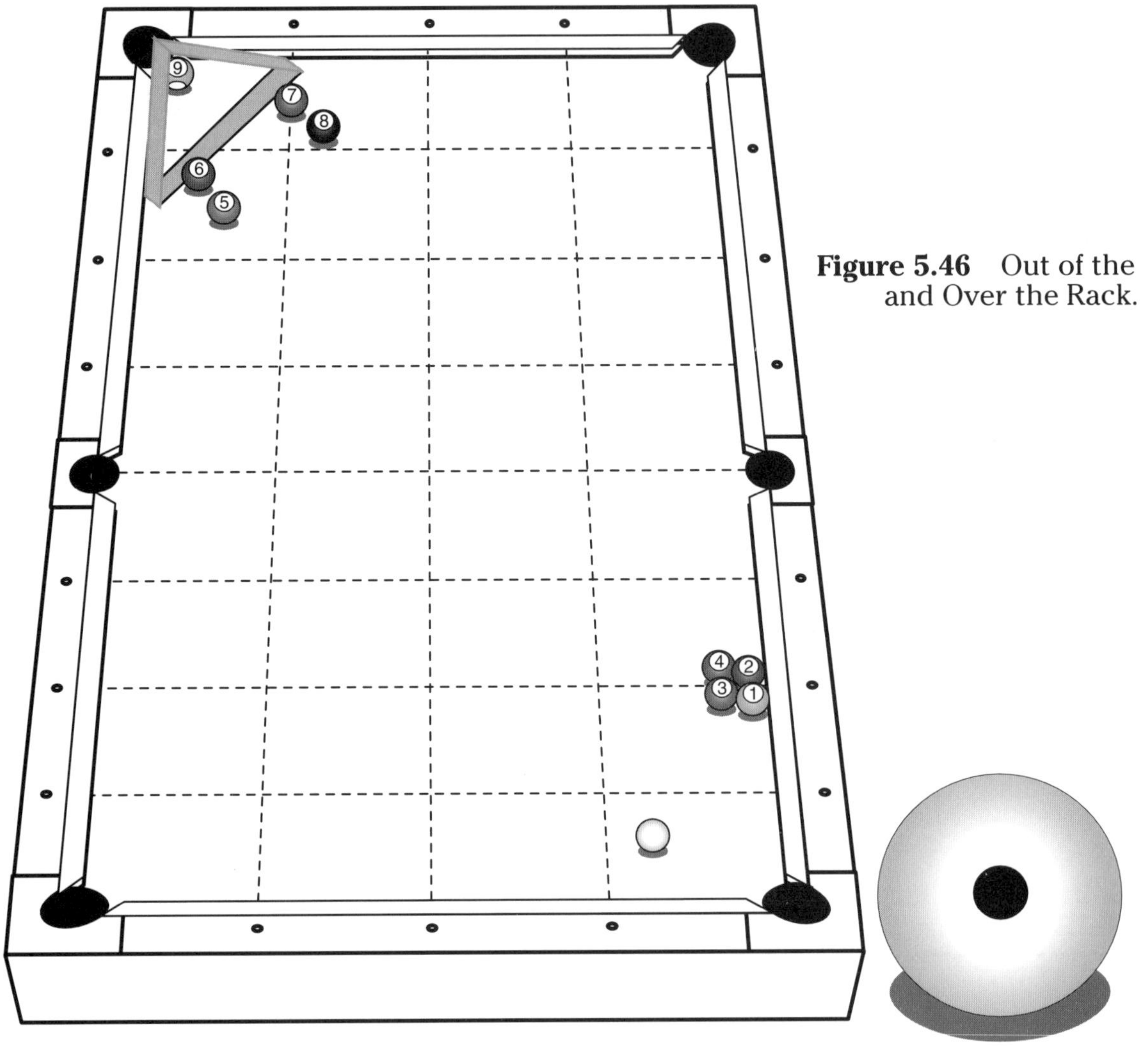

Figure 5.46 Out of the Pack and Over the Rack.

From stop shots to jump shots, all the critical shots we've discussed can greatly improve your chances of game and match wins. Nevertheless, even the best shotmakers cannot rely solely on their expertise with crowd-pleasing critical shots to win games. Up until now, we've focused on developing your skills to make a single shot. But perfect pool is really about continuing to shoot, ball after ball, while keeping your opponent in a chair! Master your single-shot skills and you're ready to turn these single-shot successes into multiple-ball runs.

Chapter 6

Pattern Plays

Now that you can move your cue ball around the table and have learned all the critical shots that can make or break your game, it's time to find out what all the fuss is about! We're ready to use all that knowledge to develop a keen position game, which requires the recognition and use of basic pattern play.

Position play, simply put, is making your first shot with the intention of placing the cue ball in an advantageous position for your next shot, with an angle to get to the shot after that, and so on. In order to be able to do this consistently, it is necessary to learn basic patterns. While every pattern cannot possibly be documented, there are many that come up again and again. By simply paying attention, in no time at all you will recognize many basic patterns. Equally important, you'll know when a good pattern does not exist, so that you can plan your strategy for a well-played safety.

THE FIVE COMMANDMENTS

Our "Five Commandments" of position play apply to all the cue sport games, and will help you to recognize more patterns and opportunities no matter which game you prefer. Keep these simple rules in mind and your pattern and position play will improve greatly in just a very short time.

1. Look Ahead

In the various games of pool you get plenty of chances to be a chess player, fortune teller, and weatherperson all wrapped into one. With proper forethought and planning, your predictions will most often come true. With poor planning your opponent will be the one predicting the outcome and pocketing the win. Pattern play is where your real power comes in, where you can control your execution of the rack and leave your opponent sitting in his chair.

No matter what your game of choice, you should always be looking at least two or three balls ahead. Using Nine Ball as an example, if you are shooting at the 1-ball to get on the 2-ball, you should already be looking to get to the 3-ball, and know what angle you need from the 3-ball to the 4-ball. As you move the cue ball from point A to point B, you're constantly working on making your next shot as easy as, or easier than, your current shot. Eventually, you will know right after the break how the entire rack should be played. You'll be able to predict where each ball should be pocketed and know what angles are required to get in position for each of these balls. If balls are tied up, you'll know whether there's an opportunity to break up clusters with early shots in the rack or whether to seek a safety.

Initially you may find this difficult to do, but don't allow yourself to become lazy in this area of your game. Whether you think you can run the rack or not, keep developing good habits in your planning. In time you'll be able to break the balls and with a glance determine which pocket you will put each ball in for the entire rack. You will find players, even a few top players, who claim to only look one ball ahead in their games. Is this possible? To an extent, it can be, but only if your cue ball control is so phenomenal that your resulting position on each shot doesn't matter. To the rest of us, planning and pattern play are imperative for a solid pool game.

In figure 6.1, we've shown you a sample five-ball runout in Nine Ball. The player broke the balls and ran up to the 5-ball with the resulting position. Test yourself—plan this run in your head. Take some paper and a pencil and mark how you would play this rack. Then take a look at the series of figures labeled 6.2 a–d, which illustrate the proper method to the runout. How did you do? Were you able to quickly analyze the rack and decide how to make all your subsequent shots simple ones?

Here's the reasoning behind the run: in figure 6.2a we're shooting the 5-ball into the left corner pocket. We have well over a foot of "breathing room" where the cue ball can land to get an angle on the 6-ball, giving us the best chance to get back down table for the 7-ball. If you play the 5-ball too weakly and end up in the shaded area, you'll have a more difficult shot on the 6-ball to get back to the 7-ball.

Fig 6.2b, then, represents the ideal area (shaded) to be on the 7-ball. Because the 7-ball is off the rail, it's even okay to wind up straight in on this ball, but an angle will make it easier and more natural to execute. This allows you an angle to make the 7-ball and bounce off the rail toward the 8-ball.

The ideal area for your position on the 8-ball is shown in figure 6.2c. This position, close to the center of the table, will allow you to use the right long rail to bounce back across table towards the 9-ball. By now you should begin to see how easy it is to run a table if you look ahead and plan proper angles in advance.

Finally, in figure 6.2d, note where your cue ball, after pocketing the 8-ball, can cross over the table into the shaded ideal area for an easy shot on the 9-ball. Shoot the 8-ball in the corner with a bit of low right spin. Though you are crossing over the table, this is a safe shot as long as you don't scratch in the side pocket. Plan to have your cue ball arrive below the side pocket, as this is an area where your margin for error is much greater.

If you didn't do so well on this first exercise, read on! Your errors may have resulted from not knowing the rest of the Five Commandments.

2. Be on the Correct Side

Suppose you're shooting at the 1-ball to get on the 2-ball and then the 3-ball. You make the 1-ball, and have a shot on the 2-ball, but you ended up on the opposite side of where you planned to be on the 2-ball. Uh oh! Now there's no way to get to the 3-ball without doing something difficult or unusual.

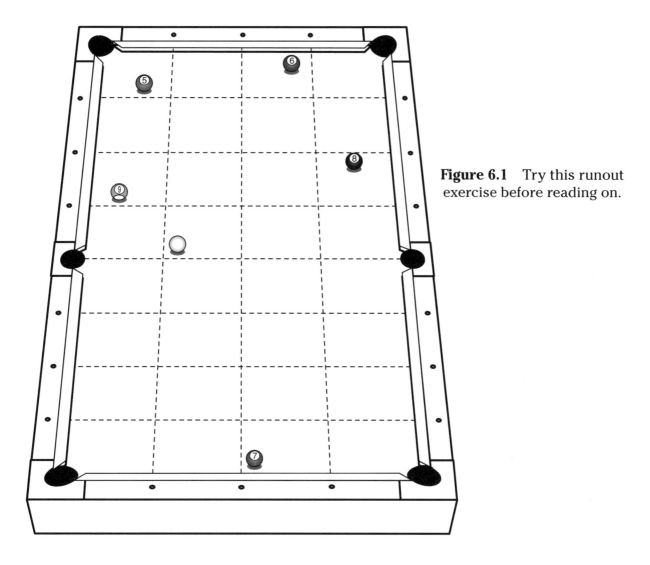

Figure 6.1 Try this runout exercise before reading on.

You're bound to hear players talk about having gotten on the wrong side of a ball. If you get on the wrong side of any ball early in the rack, it can easily throw off your position play for the remainder of the game. There's always a right side and a wrong side to be on when you are playing position, except in those rare instances when you can play all your remaining balls straight in with stop shots! By not thinking out the rack ahead of time, too many otherwise good players run the 1-ball through the 6-ball, but have the wrong angle when they get to the 7, 8, or 9 ball. They've gotten on the wrong side of the ball and now have to do something drastic to obtain position and get back in line for the remainder of the rack. This most often results in missing the ball, or getting out of position and giving up the last two or three balls to their opponent.

In figure 6.3, we've illustrated a typical situation where some poor player has gotten on the wrong side of the 8-ball! Badly calculated position was played from the 7-ball to the 8-ball, and what's left is a nasty angle going away from the 9-ball. With the balls in this position, you really have to come up with a super stroke shot to get the cue ball to go around the table to get in position for any kind of shot on the 9-ball. By contrast, if the cue ball were anywhere in the shaded area, representing

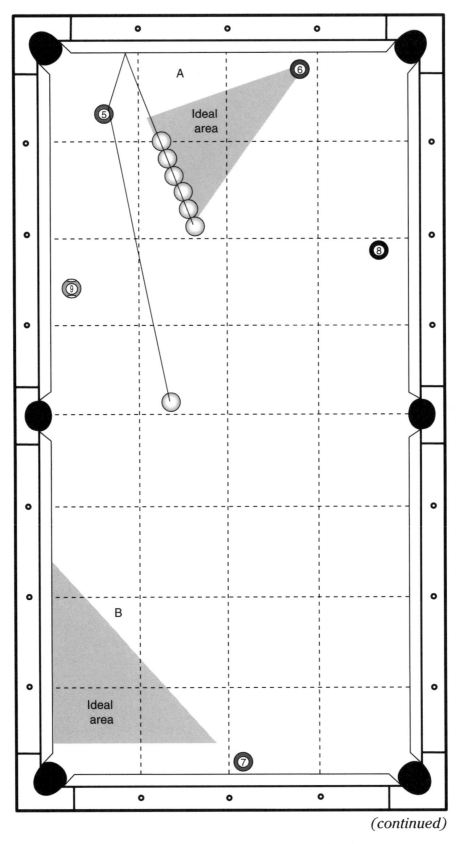

(continued)

Figure 6.2   Here's the best (and simplest) way
to achieve the runout.

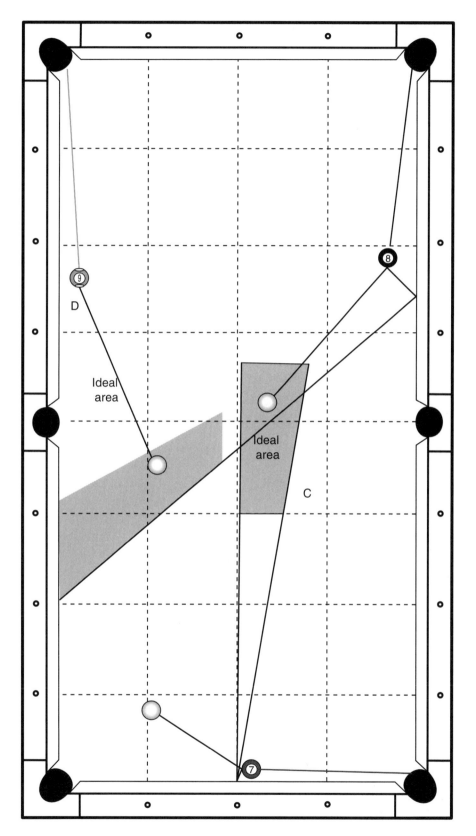

Figure 6.2   *(continued)*

the correct side, you could simply float the cue ball down to the other shaded area for a relatively easy shot on the 9-ball. And, just in case you're still not a believer in this commandment, figure 6.4 illustrates another case of ending up with the wrong angle. You're shooting the 7-ball and trying to get position on the 9-ball. Due to your poor resulting cue ball position, you'll have to go three rails to get position on that 9-ball. Even worse, you now have a greater chance of scratching, since you're turning the cue ball loose and running it around the table another 20 feet! The farther you have to make your cue ball travel, the more control you lose. That's really a shame, since the shaded area represents the best (and vast) area where you could have planned to arrive on the 7-ball for an easy position play to the 9-ball.

3. Don't Cross the Line

The line we're referring to is the line from the pocket through the object ball and extended out across the table, as shown in figure 6.5. As you'll note in this shot, even after the cue ball crosses the line of the 9-ball to the pocket (but not until after contacting the rail), you have a makable shot at the 9-ball, with a much greater margin of position than if you were to try and go back and forth across the table. When the cue ball has to cross over this line too soon in order for you to get position on the shot, it means you're undoubtedly sending the cue ball back and forth across the table to get there. Your speed control on the cue ball must be excellent for you to be able to control that shot. If you think you have no choice but to cross over the line, look for another option. In figure 6.6, the obvious shot on the 3-ball results in crossing over the line to get on the 4-ball, as shown by line a. Instead, use the natural two-rail shot option to go *away from* the line of the 4-ball, as illustrated by line b.

As you plan the path to your next object ball, you will always be looking for a path *to* the angle you want on that object ball or *away from* the angle you want on that object ball. When you go away or toward the line, your margin for error can be measured in feet. Conversely, crossing over the line can cause a margin of error measured in inches. Figure 6.7 shows two possible ways to get on the 2-ball from the 1-ball. But, knowing the angle you want on the 2-ball to get to the 3-ball, shot A is the way to go; you are again coming into the angle of the shot you want on the 2-ball. Your margin for error is indicated by the entire line to the 1-ball. In shot B, you are crossing over that angle, with your error zone indicated by the broken line. Notice how much smaller your position zone is when you cross over the line.

Heading into or away from the angle obviously gives you the best chance to be in line for your next shot. Even if your speed control is off a little one day, your position play won't suffer as much. Optimally, on each shot, you would like to be no closer than a foot away from your next object ball, and no farther than two feet away. And, it's easier to control speed for position play on the next shot if you always have a 45-degree angle or less on your current shot. If you can achieve this, you are playing perfect pool.

Sometimes the lay of the table won't allow you to do that, especially when you aren't left with an angle on your first shot at the table. When you get straight in on a ball, your options will be fewer. You can go forward, but obviously not too far without scratching. You also can go backward. It may be possible to cheat the pocket or spin the ball. However, now your chance of making the ball has decreased

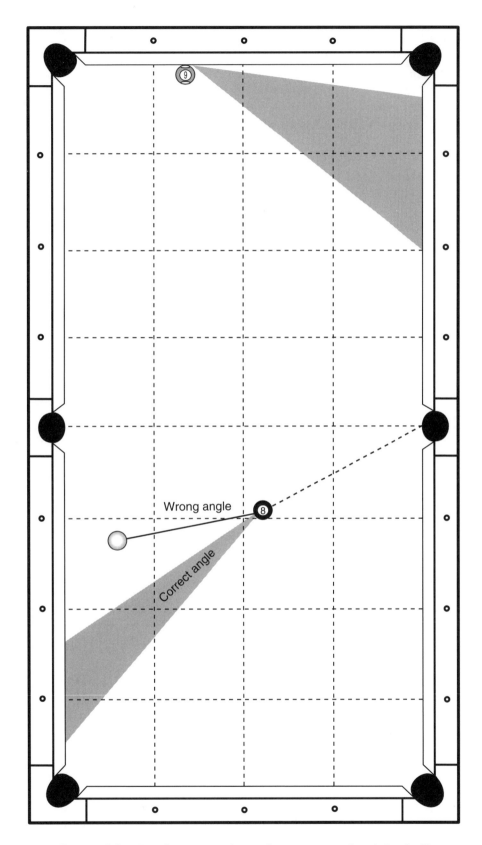

Figure 6.3 Don't get stuck on the wrong side of the ball.

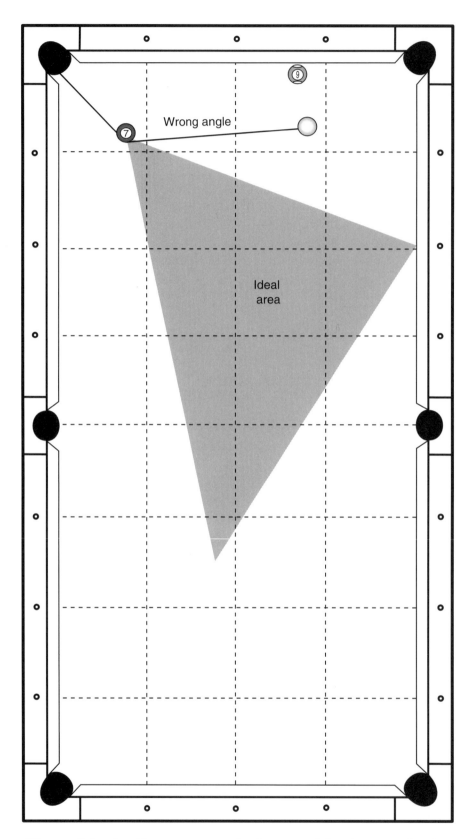

Figure 6.4 Another wrong angle shot, resulting in a tough trip to the 9-ball.

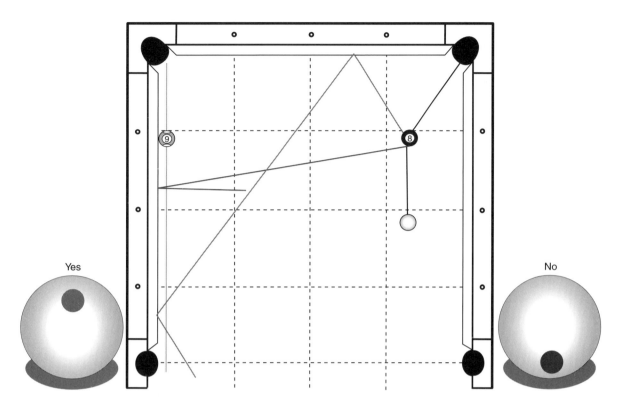

Figure 6.5 The line you don't want to cross!

75 percent or more. This is because any form of sidespin on a straight-in shot is transferred to the object ball, which has a tendency to bounce around the pocket and hang there. In the case of the straight-in shot, know the range of forward and backward motion and what can bring you into the best range for either a makable shot or a safety maneuver on your next object ball.

4. Let the Table Be Your Guide

The lay of the table will regularly dictate patterns to you, especially if the balls are wide open. The way in which the balls lie will tell you how to plan your attack. Your goal is to move the balls as little as possible. Even if you have a cluster that you can break up early in the rack, you'll want to move these only a little. In this way, the lay of the table will remain similar to how you began, which means less revision of your plans in the middle of the rack. If the rack presents several shots that you must travel back and forth down the table for, this tells you that your cue ball will be traveling a lot in this rack. You will immediately look for patterns up and down the table, using the rails to control your speed. The longer the distance from shot to shot, the easier it is to control your speed using the rails. Look to go one rail instead of none, or two rails instead of one, so long as you can still head into or away from the angle of your next shot.

If most of your balls are grouped together at one end of the table, your plan will automatically adjust to stop shots and very little movement of the cue ball. Staying on the correct side of subsequent balls will become critical. The wrong side could result in forcing you to send your cue ball all the way around the table to get

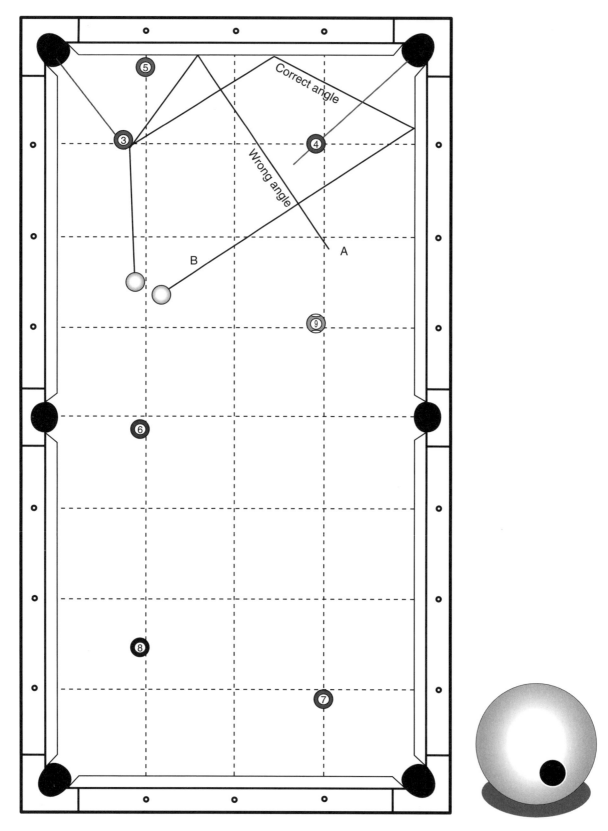

Figure 6.6 The better option for position without crossing over the line.

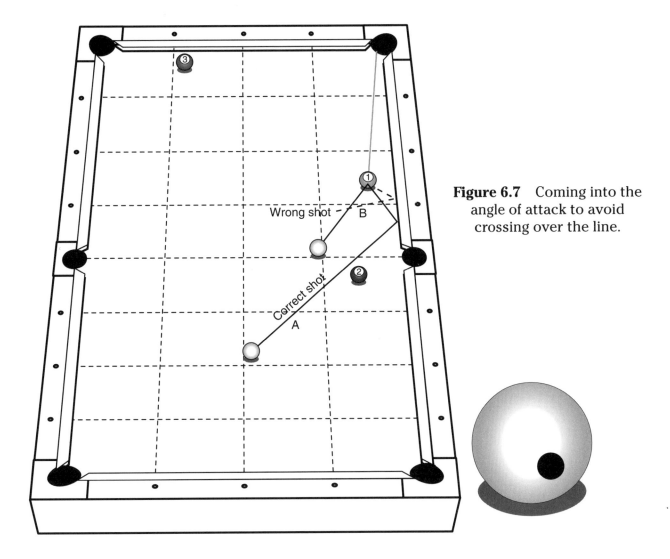

Figure 6.7 Coming into the angle of attack to avoid crossing over the line.

back to your next shot. If several balls in the rack are clustered, with very little chance of a breakout, the lay of this table indicates a safety.

In other words, don't fight what the table is trying to tell you. In figure 6.8, you can see that you are straight in on the 4-ball. You could try to cheat the pocket, heading into the short rail, then the long rail, and coming down to try breaking up the 5-6 cluster. Let's face it, though—that's tough enough to explain, let alone shoot, even for a pro. The table offers you another option. The most prudent play stops the cue ball after contact with the 4-ball. Then you can simply shoot the 5-ball as a stop shot or roll up slightly to allow your cue ball to freeze to the 6-ball, letting your opponent kick at the 5-ball. If you ignore what each table situation tells you and go for the crazy breakout, or take flyers at shots because you didn't plan closer position, you've lost the advantage of the table being your ally. Your opponent will be the one who listens and wins.

The size of the table will immediately affect the lay of the balls and thus dictate different patterns and strategies. With the smaller bar tables (3½ by 7), less surface area means less room to work. You're better off playing pinpoint position, and must have a definite destination in mind before you actually execute the shot. Bigger tables and fewer balls allow the use of more area position play. Complicating

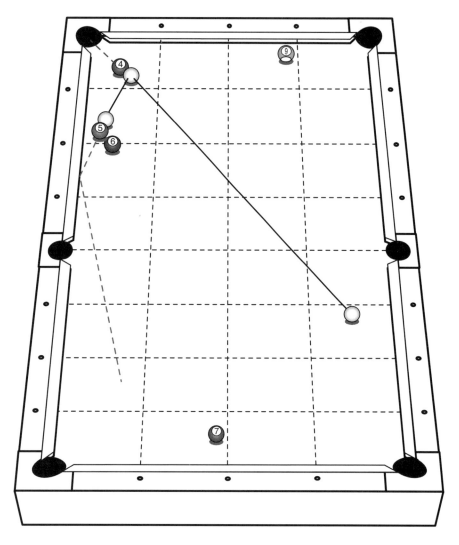

Figure 6.8 Every table tells a story; don't fight what the table is telling you.

the size of the bar table is the game of choice usually played on this table— most often Eight Ball in league play, which involves the use of all 15 balls. This will result in more clusters and more shots that are difficult to get at, which will dictate not only pinpoint position play, but stealth and planning in your execution.

5. Think Backward

This commandment works especially well in the games of Eight Ball, Nine Ball, and Straight Pool. In Eight Ball and Nine Ball, you begin with the game-winning ball (the 8 or 9). In Straight Pool (14.1), you begin with the shot you want left on the table as your break shot for the next rack to continue your run. Thinking backward is not a commandment that will work well in the game of One Pocket, since you may never know which ball will be your game ball. (The most manageable way to play your patterns in One Pocket is to think three balls ahead!)

Thinking backward is rather like working a crossword puzzle. You complete the words you know first, using them as clues to the next words. In the same fashion, by beginning with the last ball you intend to pocket, you pick the pocket it will go in, and proceed from there.

Nine Ball is the simplest game in which to think backward, since you know every ball you need to make and in what order. You'll never need to decide which ball to play first, only how to play the ball to get to the next ball, right up to the 9-ball. But at the same time, thinking backward is critical because you don't have the luxury of changing your mind about which ball to shoot first, as you may do in Eight Ball or Straight Pool.

In figure 6.9 your opponent has been kind enough to miss and leave you a possible runout. Of course, it becomes a probable runout if you first establish where you want to pocket the 9-ball. Looking at the lay of the table, you decide to pocket the 9-ball in the left corner pocket. So, how will you get from the 8-ball to the 9-ball? Then, how will you get from the 7-ball to the 8-ball? Finally, where must you go from the 6-ball to be on the 7-ball? As you look at these balls, you should realize that you must begin by shooting the 6-ball in the upper-left corner. Draw the cue ball off the long rail, attempting to get straight in on the 7-ball in the side. Shoot the 7-ball as a stop shot; then shoot the 8-ball in the corner and allow the cue ball to go three (or four rails). The biggest mistake players make in a runout like this is not getting on the 8-ball correctly to have the easiest and most natural path back

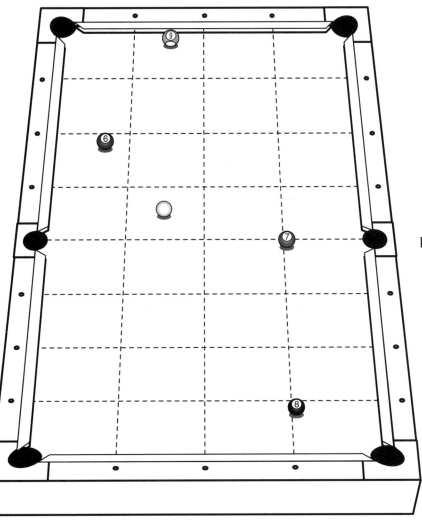

Figure 6.9 Thinking backward through the rack, beginning with the 9-ball.

to the 9-ball. It is critical in the game of Nine Ball to be able to play the correct patterns as they come up in game situations.

Thinking backward in the game of Eight Ball requires you to pick the pocket for the 8-ball, then decide how you will manage the trouble balls on the table, then pick a key ball (the ball before the 8-ball) and work backward from there. This may often present a slightly more difficult first shot, but it will be to your advantage to take the tougher shot first in order to run the rack the right way. Figure 6.10 illustrates this. Your opponent missed her last ball before the 8-ball (the 10-ball). She did you a big favor in the process by removing all the clutter of her own group of balls. As you can see, the 8-ball is in a relatively difficult position near the left side rail. Now you need to make a pattern-play decision. You have a few key balls to choose from—the 7, 3, or 4 ball. We'd opt for the 4-ball in the side, because this will allow you to work from one end of the table to the other, and give you the easiest route for a resulting easy shot on the 8-ball. Begin with a stop shot on the 1-ball, which will leave you fine for the 5-ball. You'll want to come off the rail for the 6-ball, and when shooting the 6-ball, bring it out for the 7-ball. You shoot the 7-ball, and then the 3-ball, bringing the cue ball up the table for a straight-in or slight

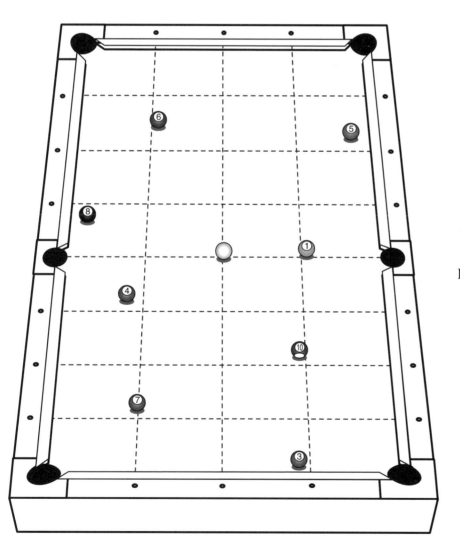

Figure 6.10 Thinking backward is very important in the game of Eight Ball.

angle shot on the 4-ball. A simple shot on the 4-ball will result in another simple shot on the game ball!

The run was made easy by first looking at the 8-ball, then determining your best key ball to the 8-ball (the 4-ball), and then finding the least difficult way to click off the other balls, slowly working your way to the bottom end of the table.

Figure 6.11 illustrates how you might manage a Straight Pool run, again by thinking backward. There are six balls remaining on the table. Unlike Eight Ball or Nine Ball, where you always know the 8-ball or 9-ball will be your game ball, in Straight Pool you must choose which ball will allow you a break into the next rack. We've shown two balls that would make good break shots here—the 5 and the 14. Either will work fine, but if you have this luxury, know that this is where being right- or left-handed can come into play. If you're left-handed, the best ball for your break shot would be the 14. Right-handed players will be more comfortable shooting the 5-ball. If you are left-handed, you'll use the 9-ball as your key ball for the 14 break ball. If right-handed, you'll use the 2-ball as your key ball to the 5-ball.

Continuing to work backward from here, you would shoot either the 1-ball or the 12-ball. Let's assume the player running this rack is right-handed. In this case

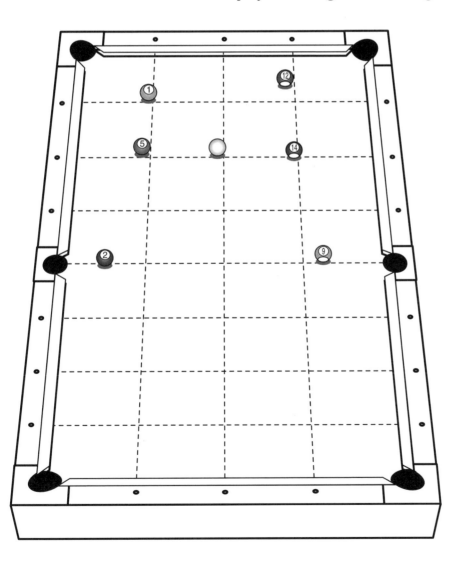

Figure 6.11 Thinking backward in a Straight Pool runout.

he begins with the 12-ball, bringing the cue ball back to the center of the table for a stop shot on the 14-ball. This will allow a shot on the 1-ball, playing the cue ball off the long rail for the 9-ball in the side. Again, a stop shot for another stop shot on the 2-ball in the other side, and you're left with a perfect angle to pocket the 5-ball. Send the cue ball into the next rack of 14 balls and continue the run!

COMMON PLAYING PATTERNS

At a certain point in your game, pocketing balls becomes second nature. This is when your position play will flourish. When you don't have to concentrate so much on just making the ball, you can focus on where your cue ball is headed. This is when patterns, position play, and speed of the cue ball will really begin to come into play.

As your pool game develops, you'll notice different tracks for one- and two-rail position—for example, the cue ball coming off the object ball, into the short rail, then into the long rail and back into the middle of the table. As you take note of these tracks, you'll use them more and more as time goes on. Your use of patterns and position play will depend, to some extent, on whether you are right- or left-handed. For instance, a cue ball on the upper-right side of the table presents a better shot for the left-handed player. A right-handed person likes the left side of the table; therefore, they will play different patterns than left-handed players.

Be aware of a couple of pitfalls that could mar your progress. First, too many players begin playing poor patterns early, but they win a game or two, and mistakenly continue to believe they executed the rack correctly. This will hurt you down the road. You'll remember that the incorrect pattern worked and you'll think it's going to happen again and again. When it doesn't, you won't know why.

The second pitfall arises if you become inflexible in your pattern play. You have to be willing, when necessary, to change your mind. Say you're playing Nine Ball, and you have a good shot on the 1-ball. No balls are tied up. You plan your runout, run to the 4-ball, and discover that you're out of line on the 4-ball. At this point, you have to be ready to change your pattern plan, since you can't get to where you want to be on the 5-ball. Take advantage of the fact that you are the player still at the table, and make a new plan. Start over. There's no point in doing all the work and giving the win to your opponent because you were caught in one particular pattern and were unwilling to do what had to be done to regroup!

The following information will give you a bit more insight on how to develop your knowledge and pattern-play skills in four of the most popular games: Nine Ball, Eight Ball, Straight Pool, and One Pocket.

Nine Ball

In Nine Ball, because you are required to hit and/or pocket the balls in connect-the-dot order, all your decisions as to which ball to make next are made for you. Once you break the balls, you will always plan your entire rack at the moment the balls have stopped rolling. True, balls may be tied up, in which case you'll plan a safety, or you may get out of line at some point and have to replan your strategy. Regardless, always start with a plan that will take you as far through the rack as you are able to or want to go.

While patterns are endless in every game, your Nine Ball game, because you get used to the order of pocketing the balls, will present typical patterns that connect over and over again. If you have a good memory for situations that have come up in the past, your pattern play will pick up speed in leaps and bounds. It won't be long before your mind already knows what to do and you realize that a particular situation has come up before. The more you pay attention to Nine Ball patterns, the more automatic your response will be to the table layout in front of you.

While you may be able to get away with straight-in or relatively straight-in shots early in the rack of a Nine Ball game, having angles at the end of the rack are crucial to running out consistently. This is always where less-experienced players will fall down in Nine Ball. They have no problem with the first five or six balls on the table, but are suddenly out of line for the remainder of the rack.

In figure 6.12, you are left with the remainder of a Nine Ball rack. You are presented with a straight-in shot on the 4-ball. Using your five commandments, what would be the best and most common way to play this rack? Begin by asking yourself how to get from the 8-ball to the 9-ball. Play the rack yourself to see what you come up with, then try this. Shoot the 4-ball with draw, attempting to get straight in on the 5-ball in the side pocket. Shoot the 5-ball, and roll the cue ball up just a bit to get straight in on the 6-ball. Play the 6-ball with draw on the cue ball, back into the long rail on the left side of the table. This gives you a natural angle on the 8-ball (the 7-ball was pocketed earlier in the game) to come around the length of the table with a nice, easy stroke, leaving you a makable shot on the 9-ball in the lower-right corner pocket. If you had gotten straight in on the 8-ball, you'd be in a tougher position to make the 9-ball. You could end up on the other side of the 8-ball and draw the ball down table, but this is a tougher shot, and you want the easiest shots toward the end of your rack.

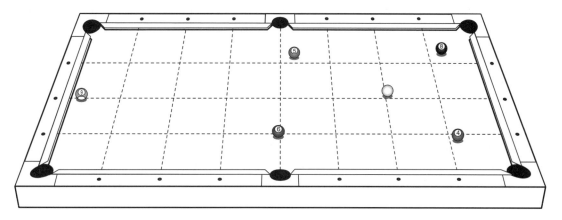

Figure 6.12   Which is the best way to play this rack?

The other big element to Nine Ball pattern play is recognizing key balls in the rack. Figure 6.13 offers a simple example of this. Your opponent has broken the balls without pocketing a ball and has left you a great runout opportunity. In fact, this pattern is so simple that the cue ball doesn't even have to hit a rail, but let's play it correctly. Begin with a stop shot on the 1-ball. Pocket the 2-ball and allow the cue ball to swing off the long rail on the right side for a straight-in shot on the 3-ball. This will allow you to roll up slightly for another straight-in shot on the

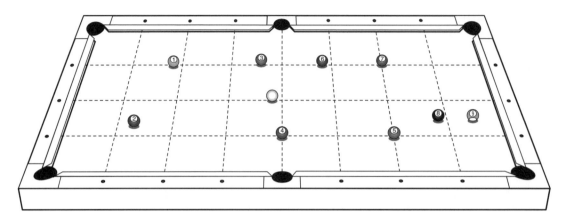

Figure 6.13 Recognizing the key ball in any rack
takes a bit of practice.

4-ball in the opposite side. Stop the cue ball, and shoot the 5-ball in the corner. Stop again, and shoot the 6-ball in the side. Stop again, and shoot the 7-ball in the corner. Depending on exactly where your cue ball landed after you pocketed the 7-ball, you have two options on the 8-ball to get position on the 9-ball. You can either allow the cue ball to contact the long rail on the right side and come back for the 9-ball in the same corner pocket you just made the 8-ball (the right corner), or roll up for the 9-ball in the left corner pocket.

Did you recognize the key shot in the rack? Probably the toughest part of this rack is to watch for being on the correct side of the 3-ball. If you get on the wrong side of the 3-ball, you may need to change your plan, since it will be impossible to just roll up for a stop shot on the 4-ball, and consequently the 5, 6, and 7 balls! It pays to keep your attention on this type of pattern, as you can see just how easy a rack can be with the proper angle on the key ball, and how difficult it will be without the proper angle.

In figure 6.14, you actually have two key shots. You'll need the correct angle on the 6-ball to get to the 7-ball, and the correct angle on the 7-ball to get to the 8-ball. Think ahead! When shooting at the 4-ball, make absolutely sure to get on the 5-ball with a proper angle on the 6-ball. This way, you can roll up for a shot on the 7-ball, and roll up again for a shot on the 8-ball. From here, it's conceivable that the 9-ball can be made in any of the six pockets, but make sure you pick one *before* you pocket the 8-ball. Never make the mistake of not having a destination for the cue ball. Always remember to allow yourself correct position on the key balls in each rack, as they will be crucial to your successful execution of runout patterns.

The best way to begin seeing more common patterns in Nine Ball is to practice first with just the 8 and 9 balls. Throw them out on the table, and make the 8-ball to get shape on the 9-ball. Then add the 7-ball. Shoot the 7-ball to get an angle on the 8-ball to get to the 9-ball. Then add the 6, 5, 4, and so on. This forces you to develop a keener insight into what angles are necessary and useful, what key shots will make or break a rack, and how to plan your pattern from the very beginning.

Eight Ball

Figuring out your pattern in a game of Eight Ball will present a few more challenges than in Nine Ball, where at least you know which ball you must shoot to hit! On the

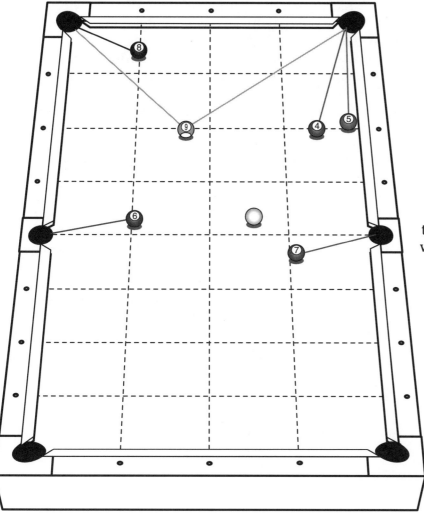

Figure 6.14 In this rack, there are two key shots that will get you on the right side of each ball in the rack.

other hand, in Eight Ball you will have options for shots that you won't have in Nine Ball, giving you a bit more latitude in your pattern selection. As a result, a great deal more strategy is involved in Eight Ball. You may have a choice of six or seven balls of your group (stripes or solids) to shoot at, but there is always the one right shot that will lead to the most productive runout, breakout, or eventual safety attempt.

Pattern play in Eight Ball is also a matter of timing—of knowing when to run out. This is where thinking backward plays heavily. You'll more readily know when you have a pattern to work with, or if you will need to play safe, break out a cluster, or create trouble balls for your opponent before continuing your run.

Begin your Eight Ball rack by figuring out where you want to play the 8-ball. Is it in a good spot, or tied up? In the center of the table, or on a rail? Then pick your key ball that will get you to this ball. If there are trouble balls, you'll try to get to those balls as soon as possible, but exercise caution in this area. You're not trying to hit the clustered balls too hard. If you head into them with too much force, you'll likely end up creating a cluster somewhere else on the table. Instead, your plan will be to open them up to have a shot at each of the balls in the cluster.

Smart Eight Ball players will also attempt to have a "safety ball" positioned near a pocket or hung in the pocket. Even with a great breakout plan, sometimes the unexpected can happen. The balls can freeze up against each other or the cue ball gets stuck between them. With a safety ball, once you send the cue ball into the cluster, a ball located near the pocket will give you something to shoot at if you didn't end up with a practical shot resulting from the cluster you broke up.

Let's take a look at a couple of Eight Ball racks that demonstrate these skills. In figure 6.15, you have solids. The 4-ball is tied up with the 13 and 14 balls in your opponent's group of balls, but you are still in a fine position for the runout. Do not shoot the 3-ball or the 5-ball first, even though they are attractive shots at first glance! Instead, you'll want to shoot the 6-ball in the side pocket. With this shot you have a natural angle on the 6-ball to go into the cluster. Remember, don't head into the cluster with too much force, as this can result in other clusters on the table. The real advantage of this table layout is the fact that you have two safety balls, the 3-ball and the 5-ball. Should you get stuck somewhere in the cluster, you will still have a shot at one of these balls. The remainder of your runout will then depend on the resulting position of your 4-ball. Give this one a try and see what works for you.

Figure 6.16 illustrates an Eight Ball table layout in which your opponent, despite a powerful break shot, has pocketed nothing, leaving you with an open table.

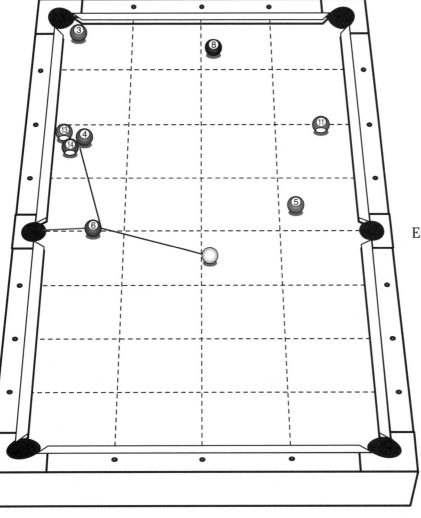

Figure 6.15 Running an Eight Ball break with the use of safety balls.

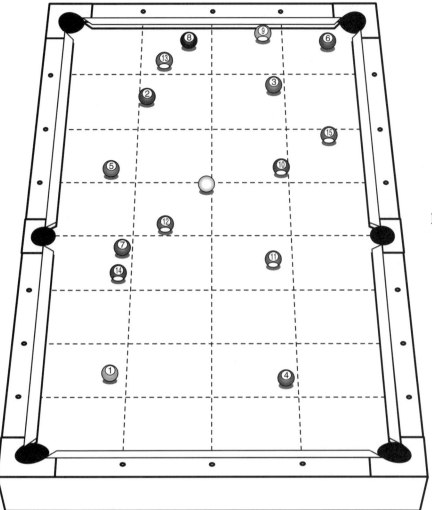

Figure 6.16 Which group would you choose in this Eight Ball rack?

This means you have the luxury of choosing whether you would rather play the solids or stripes. The cue ball has been left in a most advantageous position in the center of the table. Which group do you choose?

To decide, you must establish a pattern before you shoot your first shot. Are there any problem areas on the table? You should first notice that the 15-ball is tied up for the upper-right corner pocket because of the impeding 6-ball. Worse, the 9-ball cannot be made in either corner, with the 6-ball blocking the right side and the 8-ball blocking the left. Since you can't see the 9-ball in any pocket, your most prudent move is to take the solids.

If you plan to run this rack, take the 6-ball early, in order to be able to pocket the 3-ball in the same pocket later. If you don't plan to run out, leave the 6-ball as a blocker for the 15 and 9 balls, creating problem areas for your opponent.

Let's assume you do plan to run out. The pattern is relatively simple: pocket the 2-ball, then the 6-ball, and swing down table between the 6-ball and the rail to shoot the 1-ball in the corner. Then play the 4-ball in the other corner, and swing up to shoot the 7-ball straight in the side. This will give you a straight-in 5-ball in the corner, followed by the 3-ball in the other corner. When you play the 3-ball, use follow on the cue ball to roll up for a shot on the 8-ball in the left corner.

What happens if you absolutely cannot run out? Figure 6.17 illustrates a rack that cannot be run. Though it's unlikely that you will face a rack quite this tough, you will face racks with two or three clusters involving your group of balls. This is when it's prudent to plan a safety pattern. The best safety in this particular diagram is to send the cue ball into the 5-ball (allowing either the 5-ball or the cue ball to contact the cushion for a **legal hit**). With a gentle hit, this shot will still loosen the 15-ball from this cluster, while at the same time leaving no good shot at either group of balls. Your opponent will be forced to counter with a safety of his own.

Keep in mind that when you are forced to plan a safety or series of safeties, it helps to slowly break up clusters with each subsequent shot. In this way, you've given your safety play a plan, continuing to maneuver the object balls into a favorable position for the eventuality of an offensive opportunity.

If your opponent is knowledgeable about the game, you can assume he will be doing the same things, with the same intentions. In this case, you will most likely engage in a safety battle in which the more patient player will have the edge. Don't take a risky shot simply out of boredom or a misconception that you're not accomplishing anything proactive in the game. Continue to plan your eventual pattern and strategy. Far too many games are lost because a player tires of what

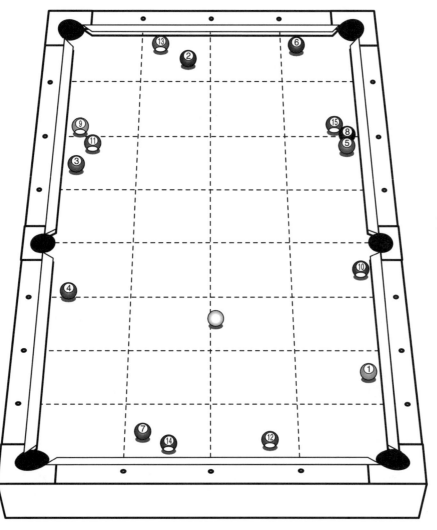

Figure 6.17   This rack is not likely to be run; look for an alternative.

When in Doubt, Head for the Center of the Table!

No matter how well developed your pattern play game becomes, there will be occasions when you're just not sure where to head next, or where what you perceive as ideal position now may present potential danger a few shots down the road. When in doubt, head for the center of the table!

As the games of Nine Ball and Eight Ball have evolved over the years, it has become crucial that you hit the correct ball on the table first, or suffer the consequences of the one-foul rules and give your opponent ball in hand. In Nine Ball you must always hit the lowest numbered ball, driving it to a rail, or hit the ball and drive the cue ball to a rail. In Eight Ball, you must always hit a ball from your group of balls (stripes or solids), there again making a legal shot, safety, or pocketing a ball by hitting your ball first and then pocketing one of your opponent's balls.

Whenever you're in trouble, think you're in trouble, or just plain don't know what to do next, the best place to have your cue ball arrive is at or near the center of the table. From the center you will always have more avenues and paths available from the cue ball to other object balls and better access to a wider array of shots on the table.

From the center of the table you'll naturally have a shorter shot. What you're basically doing is cutting the table in half. For example, say you're playing on a 4¹/₂ by 9 table. With the cue ball in the center of the table, your next shot will never be more than 4¹/₂ feet away, making it much easier to see and hit your next object ball. If you end up with a straight-in shot, you are close enough to the ball to have a better chance at cheating the pocket and creating an angle for your next shot. This means you won't have to worry as much about using the rake or stretching for a shot. Being closer to the ball means you will probably be able to assume your normal stance and use your normal bridge. Keeping the cue ball in the center of the table also automatically avoids the difficulty of being frozen on any rails, which allows you to retain control of the full range of draw, follow, and english options.

But the list of benefits doesn't stop there! Shooting from the table center also gives you an unlimited number of options to hit the ball if you're playing safe. Again, you are able to use any english in your repertoire, it's easier to see the actual shot and the hit, and with the table cut in half it's much easier to control the cue ball. If you're stuck with a bank or a kick, your options are still greater from this position.

Best of all, learning to maneuver your cue ball to the table center is an easy and fun way to practice. Begin by placing the cue ball in the center of table. Throw the remaining balls in the rack (9 if you are practicing Nine Ball, 15 if you are honing your Eight Ball or Rotation skills) and shoot every shot with the intention of having your cue ball arrive back in the middle of the table. This exercise will allow you to work on your use of english and speed control and give you a feeling of real power and control.

This is also a good exercise for working on your kicks and banks, since these critical shots are much easier to develop and practice from shorter distances. Beginning the same way, attempt first to bank every ball in from the table center—again, trying to get your cue ball back to center. This will help you to focus not only on your banking skills, but also on your cue ball control. (The same goes for kicking at balls, though you won't be able to bring the cue ball back to center as often, especially with softer kicks.) By "shortening the table," banks and kicks that you previously thought mysterious and intangible will suddenly become well within your reach!

seems like an interminable waiting game. And remember this: even the most vicious of predators must sometimes patiently wait for the right time and place before pouncing on their victims!

Straight Pool

The first rule of basic pattern play in Straight Pool is to try and cut your Straight Pool game down to a "half table" game. This simply means that you will do your best to play on the upper half of the table, keeping all the object balls in this area. Use the upper-left and upper-right corner pockets, along with the side pockets, as your destinations for all or most of the object balls in your run. Avoid the two bottom corner pockets as much as possible. These pockets translate to longer shots and less cue ball control. You'll find that top Straight Pool players very seldom use the lower corner pockets—perhaps once or twice in a 100-ball run.

The other rule to remember is to open up "the pack" (the rack of 14 or 15 balls) a little at a time. Your goal will be to make a ball and break out a ball or two before the next shot. Visualize continually whittling away at the rack and slowly spreading it open bit by bit, like you'd work a piece of clay or dough from a small lump to a larger, more flexible shape. In the same way, your rack will slowly take on a more manageable shape, allowing you to continue your run and position an eventual break ball. Slow and steady rack management will keep the balls toward the upper end of the table. This will also leave a bit more work for your opponent should you miss, by not having the balls spread wide open.

Figure 6.18 shows you a typical rack that has been broken open and spread out a little. You'll want to open the balls a bit more as you continue your run. To begin this tactic, shoot the 1-ball in the upper-left corner pocket with low right english. This will bring the cue ball in between the 7 and 5 balls. The low right english will spin the cue ball to a point where it will throw the 7-ball and 5-ball away from the cue ball, freeing it up for another shot. This is a very good play, since you have a safety ball. Your safety ball in this case is the 6-ball in the side. It helps to have a safety ball in Straight Pool as well, since sometimes your careful planning can still result in the cue ball getting too close to other balls in the pack and leaving you very little in the way of shot selection.

As you practice your Straight Pool patterns, breaking up racks and setting up safety balls and break shots, you'll want to follow a certain order of attack that has served Straight Pool players well throughout the generations. You'll first want to clear the pockets on the lower end of the table, more specifically the corner pockets. If there are balls lying at or near the pockets, play them first, clearing the path for other balls closer to the center of the table to be pocketed. Then concentrate on breaking open troublesome clusters. If they can't be broken apart immediately, have a plan for when they will be attacked. Third, try to clear off balls that have gotten positioned near the rails. Unlike in Nine Ball or Eight Ball, thinking backward in Straight Pool won't come into play as often at the beginning of a rack. When you get to the final six or seven balls remaining on the table, this is the proper time to determine a break shot, and the key ball from the break shot, and then work backward from there. This sequence of events will make it easier to develop proper patterns and continue your run.

Figure 6.19 shows another Straight Pool layout. As you can see, the balls are a little more wide open. Following the sequence, there aren't really any balls completely

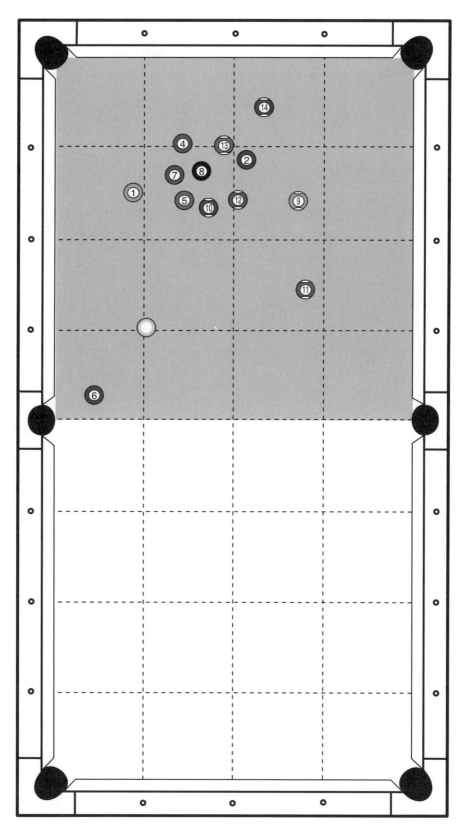

Figure 6.18 Begin slowly opening the balls in a Straight Pool rack, working them apart for your best chance at a runout.

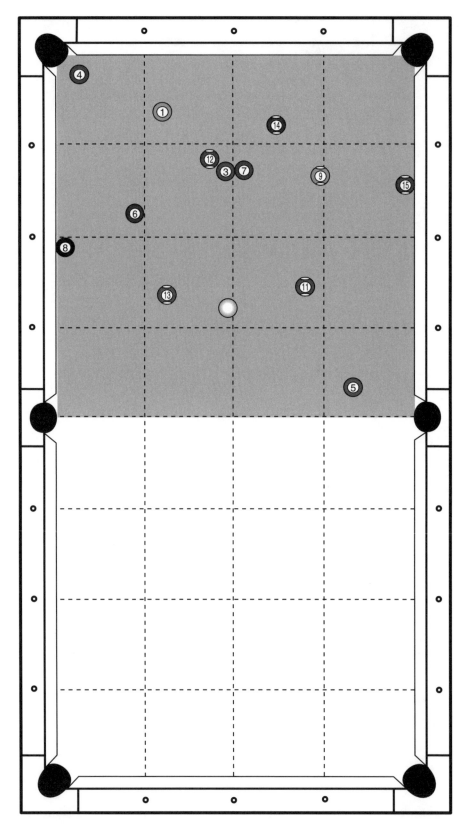

Figure 6.19 Completing a Straight Pool run using just four pockets.

blocking the pockets, though the 7-ball could be a problem on the left side of the table. The 8 and 15 balls are on the rails, and will soon need your attention. As you slowly pick off balls, work your pattern play towards the center of the table. Nudge balls as you pocket others, keeping them on one end of the table and allowing yourself to complete the run without using the two lower corner pockets.

Even if you are not normally a fan of Straight Pool, you may find that a short Straight Pool game with a partner makes a great warm-up for a set of Eight Ball or Nine Ball. This game focuses on key areas, including cue ball control and pattern and position play, along with the mental benefits of patience and proper planning. It was quite an art of the legendary cueists—players like Willie Mosconi, Jimmy Caras, Irving Crane, and Steve Mizerak—to be able to effortlessly run ball after ball, well into the hundreds, while making the cue ball dance from one shot to another. Amateurs not well versed in the art might comment: "So what? Every shot they make is so easy, I could do that. . . ." While the more astute smile knowingly and patiently explain that, in fact, making every subsequent shot simple is the art itself.

One Pocket

The pattern play options are endless in the game of One Pocket. The different types of shots and layouts are limitless. It is a game where there are very few hard and fast rules, and pattern play is anything but common. For this reason One Pocket is definitely the game to play if you want to use your imagination and creativity to its fullest. One Pocket is also the most difficult game to play because every skill you will ever develop comes into play: shooting straight, controlling the cue ball, controlling object balls, safety play, kick shots, bank shots, caroms. And every conceivable type of shot can come into play at least once in a single game!

The rules we can outline for pattern play, therefore, will focus on common threads that can run through any particular game. First, because of the unpredictable nature of the game, you will never be able to think a full rack ahead. Too many situations change; the balls get moved around, and you never know what your last ball will be. Second, there is always one excellent place to leave the cue ball—and that is as near as possible to your opponent's pocket, shown by the shaded area in figure 6.20. In this case, your opponent has the left corner pocket, you have the right corner. Whenever possible, you will do your best to leave your cue ball in the shaded area. Leaving your opponent here leaves them no straight-in shot options. The best option they will have is a bank, and they'll have to be able to bank very well. Consistently having to shoot from this area will be frustrating and counterproductive for them. It's also a great pattern play and strategic move to fall back on whenever you're just not sure what your next move should be.

The intricacies and highly defensive characteristics of One Pocket make it analogous to a chess game. Like chess, One Pocket can be broken into three basic components: the Beginning Game, consisting of some typical and not so typical opening moves; the Middle Game, where balls tend to get shifted to the other end of the table; and the End Game, where one or both opponents need just one ball for the win and play becomes extremely defensive.

Figure 6.21 illustrates one example of the beginning of a One Pocket game. Your opponent has broken the balls and left you in a difficult situation. While no

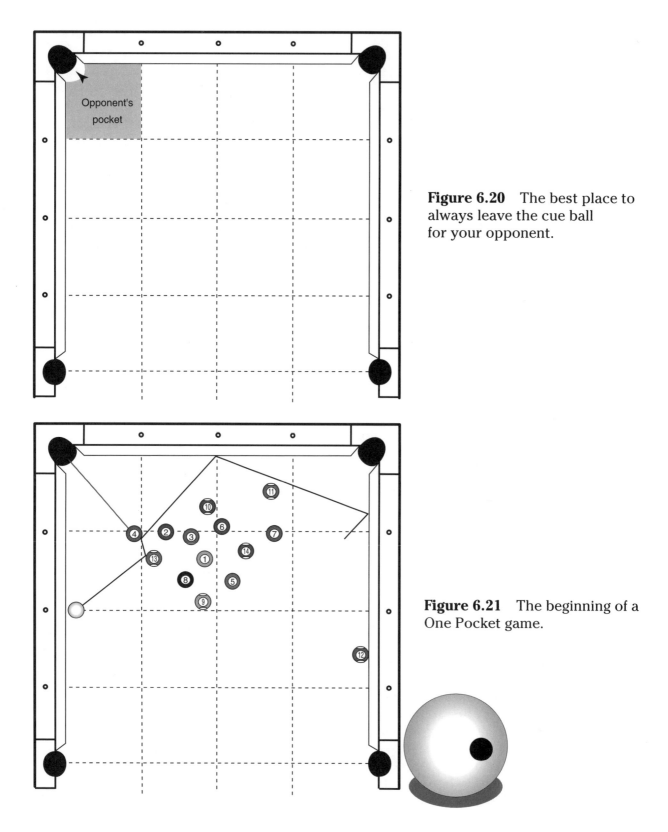

Figure 6.20 The best place to always leave the cue ball for your opponent.

Figure 6.21 The beginning of a One Pocket game.

straight-in shot exists, a carom shot is available, indicative of the sort of shot for which you will always be on the lookout. Shoot the cue ball with right english off the 13-ball to pocket the 4-ball, spinning the cue ball with the english to get to your opponent's side of the table. As you can see, the rest of the object balls are then between your cue ball and your pocket. This is the kind of move you will often try to make, since, if you miss, you leave your opponent no shot. If you make the 4-ball, you have a better chance at another shot toward your pocket.

In figure 6.22 you are presented with another beginning game situation. Your opponent has broken well, but the 2-ball, which was the corner ball on the rack, leaked toward your corner pocket. As a result, you have been left with a very thin cut on the 2-ball. Extremely thin cuts on balls come up very often in the typical One Pocket game. This shot in particular is an important shot to practice.

After you get past the opening moves, you come to the middle of the game. The middle game occurs when you and your opponent begin a defensive battle that will gradually move the balls down table. When you start moving the balls down table, keep in mind that it will be to your advantage to keep the object balls on your half (right or left side) of the table. In figure 6.23 you will notice that the balls were strategically played to the shaded area, while the cue ball was left as close to your opponent's pocket as possible. As you might imagine while studying the layout, this makes it very difficult for your opponent to attempt a shot at his pocket, let alone make a shot. If she attempts a shot and doesn't make it, chances are she leaves you a shot to your own pocket.

At the end of the game, only a few balls will be left, and chances are good that either you or your opponent needs just one more ball pocketed for the win. An end-of-the-game situation has been illustrated in figure 6.24. Your opponent has the upper-right corner pocket, and you have the upper left. You need all three balls to win the game, but your opponent needs only one. Your best play here is to bank the 5-ball two rails, following the 5-ball with the cue ball to send it down table and up off the bottom short rail, leaving an angle to the left of the 2-ball. This will allow you a shot on the 2-ball and a natural angle to the right of the 2-ball to arrive in position for the 14-ball. Again, even if you miss any of these three balls, you will

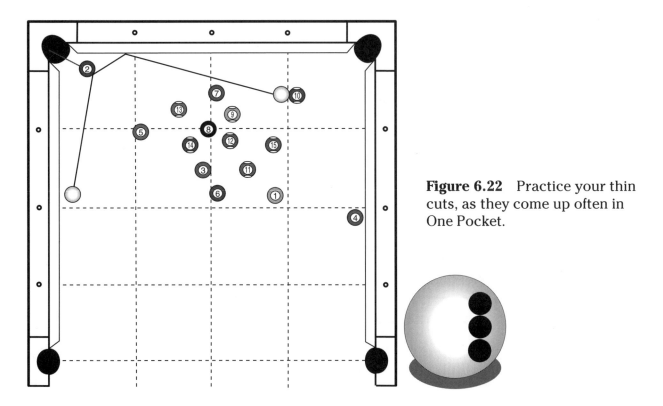

Figure 6.22 Practice your thin cuts, as they come up often in One Pocket.

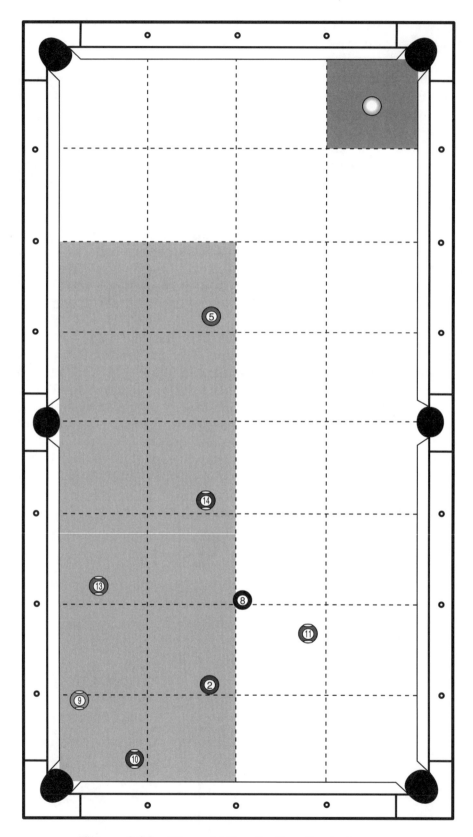

Figure 6.23 The middle of a One Pocket game.

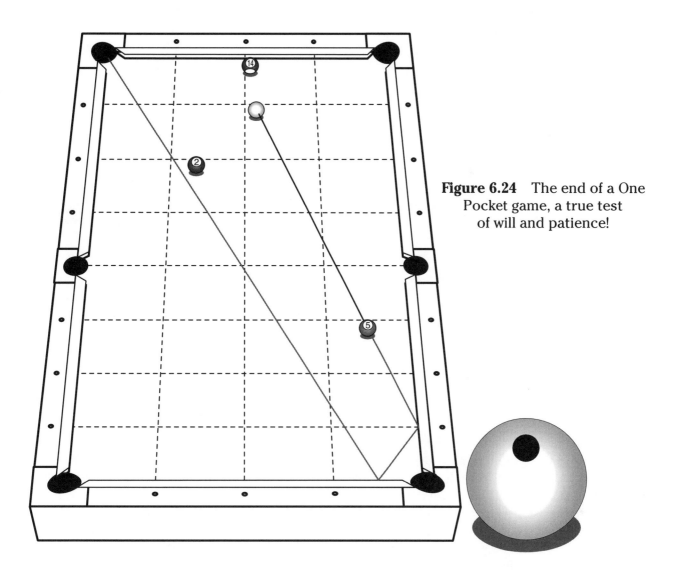

Figure 6.24 The end of a One Pocket game, a true test of will and patience!

leave your opponent very little to shoot at by keeping the cue ball on his side of the table. The two-rail bank, like the thin cut, is a valuable One Pocket tool. In fact, the best offensive and defensive shots in One Pocket involve the multi-rail bank skills. Your knowledge of banking, banking systems, and natural tracks around the table will elevate your One Pocket game immediately.

Besides thin cuts and multi-rail banks, kicking ability will also quickly advance your skills in this game, allowing offensive shot selections that are quite defensive at the same time. Upper-echelon players take plenty of time to develop strong kicking skills for this very reason. Kicking at a ball in the game of One Pocket allows you to place an object ball close to your pocket and still place the cue ball quite near or frozen to other balls. For example, in figure 6.25, your opponent has wisely left you near your own pocket with little opportunity for a shot, surely none with defensive results. You must counter his or her move. Kick into the rail first, sending the 11-ball towards your pocket, while allowing the cue ball to glance off the 11-ball and nestle itself, optimally, between the 2-ball and the 9-ball. If the cue ball freezes between these balls, wonderful; your opponent won't have a shot.

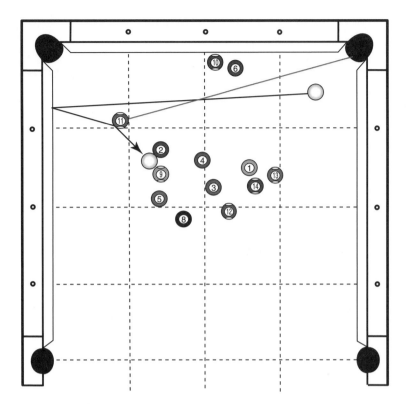

Figure 6.25   Using the critical kick shot in a game of One Pocket.

Keep in mind that you must hit this shot firm enough, since you are going rail first, to send the 11-ball to another rail or into the pocket, and avoid the foul. If you aim to hit the 11-ball thin, it will head toward the 6-ball and possibly break up this cluster, along with sending the 6-ball to a rail for a legal shot.

The vast majority of your shots in One Pocket are strictly defensive, to the point where you are attempting to control both the cue ball and the object ball or a multitude of object balls. You'll constantly be trying to send balls toward your half of the table and at the same time try to snooker your opponent from actually making an offensive shot for his pocket. One Pocket is a move and countermove game, yet sometimes your focus will rest more on the offensive, and sometimes more on the defensive game. If your opponent is a very good One Pocket player, you will need to play a more offensive game, as he or she will be experienced in countering defensive moves and accomplishing shots that you might not immediately see. If you are the stronger player, a more defensive game is in order, since you will have the added luxury of forcing your opponent to make the mistakes.

THE THREE-BALL PATTERN

Throughout this chapter we've mentioned thinking at least three balls ahead during your pattern and position play. The reason this works is quite simple. If you are, for instance, looking at the 1-ball and trying to get to the 2-ball, it will help knowing which side of the 2-ball you want to be on to then get to the 3-ball. Once you are on the 2-ball, you will be looking ahead to the 4-ball, and so on. Because angles come into the game of pool so often, thinking a minimum of three balls ahead will keep you safe from many poor pattern decisions.

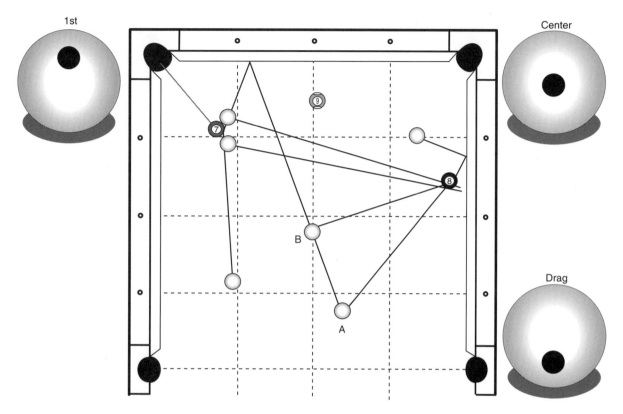

Figure 6.26 A three-ball pattern with all three balls
at one end of the table.

The most common three-ball patterns will come in one of three variations: working the three balls close together (usually at one end of the table or the other), working the balls from one end of the table to the other end, and working back and forth between the ends of the table. Each of these situations has been illustrated to show you how they are likely to appear, and how to tackle them when they do.

In figure 6.26, all three remaining balls in a rack of Nine Ball are at one end of the table. Typically, a three-ball pattern such as this allows the luxury of not having to move the cue ball very far. At the same time, the pressure will be on you to stay on the right side of each ball, or you'll have to send the cue ball all the way around the table to get back to your group of balls! If you shoot the 7-ball with straight follow, you can bring the cue ball off the short rail and back down toward the center of the table, as shown in shot A. If you are going away from the line of attack to make the 8-ball in the corner, you'll need to get the cue ball past the second diamond. Then a straight drag shot or center-ball hit will allow you to play the 9-ball in the left corner. If you come up short, you'll need to come back across the table to play the 9-ball in the right corner pocket, as shown in shot B.

In our next situation, illustrated in figure 6.27, you will be working the balls from one end of the table to the other. The 7-ball stands at one end of the table, the 8-ball is in the center, and the 9-ball lies at the other end of the table. From where the cue ball is, your best angle into the 8-ball will result from using a touch of low left english on the cue ball as you pocket the 7-ball. This will allow you to use the short rail and the long rail to get an angle on the 8-ball. So long as you use the second rail, you will get a great angle coming up the table.

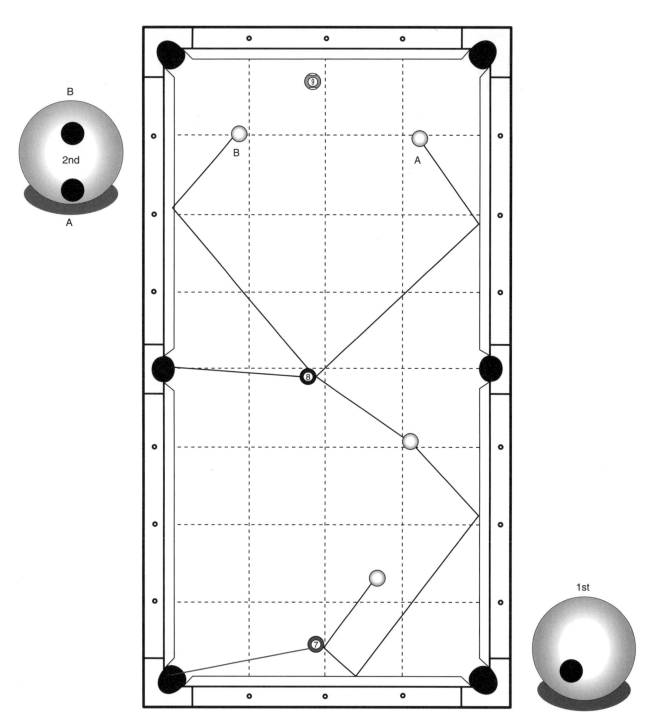

Figure 6.27 Working a three-ball pattern from one end of the table to the other.

Let's say you barely hit the second rail and come up a little short on the 8-ball. In this case, you can use straight draw to bring the cue ball to the right side and shoot the 9-ball in the left corner pocket, illustrated in figure 6.27a. If you come up a little farther, you will have the natural angle to follow the cue ball up into the rail near the second diamond, and off the rail again to shoot the 9-ball in the right corner pocket (figure 6.27b).

This brings us to moving back and forth down the table. In figure 6.28, the 7 and 9 balls are at one end of the table, and the 8-ball is at other end. This type of pattern forces you to move the cue ball a greater distance. Your speed control will have to be a little better, but planning a correct pattern play in advance should eliminate any problems. Hit center ball on the cue ball when you pocket the 7-ball to come down table, passing the angle of attack on the 8-ball in the corner. If you

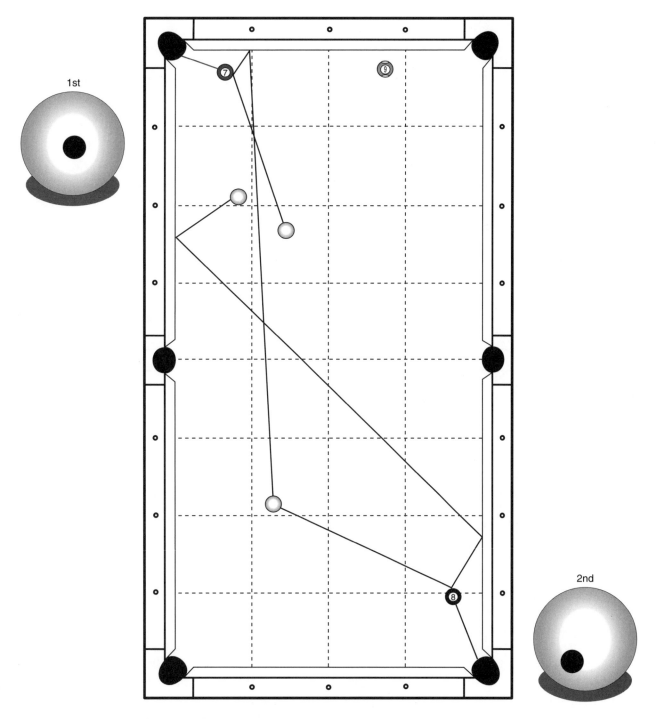

Figure 6.28 Working a three-ball pattern back and forth
on the length of the table.

come down table short on the resulting position for the 8-ball, you could have a long straight-in shot, in which case you'd have to put more force into the cue ball and draw it the length of the table to get back to the 9-ball. As long as you come down table past the side pocket, you'll have an easy shot on the 8-ball, which will result in easy position play for the 9-ball. Play the 8-ball using low left english, using the long rail on the right side, crossing over the table, then into the long rail on the left side, and out again toward the 9-ball. Now you can shoot the 9-ball in the upper-right corner pocket. The key shot in this pattern is the 7-ball and your speed control on the 7-ball for a good angle on the 8-ball.

The next series of three diagrams shows just how much thinking three balls ahead can affect your pattern-play decisions. In figure 6.29, you have a relatively easy shot on the 5-ball in the side pocket. Stopping the cue ball or rolling up would give you a fine shot on the 6-ball. However, looking ahead, you'll see that you want a bit of angle on your third ball in the pattern, your 7-ball. So instead, create an angle, using low ball, to pocket the 5-ball.

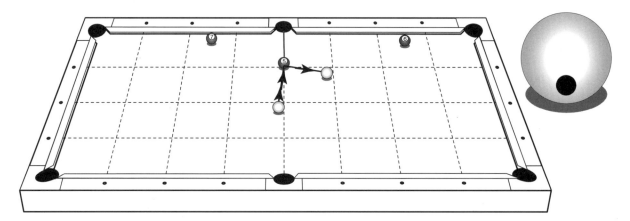

Figure 6.29   Thinking ahead will keep you ahead of the game in this three-ball pattern.

In figure 6.30, now that the 5-ball is gone, your three-ball pattern includes the 6, 7, and 8 balls. You'll note that the angle you gave yourself on the 6-ball will give you an easy way to get an angle on the 7-ball, so that you can draw back off the left long rail for a shot on the 8-ball.

Once you pocket the 6-ball, your three-ball pattern will include the 7, 8, and 9 balls. Draw off the 7-ball (per figure 6.31) for a simple shot on the 8-ball that will leave you in a perfect spot for the 9-ball.

But don't stop there! Despite the fact that your 9-ball is the last ball on the table, let's pretend you have pocketed the 7-ball. Play a three-ball pattern for the 8, 9, and an imaginary 10-ball. You don't need to imagine anything crazy; just pretend the 10-ball is somewhere near the 9-ball. You will either stop the cue ball upon contact with the 9-ball, or roll up just a bit. Why add the imaginary ball? Quite simply, the reason so many players miss game-winning balls, especially in the games of Eight Ball and Nine Ball, is that they get down to the last ball and don't have a destination for the cue ball. This often causes too much focus on pocketing the object ball, and leaves no clear thought about where to put the cue ball. The result—not stroking, or overstroking, the shot, and consequently giving your oppo-

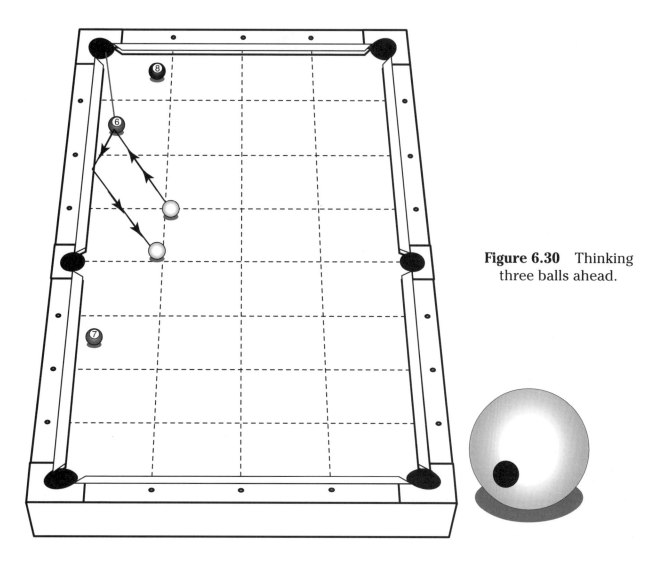

Figure 6.30 Thinking three balls ahead.

nent the game. This is a silent rule of thumb among most professionals: always have a destination in mind for the cue ball. Learn from them!

SHRINK YOUR TABLE

A final word about developing pattern- and position-play skills. As you are examining the Five Commandments, common playing patterns, and three-ball patterns, you can reduce the surface of the table you are playing on by a foot! No magic here; just think about placing your cue ball six inches in from each of the cushions on whatever size table you practice on. If you think about playing position inside this area, you will always have the full complement of cue ball control options at your disposal. Playing position to one cushion or another will drastically limit your options, as you will be forced to shoot high on the cue ball. Center ball, stop shots, and draw shots are virtually impossible with the cue ball adjacent to the cushion. If you find, when attempting to keep the cue ball off the rail, that you are landing there quite a bit, you'll know immediately that your speed control needs a

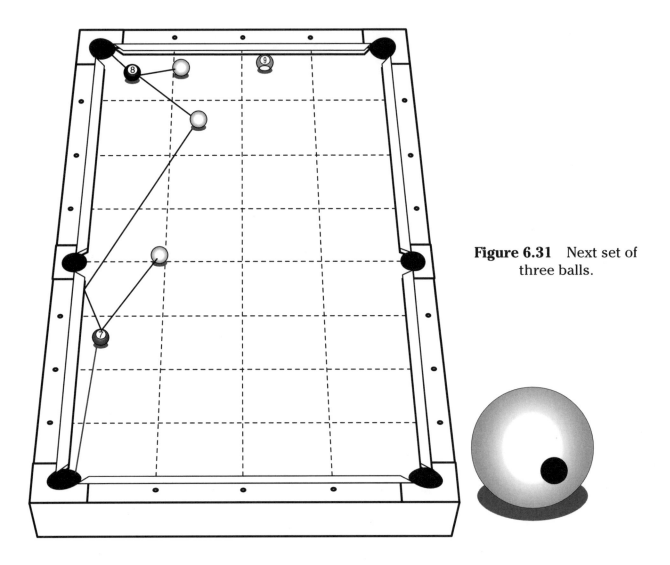

Figure 6.31   Next set of three balls.

bit of work. This could be leaving you in increasingly difficult positions through-out each rack. It could also mean that you are using one rail when you should be using two, or two rails when you should be using three. When using the rails, plan to come into a rail and out again, not just to the rail, increasing your chances of being at least six inches away.

You are now equipped with the knowledge to execute pattern plays for better position. The Five Commandments we've provided are key to developing your own sense of the game. The more you play, the more you'll recognize basic pat-terns, and observe what works for the games you play most frequently. Be open to learning as much as you can, but always keep in mind the keys you've learned here in order to avoid poor pattern habits in the future. As you play and practice, continue careful observation in your pattern play to recognize when a good pat-tern does not exist. Once you can easily see that a runout isn't possible, you'll be ready to execute a clever safety and still turn most games to your favor.

Chapter 7

Safety Play

In the movie *The Hustler,* Eddie Felson (Paul Newman) says to Minnesota Fats (Jackie Gleason), "You don't leave much when you miss." Fats retorts, "That's what the game is all about."

How true that statement is in today's most popular games.

Years ago, in games like Eight Ball and Nine Ball, the rule was two fouls, ball in hand, also commonly referred to as "one **rollout**." That meant you could roll your cue ball to a more favorable position if you did not have a clear shot at your ball. It was then your opponent's option to have you shoot again or take control of the table himself. If you took the shot and either didn't send a ball to the rail, or scratched the cue ball, your opponent then had cue ball in hand. In other words, the cue ball could be placed anywhere on the table for the incoming shot. Playing under these rules, there seemed to be a tendency for players to play a more aggressive game and make more spectacular shots. In fact, before the jump cue was the norm, top players who could jump the ball with their regular playing cue would roll out to jump shots. If your opponent couldn't jump over a ball, he had to give up the shot option.

The rules changed to one foul, cue ball in hand for television, so that the games would be played faster. As the rules of Eight Ball and Nine Ball have changed over the years to one foul, ball in hand, a solid safety game has become more important for a winning pool game.

TYPES OF SAFETIES

Safeties can be broken down into a few different categories. The lay of the balls on the table will dictate to you which of these safety categories is best. The first kind of safety involves either hiding the cue ball or hiding the object ball, and on rare occasions, you will be able to hide both balls. You'll soon learn that the easier of the two common safeties to execute is that which hides the cue ball. Since the game of pool is all about controlling the cue ball, it is more natural to place the cue ball in an awkward place on the table for your opponent. The other option, placing the object ball where your opponent will have a difficult time even hitting it, is considered more difficult. Very few players practice controlling the speed of the object ball. They are usually thinking about pocketing the object ball, and so focus on speed that will get them to the pocket, not on the fine gradations in speed that can simply get them close to the pocket, or close to another ball. Because of this, safeties that involve object ball speed control are considered more difficult to execute.

A third type of safety involves hiding both the object ball and the cue ball. This shot requires excellent speed control on both balls. Again, you will need to spend a little time learning about object ball speed to become proficient with these kinds of safeties. Then there are safeties that appear to be aggressive shots and not safeties at all—what we call two-way shots. In the two-way shot, you attempt a difficult bank or combination, but are hiding the cue ball from the intended object ball in the process. Should you miss the difficult shot, you still leave nothing for your opponent. These are also often referred to as "free shots."

Finally, yet another form of safety play is to lock up balls, or create a cluster. This is used when there is no way that you can hit the intended object ball. This is explained in greater detail in chapter 8 on strategy and intentional fouls.

When the need to play safe arises, a vivid imagination and creativity can be your greatest assets. Imagine the cue ball exactly where you want it to be. Optimally, you will attempt to freeze the cue ball to another ball or to the rail. If the cue ball is frozen behind another ball, it is very difficult to execute a simple one-rail kick at the hidden object ball. Your opponent will be faced, at best, with a multi-rail kick, which has a much greater degree of difficulty. And, when the cue ball is frozen to, or very near, the rail, your opponent has limited options because you have taken away any shot that must be hit below center on the cue ball. Any hit on the cue ball above center is harder to control, which increases your chances of getting back to the table.

A solid safety game can be enhanced by practicing shots that are easy to execute, and easy to see in regular game situations. When you learn each type of safety we've outlined, look for the opportunity to play them every time you practice, even if you're playing by yourself. Looking for such safety opportunities will help build your safety game through increased use of that imagination and creativity!

Controlling the Cue Ball

The first safety option we've brought to your attention involves a light touch on the cue ball. Your intent will be to move the cue ball a very short distance, and at the same time try to move the object ball a short distance. Figure 7.1 illustrates a one-set shot. To accomplish this shot, begin by hitting just a little below center, with a touch of left english. You're attempting to drive the object ball forward, past the 9-ball, and send the cue ball behind the 9-ball. This is an excellent shot to practice, as it will give you a feel for moving the cue ball only a short distance. This sort of light touch is a skill you won't encounter on most of your regular shots, but is invaluable to have when the occasion does arise!

In figure 7.2 we have a similar shot in a Nine Ball game. To execute this, send the 2-ball down the table and "squeeze" the cue ball in between the 6-ball and the 3-ball. Again, once you learn this shot, it's quite simple to execute.

Let's say you're playing a game of Eight Ball and your opponent just scratched. You have cue ball in hand. As you'll notice from figure 7.3, your 3-ball and 6-ball are

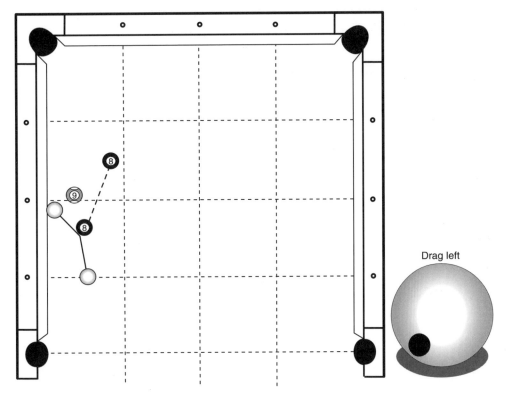

Figure 7.1 This safety requires a light touch on the cue ball,
a key skill in safety play.

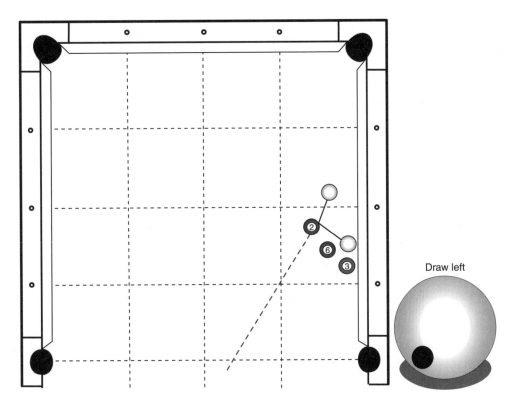

Figure 7.2 The use of the soft safety in a Nine Ball game.

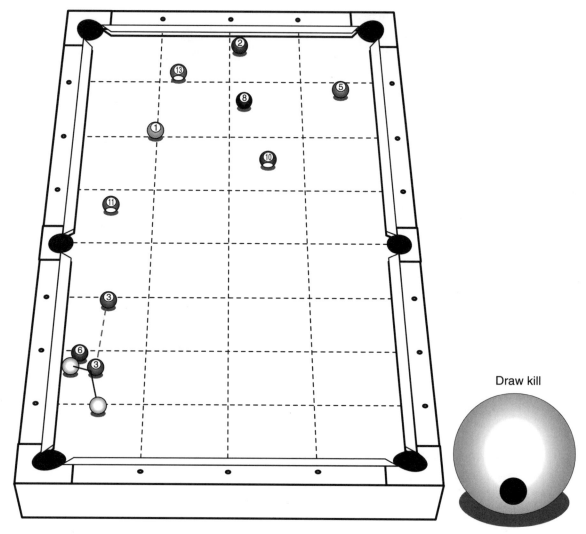

Draw kill

Figure 7.3   An Eight Ball safety play that also puts the balls in better position for your next turn at the table.

tied up. It's virtually impossible to break them up with the other balls on the opposite side of the table, and neither one has a clear path to a pocket. Instead, execute the safety shown. You'll open the 6-ball and 3-ball, and at the same time place your cue ball between the 6-ball and the cushion, giving your opponent a very difficult kick shot. Should he foul again, you'll have cue ball in hand with a much easier chance of running the table.

Another type of safety shot that comes up quite often is illustrated in figure 7.4. In this situation, the incoming player has cue ball in hand, but there's no open shot at the 1-ball to make it in any pocket, since the 6-ball is blocking its path. Rather than try to bank the ball or take a high-risk shot, a safety is your best bet. To accomplish this, you'll need to stop the cue ball dead after it makes contact with the object ball, sending the 1-ball down table. The closer you leave your cue ball to the 6-ball, the better off you'll be.

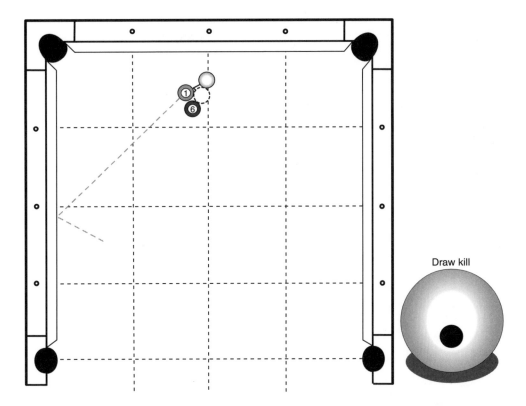

Figure 7.4   Stopping the cue ball, while sending the object ball
down table.

There are endless possibilities of stopping the cue ball with cue ball in hand
and trying to freeze it on a ball or stop it behind a row of balls. Take a look at figure
7.5, which shows another Eight Ball situation. Your opponent just missed and you
have no open shot at the 1, 2, 3, 5, or 6 balls. Rather than take a flyer, simply shoot
on the left side of the 6-ball with a touch of follow, using either straight high ball or
a bit of left english. This will send the cue ball into the short rail and back into the
3-5 cluster. Hit the cue ball hard enough to barely glance off the 6-ball and open the
3-5 cluster just slightly, while leaving the cue ball behind these balls.

In figure 7.6, you will be sending the 3-ball down table, but you have to hit it
pretty firm to get it there. At the same time, you're trying not to let the cue ball
travel too far once you hit the 3-ball. To control this, use a below-center shot, with
a thick (three-quarter ball) hit on the 3-ball. You'll need to take as much speed as
possible off the cue ball in order to park it behind the 5 and 6 balls. This is a shot
that comes up quite frequently, especially in the game of Nine Ball.

In figure 7.7, you came up a little short for your position on the 9-ball. You're left
with a decision. Take the "flyer" bank or play safe. Taking the bank probably isn't
advisable for a couple of reasons. First, if you don't know conditions of the table,
it could play short or long on you. Plus, you must know where your cue ball is
going and how to get it out of the way. Finally, if you miss the bank, chances are
you will sell out, leaving your opponent an easy shot for the win. Better to play
safe by cutting the 9-ball on the left side. Hit it very thin and send the cue ball two

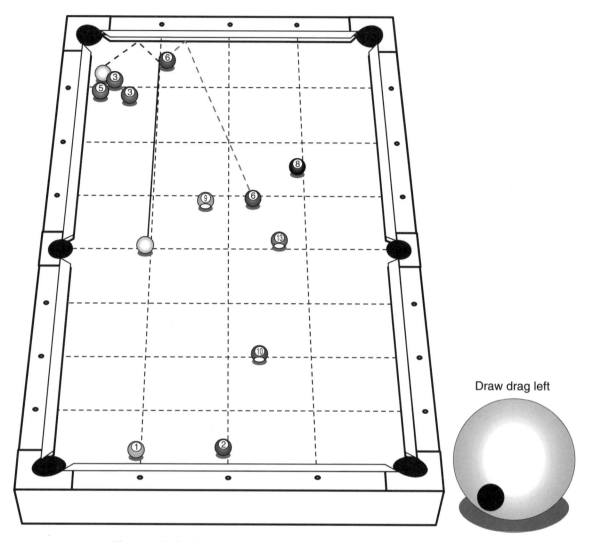

Draw drag left

Figure 7.5   Sending the cue ball into a cluster of balls.

or three rails down table. If, for example, you want to come short on the second rail, you would use a little low left english. If you want to come longer, you would hit the cue ball with high left english, hopefully driving the cue ball at least three rails on its way to the other end of the table. This will give your opponent a very difficult shot, even to execute a safety of his own.

Being able to hit an object ball very thin is vital in great safety play, and definitely worth the practice time invested. There will be plenty of times when you're presented with a shot situation involving a length-of-the-table thin cut on a ball. You're better off trying to overcut the ball than to undercut it. The overcut shot will send your object ball to the long rail and then back into the short rail, leaving your opponent virtually the same shot. An undercut shot will hit the short rail first, bounce out in front of the pocket, and leave an easier shot for your opponent.

In figure 7.8 your opponent left you an extremely tough shot on the 9-ball. Attempt to cut the ball in, but use a thin cut with a middle-ball hit (or a touch below center, as it will have become middle ball by the time you get all the way down the

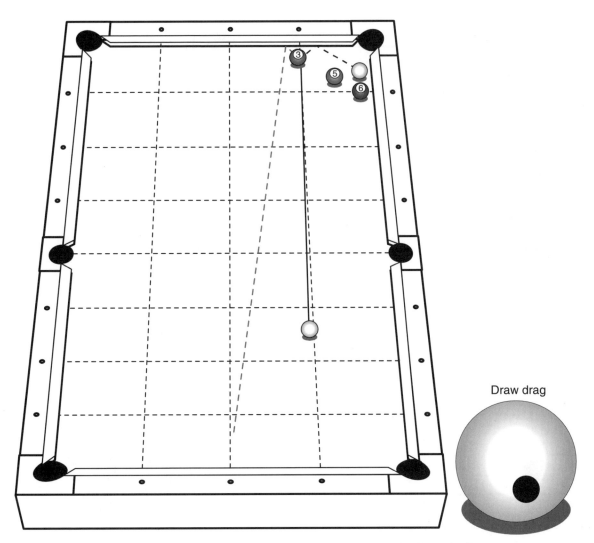

Figure 7.6 Stopping the cue ball behind blocking balls
with a below-center hit.

table to the 9-ball). If you make the shot, great, you've won. If you don't, the cue
ball, as indicated, will travel back down table, leaving your opponent with an even
tougher option!

Controlling the Object Ball

Controlling the speed of the object ball becomes a very crucial part of playing
good safeties. But, since you seldom gauge the speed of your object balls when
you're pocketing them, it will take some practice getting to know object ball speed
in relation to cue ball speed. One great practice aid to learn the speed of the object
balls is to throw a rack of balls out on the table and try not to actually pocket
them! Instead, attempt to lag each ball to its intended pocket, but not actually in
the pocket. This will give you more of a feel for just how fast the object balls go on
different tables, with different cloth, different hits, and so on. It's a very good training aid to see and feel the shot going in on the last revolution.

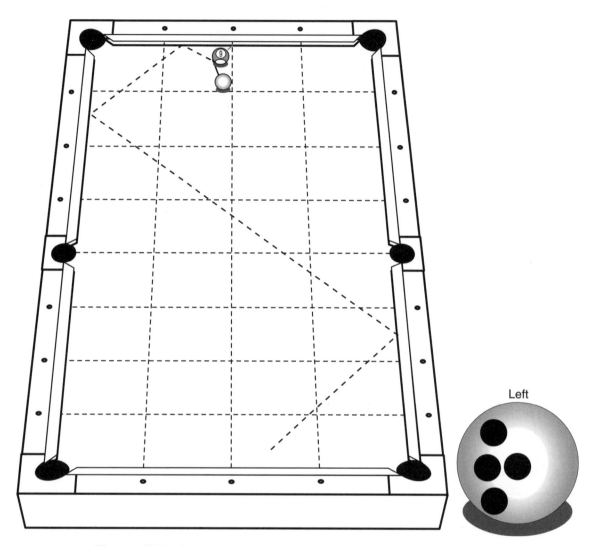

Figure 7.7   Opting for the safety leaves your opponent with
the tough shot.

Figure 7.9 is an excellent example of using speed control on the 9-ball. Attempting to play a cut shot all the way up table on the 9-ball in this illustration is a low-percentage shot. Possible scenarios include leaving the object ball hanging in the pocket and allowing the cue ball to travel back and forth between the short rails, no doubt leaving your opponent an easy straight-in shot. Or you can try holding the angle and banking the 9-ball into the side pocket; but if you do that you leave the cue ball almost in the middle of the table and sell out if you miss. The smart play is to bank the 9-ball into the long rail across to the opposite long rail to leave it in the middle of the short rail. At the same time, by using low right english on the shot, you will bring the cue ball roughly to the opposite side of the table on the other short rail. Practicing this shot will allow you to soon develop a feel for controlling the object ball.

This shot also plays very well in Eight Ball. Take a look at figure 7.10. You have one ball left on the table. The 8-ball is all the way up table, making it a low-percentage shot to bank the 2-ball cross-side because you have to hold the angle. It's very

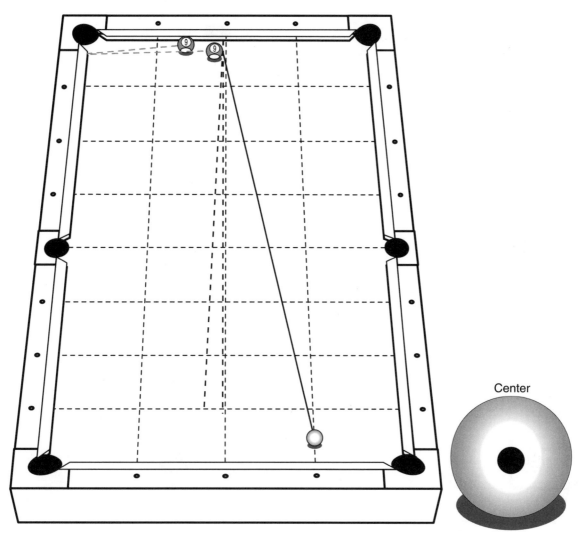

Figure 7.8 Attempting the shot on the 9-ball will still allow you a safety.

difficult to bank cross-corner. Even if you do, you won't have a very decent shot on the 8-ball. If you play a great shot and cut it up the corner, again, so what? You won't have a shot on the 8-ball! You're much better off playing a two-rail safety, trying to bring the 2-ball just in front of the 8-ball. Hit this shot with low right english, and remember that it's more important to try to keep the cue ball near the center of the short rail.

Sometimes it's not possible just to control the cue ball for a safety. It's great to try and control both balls as in figures 7.9 and 7.10, but keep in mind that it's more important here to control the 9 and 2 balls than the cue ball.

Let's say you are executing a safety and you've contacted the object ball. Now your cue ball is approaching a blocker, in other words, another object ball on the table. You should keep in mind that the closer the cue ball comes to the blocking ball, the fewer options your opponent has to execute a good hit. Why? Because it takes away more and more of the table that the cue ball can directly hit. For example, in figure 7.11, the closer the cue ball gets to the 3-ball, the more difficult it

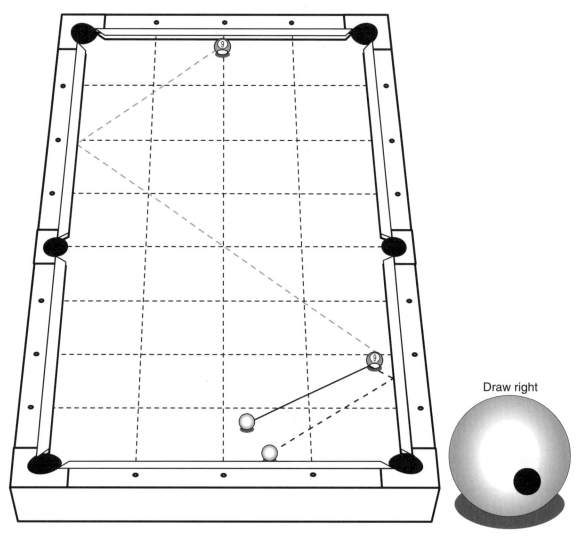

Figure 7.9   Controlling speed on the object ball requires
a bit of practice.

will be for your opponent to hit the 2-ball. This is because the closer the cue ball
comes to the 3-ball, the greater the area on the table is hidden from your opponent
for a straight-in hit, no matter where on the other end of the table your 2-ball
should land. It would now take a multi-rail shot to hit the 2-ball. Thus, it's more
important in this situation to control the cue ball, and the more you want to control the cue ball, the more difficult it is to control the object ball. So remember
where to keep your focus.

THE TWO-WAY SHOT

The two-way shot is a favorite among all players. Two way refers to the fact that
the shot you are playing is offensive and defensive at the same time. The offensive
shot will tend to be a lower-percentage shot, but, if it's pocketed, you can continue

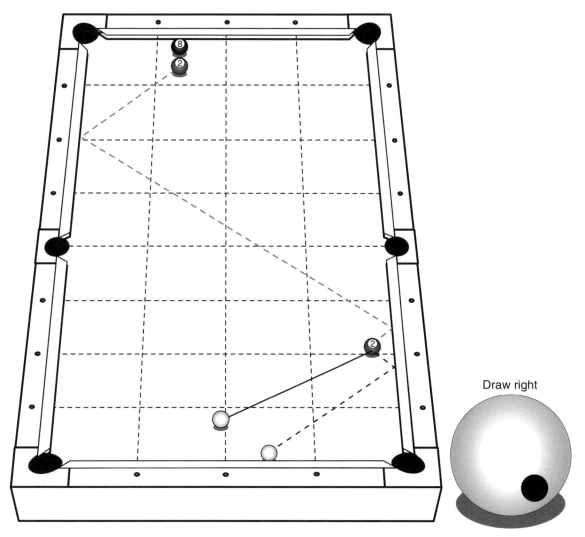

Figure 7.10 Another example of controlling the speed of the object ball, this in a game of Eight Ball.

play. On the other hand, if the low-percentage shot is missed, you have still played safe! In figure 7.12, the cue ball is placed in a situation where you're almost straight in on the 1-ball. It would be very difficult to draw the ball straight back to get on the 2-ball. Instead, you'll attempt to bank the 1-ball cross-corner and, at the same time, send the cue ball down table to get position on the 2-ball. It's a much easier shot to execute and you can hit it either way. Whether overcut or undercut, you won't give your opponent a decent shot. You're more apt to overcut this one, but it doesn't matter; you still have the 6-ball as a blocker at the other end of the table. And, by banking it cross-corner, you'll wind up with a better shot on the 2-ball, with angle to get on the 3-ball to boot!

In figure 7.13, you're in a situation where you have no straight-in shot on the 1-ball. However, it's a very easy shot to bank the 1-ball cross-side and hold the cue ball where it's at, or draw it back just a hair to have a shot on the 2-ball. Once more, if you do miss the 1-ball, you have the 5-ball and the 6-ball as blockers. The

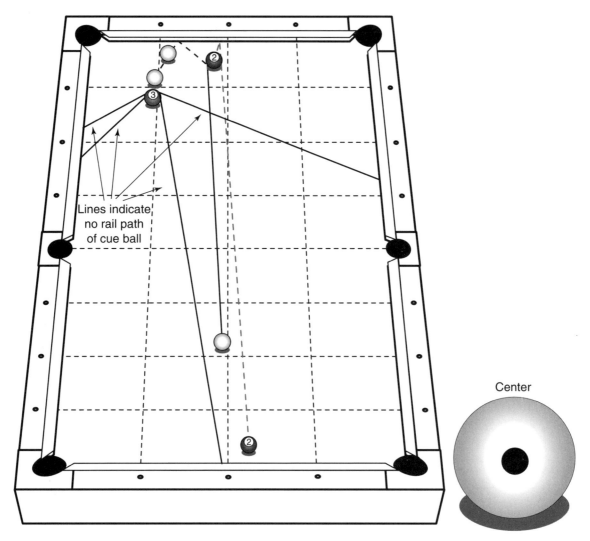

Lines indicate no rail path of cue ball

Center

Figure 7.11   The closer you can leave your cue ball to an impeding ball, the fewer options your opponent will have to kick at the ball.

bonus—if you go too far, you leave the 1-ball long and make it more difficult for your opponent to get back down table for the 2-ball. This requires executing the simple stop shot shown earlier, and becomes an excellent two-way shot to have in your arsenal.

Figure 7.14 shows basically the same situation. However, this shot requires a length-of-the-table bank. Once again you have two potential blockers, the 5-ball and 6-ball. All you have to concentrate on is getting the speed of the 1-ball down and swinging the cue ball behind the 2-ball. People have a tendency to overlook these shots. Beginners would try to cut the 1-ball thin on the right side and bring the cue ball down two rails, which is a difficult shot with which to hook your opponent.

Caroms and combinations (which come up more often in Nine Ball than in Eight Ball) also provide excellent two-way shot possibilities. Take a look at figure 7.15. You may be able to clear the 1-ball to the corner pocket, but it will be extremely

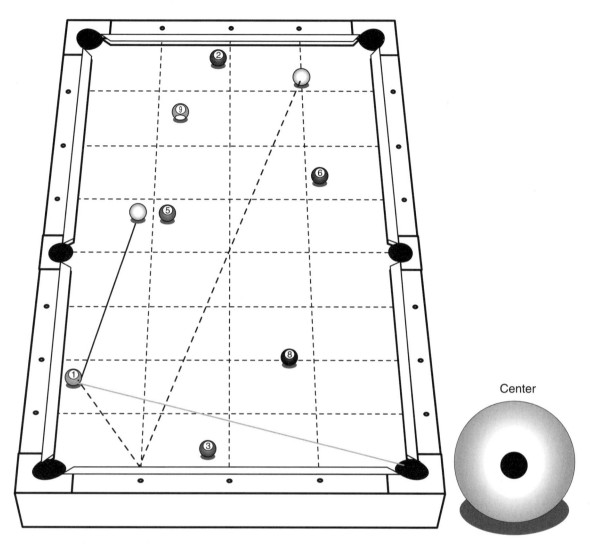

Figure 7.12 This two-way shot allows a possible made shot with position, but also allows a safety should you miss.

difficult to get a shot on the 2-ball, as it is clustered with the 5-ball on the rail. However, you can attempt the 1-9 combination, while parking your cue ball by the 3 and 4 balls. If you pocket the 9-ball, you've won the game. If you didn't and you've kept the cue ball very near or (better still) frozen to the 3-ball, your opponent will have a very difficult time getting a good hit on the 1-ball, probably resulting in cue ball in hand for you on your next turn at the table!

In figure 7.16, you have a low-percentage shot on the 5-ball, but the 9-ball is sitting close to the pocket. Pocket the 9-ball by caroming your cue ball off the 5-ball and into the 9-ball, meanwhile sending your 5-ball up toward the other end of the table. Again, this is a potential game winner, resulting in a safe shot should you miss. If you enjoy the game of Nine Ball, the opportunity to shoot a carom shot, involving the 9-ball or many other balls, will come into play quite often. It is definitely worth practicing!

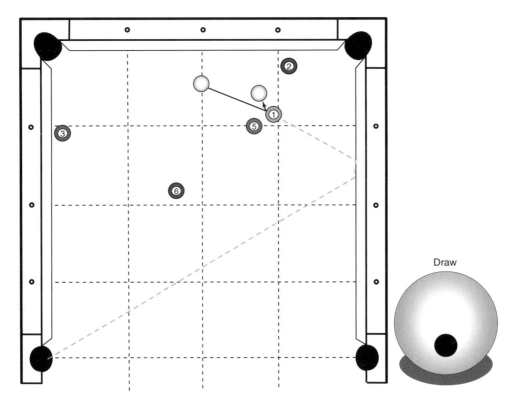

Figure 7.13   This two-way stop shot is a critical shot to have
in your safety arsenal.

COUNTERING SAFETIES
WITH SAFETIES

Let's say your opponent is at the table. He shoots at a ball, misses, and leaves you
hooked, or he plays a safety and hooks you, meaning he's left you an obstructed
path to your object ball. Now your only alternative is to try and kick at the ball to
make a legal hit. While you may think that your opponent is now in control, in fact
you have the edge in the safety battle, if you know a basic strategy—try to control
the cue ball after the kick. In other words, you'll often be aiming for one side of the
object ball to enhance your possibilities of winning that game, rather than just
trying to get a hit and sit down again.

Too many players try to slam into the object ball by kicking it as hard as they
can, hoping they can slop a ball in, create clusters down the table, or change the
whole table layout. This is not the thing to do. What you try instead is to control
the cue ball. In the last five to ten years, we've seen a real renaissance in kicking at
balls. Many of the top players in the pro ranks have become so proficient at kicking balls that they will actually roll out to a kick shot, rather than leave their opponent any direct shot. They are hoping to have the push (or rollout) returned to
them, where they can execute the shot by kicking at the blocked ball and still

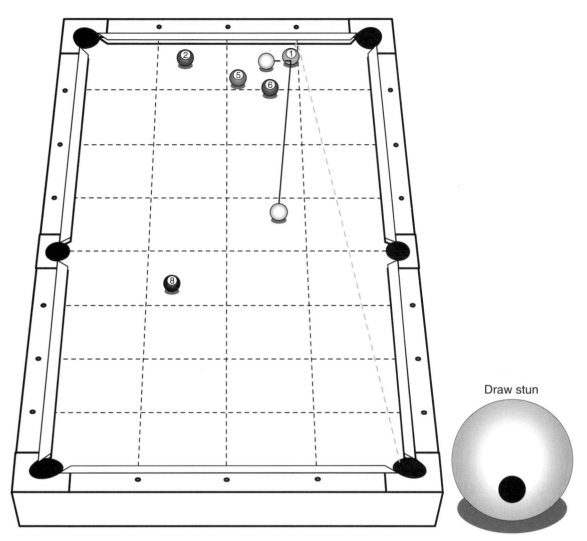

Draw stun

Figure 7.14   Don't go for the tough shot and overlook
a potential safety situation.

leaving their opponent in a tough spot. If you're attempting a kick and there's a cluster of object balls around your target ball, it's much easier to hook your opponent just by hitting the correct side of the object ball.

When you start learning to kick at balls, practice trying to hit one side of the ball and then the other. Only in rare instances (such as when your object ball is hung in the pocket and you're kicking to play position off that ball) will you want to kick full into an object ball. In safety play, though, hitting one side or the other will be what is most often required of you to return a safe play to your opponent.

In figure 7.17 you'll find an excellent example of an opponent's safety. You're going to use high ball (follow) and kick rail-first into the 5-ball. Using follow on the cue ball will actually produce the reverse (draw effect) on the cue ball as it leaves the rail and contacts the 5-ball, allowing you to hit the 5-ball and park the cue ball somewhere between the 6-ball and 8-ball. And, by contacting the 5-ball on the

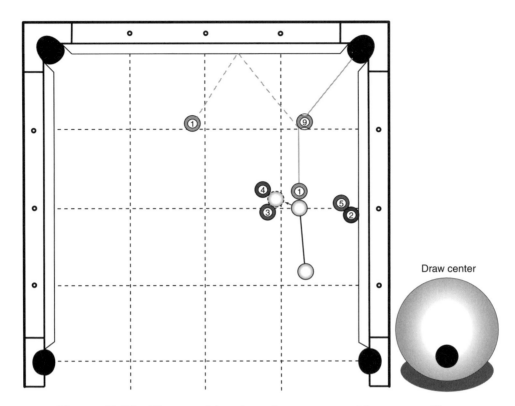

Figure 7.15   The combination shot can provide an excellent
two-way shot possibility.

side, you will send it into the rail and back out, leaving less chance of the cue ball
having a clear path to the 5-ball for your opponent. Practice this shot. Variations
of it come up more often than you would think.

PLANNING A SAFETY

When you're playing Nine Ball, the opportunity to plan a safe in advance comes
up quite often. You'll recognize it more easily when you have balls tied up that
you just can't break up with earlier shots in the rack. For example, say you break
the balls and you notice that the 6-ball and 7-ball are tied up but the rest of the
balls are straight into the pocket. There's no way to break up these balls with the
shots you have leading up to them. In this case, the best thing for you to do is to
run down to the 5-ball and make it very easy for yourself to play a safety on the
6-ball. You'll want to get the angle to kill the cue ball after hitting the 6-ball and
freeze it to the 7-ball. With one foul, ball in hand rules, you should always run up
to your trouble balls and try to place the cue ball in position where it's relatively
easy to play a strong safety. Simply stated, if you cannot bust up that cluster
before you get to it, you're better off playing a safety from that cluster.

In figure 7.18, you are presented with a situation where the 6-ball and the 8-
ball are tied up. You have no realistic way of breaking up the 6-8 cluster from

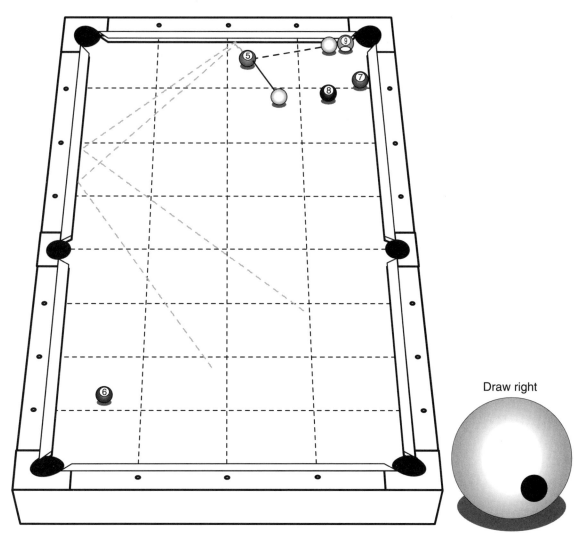

Figure 7.16   The carom shot is a common two-way
shot in Nine Ball.

the shot you have on the 5-ball. Make it easy on yourself by playing correct shape on the 5-ball. Go two rails on the cue ball after contact with the 5-ball (short rail, long rail, as illustrated), giving yourself a straight angle shot on the 6-ball. Now you can contact the 6-ball, sending it into the rail, while just sliding the cue ball over and freezing it on the 8-ball. If the cue ball is very close to the 8-ball, your opponent will have few options. If it's frozen on the 8-ball, so much the better!

WHEN TO PLAY SAFE

As time goes on, you will become more and more proficient at these simple safeties, and your safety game can become more and more elaborate. You will learn to

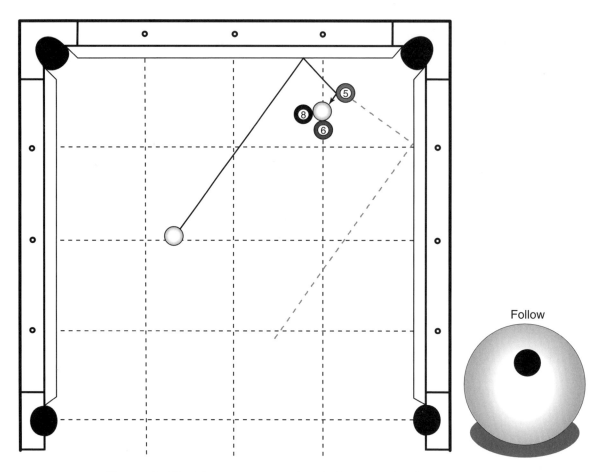

Figure 7.17   Your opponent has left you safe. Counter with
a safety of your own.

immediately recognize a great safety opportunity and begin creating more imaginative safeties on your own. In fact, some of the most imaginative players actually
prefer to play One Pocket. This is a game, when played well, that becomes virtually all creative safety play until your opponent makes that one mistake that will
allow you to run out.

In today's most popular games of Eight Ball and Nine Ball, keep a few simple
safety rules in mind. If you can't make the shot you're presented with at least 75-80
percent of the time, try and find some place to play a safety. If you're playing an
opponent whose game is far superior to your own, raise that percentage to 90
percent of the time. In this way, you take the least amount of risk in allowing your
opponent a runout, and give yourself the best chance for an easier runout when
you get back to the table. It's always better to play the smart safety shot and let
your opponent make the first mistake!

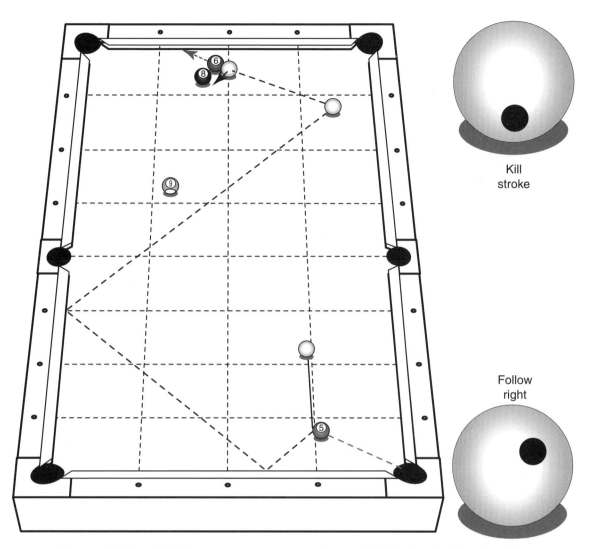

Kill
stroke

Follow
right

Figure 7.18 Safeties may not come up immediately, but with a tough
rack it's wise to plan a creative safety in advance.

As you can see, safety play can become a very big part of your game. The more creative you are and the more willing you are to use your imagination, the better your safety game will become. It is in this creation and execution of safeties that your precision pool game will advance to a higher mental awareness. The intricacies and options available to you, each time you play, are endless; and that's what makes the cue sports such a challenge! Add to this all the strategies and tactics involved in rules of game and match play and we can assure you that you'll remain challenged for years to come.

Challenging Safety Games

One of the most difficult tasks in safety play is figuring out a way to practice! Safeties may not come up often enough in your regular playing for you to really learn them, and drills just don't cut it in this area. Since the true secret to great safety play is imagination and creativity, you need to practice creating safeties where you don't naturally see them. Here are a few easy ways to make safety practice productive and interesting!

Practicing by Yourself

Start with a rack of six balls (the 4-ball through the 9-ball) racked in a small triangle with the 4-ball in front. Break the balls wide open. Now, whether or not you have a shot on the 4-ball, play safe instead. You can attempt to hide the 4-ball, or try and hide the cue ball. If the option exists, hide both balls. Even if the 4-ball is straight in the pocket, you must play a safety. Following your first safety, if you can't see the 4-ball, try to kick at it and leave it safe again. You continue to play safe on this ball until you leave yourself a shot on it. Then pocket the 4-ball and play safety on the 5-ball.

This simple exercise will force you to practice your cue ball and object ball speed as well as your tactical play. As you play, you'll soon realize that there are some places that work better than others for **ducking** purposes. You will constantly have to create a safety where you don't automatically see one. Practice freezing the cue ball to other balls and leaving yourself absolutely no shot. We see a great many pro players doing this in warm-ups—testing the speed of the cloth and trying to knock an object ball to a rail while freezing the cue ball to another ball.

Once you get proficient at this, try a full rack of nine balls. Or, if Eight Ball is your game of choice, rack all 15 balls. In each safety attempt, try and hide yourself from all the balls in the other group. From here, expand to playing safe and then trying to maneuver your way out of your own safety.

Here's another interesting exercise to try. Throw a few balls on the table and simply aim with your cue ball to cut an object ball as thinly as possible, sending the cue ball down table. Your goal is twofold. First, you want to keep the object ball very close to where it was, moving it no more than an inch or two. At the same time you are trying to control the speed of the cue ball. Very thin cuts often provide excellent safety options, but this is a shot that needs specific practice attention. Too many players see the shot, but either hit the ball too full and sell out, or try to hit it so thin they completely miss the ball and give their opponent cue ball in hand!

Practicing With a Partner

You and your partner can play what's called Safety Nine Ball. Break the balls, and play safe on the 1-ball. If your opponent can see it, she can shoot it in but then must play safe on the 2-ball. If she can't see it, she must try and kick it safe. If you can then see the ball, you may pocket it and then must play safe on the 2-ball, and so on. The better you both get at playing safe, the longer a single game will take you. You'll find that it can be quite difficult to play safe on each shot. As a result, you'll learn a great deal more about creating safeties than you would in ordinary game situations.

This is also an excellent game for developing your mental concentration and patience in your safety game. Having the mental determination to engage in a grueling safety battle not only protects your table territory, but can wear down the competition. Your opponent will become frustrated and you have the best chance of toughing it out for the first shot that offers a true offensive opportunity!

Chapter 8

Match Strategy and Tactics

Beyond basic pattern and safety play are literally hundreds of advanced game situations you should be prepared for if you plan on any sort of regular competition. Competition may be local, regional, or professional tournaments, or organized league play. In this section we will deal with little "tricks of the trade," less publicized but imperative for a well-rounded pool game. These include when to roll out or take an intentional foul, winning games via the three-foul rule, using an opponent's strengths and weaknesses to your best advantage, and team strategy.

In each case, the knowledge we are sharing with you is perfectly fair and legal. We are not proponents of shark moves and poor behavior at the pool table. A win is only a win if you've accomplished it on a level playing field. There's no voodoo here, no cheating, no shortcuts. However, advanced strategy and tactics will provide more of an edge in your competitive play than you ever thought possible. And all this just by knowing rules and key elements of the game that your opponents may not have taken the time to learn or incorporate into their own game.

ASSESSING YOUR OPPONENT

Assessing the strengths and weaknesses of your opponent can influence your game plan as you prepare to begin a match. For example, at a recent women's pro tournament, the female coauthor of this book was preparing for a match against a player to whom she had recently lost. The male coauthor (aka "Coach") advised her that the best strategy against this player was a game laden heavily with safety play. "If you don't have a shot, duck!"

The reasoning: He had watched the opponent play a couple of other matches, and noticed that, when confronted with a safety, she had very little talent kicking at balls, giving up ball in hand on virtually every kick attempt! The result: Despite less than stellar play, a defeat over this player was possible with a couple of ball in hand opportunities that might not otherwise have been planned without knowing this player's weakness.

Now you may not have the advantage of a great coach. But you will very often, especially playing local events on a regular basis, have a chance to watch other players that you will at some time be matched up against. Take the time to watch their games. Monitor whether they avoid long shots, have problems kicking at balls, can't bank balls, and so on.

Be careful not to assume that because your opponent has a certain weakness that you do not, you will automatically win. We've seen otherwise excellent players focusing so much on what their opponent is doing the first few games that they pay little attention to their own game. Worse, we've seen players obviously underestimate an opponent, and subsequently take low-percentage shots, assuming they will automatically get another chance at the table. No matter whom you are playing, never assume you will get a reprieve inning at the table, unless of course you are playing a safety.

Courtesy of Pool & Billiard Magazine

Filipino player Efren Reyes is an expert at mental toughness.

This leads us to a major rule in the games of pool: *play the table!* Always play the rack as if it will be your one chance for this game's win. This will keep you physically and mentally ready, no matter what the skill level of your next opponent. While it's to your advantage to know your opponent's game, once you step to the match, you'll need to forget the opponent, get focused on your game, and play the table. When it's your turn at the table, nothing else matters—just you, that table, and the task at hand.

Because of the challenging nature of the game, pool is probably one of the best games for bringing out competitive spirit in players. Excellence in pool requires tremendous physical control and mental discipline. Pool is an individual, noncontact sport, but at the same time you are playing the table, you are immersed in combat against your opponent. And while it's important to both assess your opponent and play the table, the most common mistake made by players is to incorrectly gauge the level of their competition and change their game to suit that assessment. Always remain aware of the fact that there is a very fine line between an excellent player and an above average player. If you take your opponent lightly, not giving him the respect deserved, even a player who demonstrates far less skill can best you.

FACING TOUGH COMPETITION

Let's change the scenario around a bit. You're playing in a local tournament, and you just found out that your next match is against John, the club's house pro. John not only dominates the local scene, but has fared well in several recent pro events. You may be feeling a little doom and gloom, since this is only your second tournament, and this win would have put you into the money rounds. Nevertheless, you need to be aware that you have a couple of advantages over John, advantages that could catapult you into the winner's circle!

First, you're an unknown quantity. You haven't played John before, and he doesn't know your game, though you've watched him play plenty of times. You have nothing to lose. John does. John is expected to win. You are actually in a great spot now, because you can relax and just have fun. John may have a harder time doing this. If you win, great. If you don't, you will have gotten the opportunity to play against a better player, measure how you fared against him, and hopefully learned something that you can take with you to your next match.

What occurs on those occasions when you're matched up against an opponent with a reputation? You have a tendency to give him more credit than he deserves. When you put a player above his ability level, it takes away from your own game. You begin anticipating what's going to happen, often predicting an unfavorable outcome. It's at this point in time that you have to just play the game, play the table, and forget about your opponent. We've all fallen into that trap of playing the opponent and not the table. But all players' games would improve rather quickly if they concentrated on their own talents and improvement of their skills. When you compete, don't take players for granted, but also don't overestimate the talent of higher-echelon players. Find your even keel by playing the table.

Another great quality to develop when facing tough competition is tenacity. You have to be like a bulldog out there. Never give up. You could be down 8-1 in a race to 9. It doesn't matter. We've seen countless matches where players have been that far in the hole and come back to win. And we've seen players who, after being up 8-1, completely lost their mental toughness as their opponent came back on them. Some players fold; the players who are mentally tough will not fold. They will want to defeat their opponents as quickly as possible. This attitude comes from developing mental toughness through practice and experience.

Try to stay really focused on the game itself, more so than your opponent. It doesn't matter what she does, or how she leaves you, or if she runs five racks. Stay focused and play your own game when it's your turn. This can be difficult to do at first, and there's often a bit of psychological warfare going on during such matches. The toughest part of the game is to watch your opponent run racks or get great rolls. You're sitting in the chair and you can do nothing about it. But rather than act frustrated or throw a tantrum (which too many players do), you will do best to show no emotion at all. This tactic, more so than outward displays of emotion, will get into your opponent's head. She can't help but wonder, "What is he thinking about?" or "Isn't he worried?" It's this kind of tough mental attitude that will wear down your opponent and give you the edge.

That's the mental side of it. What can you do physically to improve your chances? Eight Ball is an excellent game from which to draw examples of physical changes you might make in your game, depending on the skill level of your opponent. The game of Eight Ball so often comes down to timing, which is nothing more than knowing when to try and run out. If you are playing a weaker player, chances are good that he or she will not run out but instead will clear off three, possibly four balls and leave you a wide-open table.

The stiffer the competition, the sooner you must attempt to run out, because the better player will be doing the same thing. In most league Eight Ball competition today, organizers have made it crucial for the player to run out as soon as possible, because the score is dictated by the number of balls your opponent has left on the table. While it's probably better to play for the game win than ball by ball, the rules have evolved for the sake of time. Strictly going by game wins and losses would cause a lot more games to go into overtime as players became accustomed to winning via long and tedious safety battles. With the evolved rules, every ball counts; so when playing a skilled opponent, you must take maximum advantage of your inning at the table.

All things being equal, if two players are evenly matched, the outcome will usually come down to who's psychologically stronger. The player who plays the strategically sound game will be in a better position to win. For example, if it's prudent to play a safety in a match situation, the person with better strategy *will* play the safety. A player with weaker strategic skills will take the "flyer" or try something off the wall, in a desperate attempt to create something that isn't there. Those are the situations that will always come back to haunt you.

You will develop sound strategy most quickly by actually facing very tough competition over and over again. It's a process of building your mental toughness and becoming more aware of certain shots and situations. The more you play, the tougher you become. The tougher you become, the more matches you will win. You will develop mental calluses that will enable you to shake off tense situations, surrounding distractions, and the pressure of knowing what's at stake.

USING ROLLOUTS TO YOUR ADVANTAGE

The rollout refers to an option after the break in Nine Ball. Its use or misuse can vastly change the outcome of a game. The reasoning behind implementation of

Entering the Competitive Pool Arena

You're ready for league and tournament competition, but where do you begin? If your preference is for competition in your local bar, you'll more than likely be playing Eight Ball. If your favorite bar is not already involved in a local league, you have a couple of options. Try another local establishment, or find out what leagues exist in the area and convince the owner of your favorite location to get involved.

Eight Ball leagues come in two basic flavors: independent local leagues and leagues affiliated with a national organization. Independent local leagues will be owned and operated by an area player, enthusiast, or club owner. They typically feature a $5-7 weekly fee to participate, and tavern owners also pay a fee to host a team. Monies collected are put towards administration (scorekeeping, scheduling, etc.), season-end celebrations, trophies, and sometimes purse money for the highest finishing team(s). The money is a bonus—if you're looking to make a score, independent leagues won't make you rich quick. If you're looking for camaraderie, competition, team spirit, and the chance to play competitively on a weekly basis, this is for you.

Then there are those leagues affiliated with national organizations, such as the Billiard Congress of America (BCA), the Valley National Eightball Association (VNEA), or the American Poolplayers Association (APA). If your local league is affiliated, your team's success could take you on to regional and/or national competition. These organizations host annual national championships with six-figure purses, and feature competition by hundreds of teams who travel to Las Vegas and other destinations to meet up with other teams from across the nation. Events usually contain masters and regular divisions, and some include **scotch doubles** teams, seniors, juniors, and wheelchair divisions.

If tournament competition better suits your game, most billiard clubs offer some form of weekly (or monthly) scratch or handicap tournaments. Formats will vary, as will the games. Typically, Nine Ball and Eight Ball tournaments are the norm at most clubs, though some host Straight Pool and 3-Cushion Billiard tournaments. Many clubs also offer in-house or traveling Eight Ball and Nine Ball leagues, giving patrons the best of both worlds. Our recommendation is **round-robin** tournaments, which give you the chance to play several different people for your entry fee. These will run anywhere from $5 to $25, depending on the club. If round-robin tournaments are not readily available, the next best thing is the **double-elimination** format. In this type of tournament, you proceed through the winner's bracket until you lose, then move to the one-loss bracket. Two losses and you are out. The eventual winner of the one-loss bracket plays the winner of the winner's bracket for the title. Finally, there are **single-elimination** events; you lose, you're out.

Promotionally-minded clubs will also host events on regional tours, open to amateur and professional players, along with state championships and sometimes even professional events. If you have the opportunity to play in a regional tour or state championship event—do so! You'll get to see quite a few accomplished players, and many of these events are qualifiers for bigger tournaments. Some of the regional tours also offer point formats and rankings, with rewards and recognition to top point getters at season's end. These tournaments will happen less regularly (every two to six weeks) and require entry fees from $25 to $65, but they tend to be run more smoothly and offer purse money in excess of what has been put up by the players.

the rollout rule was that the first shot after the break was the one shot that both players could be unwittingly penalized by. For example, the player breaking the balls pockets nothing on the break, but the balls come to rest in a manner that does not allow the opponent to hit the lowest numbered ball on the table. The breaking player is unfairly rewarded for a poor break. A player could break badly, make no balls, sit down, and watch his opponent suffer with absolutely no shot. At the same time, the player could accomplish a great break, pocket two balls, and suddenly the cue ball is kissed to a point on the table where the designated object ball cannot be hit.

Putting the Rollout to Work

To avoid the situations just outlined, on the first shot after the break, either player (depending on who is at the table) can roll the cue ball to another position on the table, without hitting the lowest-numbered ball, and without it being considered a foul. You may hit a rail, but you do not have to. You may pocket a ball. You may use the shot to tie up other balls.

For example, let's say that you are at the table and it's your break. You break the balls and make a ball, but wind up with a very difficult shot on the 1-ball. You now have the option to roll out (shoot the cue ball) to a spot where you think you would have the advantage over your opponent. Your opponent then has a decision to make: to take the shot you've left him, or invent a safety of his own. Or he can hand the shot back to you, in which case you must shoot again. In either case, whether he elects to take the shot or hands it back, this shot must now be legally hit.

Unfortunately, too many players are unfamiliar with the full impact the rollout can have on a game and its most effective strategic uses. This is an incredibly useful tactic to set up a shot that you are more capable of executing than your opponent. If she banks poorly, simply roll out to a bank. If she has a miserable time with long shots, leave her long. If you are playing a better player, you'll usually find that there's more safety play early in the rack, whereas with a weaker player, more safeties will happen later on in the rack. This makes the rollout an important shot in the game when you are playing a strong player. Make one crucial mistake in the beginning of the rack and your opponent will run out; or she will turn the tables on you to a point where you will be kicking two or three rails to get a hit on the object ball. In this case, your best bet may be to roll out with a safety in mind should your opponent pass the shot back.

If you wish to roll out to a possible safety situation, you definitely have to use your imagination and visualize what you want to accomplish before the rollout. You must know where to put the cue ball, and at the same time understand what you will do with the shot if your opponent gives it back to you. Never just bump the cue ball to where you can see the object ball. Without a plan, your careless rollout could prove fatal to you.

A good rollout at the beginning of the game can be equated to a well-executed chess play. It involves strategy, predicting what your opponent will do, and alternative plans should she do the unexpected. If your opponent has the shot, and she rolls out to a certain area of the table, you have several quick decisions to make:

1. What is she trying to do?
2. Does she have the ability to execute the shot she left for herself?

3. Can she execute it with any degree of efficiency and proceed through the rack?

If the answers to numbers 2 and 3 are yes, then you are forced to play that shot. You certainly don't want to give it back to her.

Rollout Tricks of the Trade

There are several specific rollout tricks of the trade that we can share with you. It's important to know how to roll out to your best advantage, and equally important, you must know how to react to a rollout shot given to you. We've seen each of the following techniques used to great advantage by players. (So don't let 'em know who told you!)

Adding Distance

First, with all other things being equal, the longer the distance you put between the cue ball and the object ball, the greater the degree of difficulty. A difficult long shot, with the added limitation of having little control over the cue ball for the next shot, will make things tricky for your opponent. If he takes the flyer, so much the better for you. If he passes it back, make sure you have a safety attempt already in mind. Figure 8.1 illustrates such an example. By rolling the cue ball near the rail, you've left your opponent long and nearly straight on the 1-ball. (Try never to freeze the cue ball to a rail.) This is a difficult shot, but your opponent may try it anyway. If he does make it, though, what is he going to do with the 2-ball?

Looking Ahead

Let's say your opponent decided to roll out to the straight-in shot. These happen to be your favorite shots and you jump up to attack. Again, the only problem is that your next object ball is at the other end of the table. You always need to ascertain exactly where the balls are on the table and if the shot you have confidence in making actually has any future in it! In this particular situation it does not. There's no way to get back on the next ball. You're much better off, actually, playing a safety off the object ball (in this case, the 1-ball), rather than attempting to pocket the ball and draw the cue ball the length of the table or cheat the pocket and follow the length of the table. By taking the safety, you can still maintain control of the table without passing the shot back, and give your opponent a miserable situation to contend with in return. Only now, there's no longer a choice involved—she must shoot.

In our next situation, shown in figure 8.2, you break the balls, make a ball, and nearly pocket the 9-ball, leaving it hanging precariously on the lip! Worse still, you cannot see the 1-ball and there's no place to roll out to that won't result in your opponent banking the 1-ball into the 9-ball, or making the 1-ball and then a 2-9 combination. You'd be surprised how often similar situations come up; players execute a poor rollout, hoping that they'll get back to the table. That seldom happens. Your best maneuver is to pocket the 9-ball and roll the cue ball to a spot where you can see the 1-ball. In Nine Ball, all balls stay down, except the 9-ball, which will be brought back to the foot spot. This can prove to be an even greater move if there are other balls near the spot, which could create a difficult cluster for your opponent.

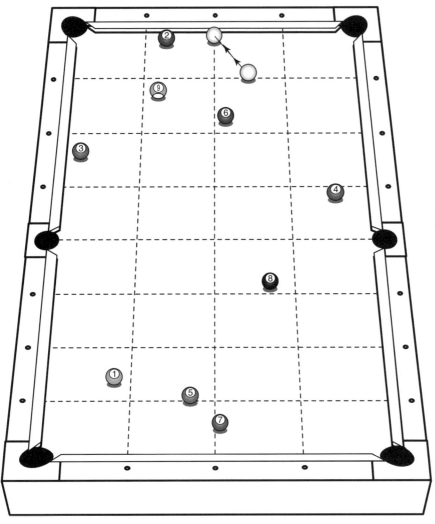

Figure 8.1 Rolling out to
leave your opponent
a long shot.

Creating Clusters

This brings us to another good rollout maneuver—creating clusters with other balls. When you create a cluster, keep in mind that you will always want to put the lowest-numbered ball of the group closer to the pocket. Figure 8.3 illustrates this. You are playing from the right corner pocket and there are a couple of balls around there. You can tie up the 3 and 5 balls, with the 3-ball closer to the right corner pocket than the 5-ball. This creates all kinds of problems for your opponent. If you put the 5-ball closer to the pocket, your opponent might have a carom or combination shot or safety opportunity, where he can also open the cluster. Remember to still have a safety option in mind for the 1-ball, as you may be asked to shoot again!

Speed Control

Speed control is an important factor in your rollout skills. Careless speed control can leave your opponent a runout opportunity, or worse, leave you in an even less desirable position should the shot be handed back to you. Creating clusters is one example of this, since careful speed control results in a cluster, while too hard a hit can break up the balls and actually make the run easier for your opponent.

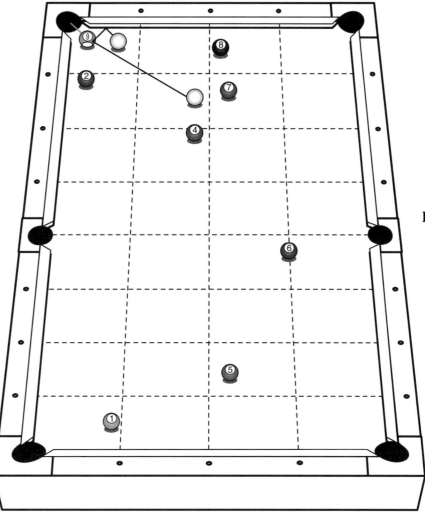

Figure 8.2 Your best move here is to pocket the 9-ball with your rollout.

Another example is when you're just trying to roll the cue ball a few inches to a certain spot on the table near a cushion. In this case you're not trying to freeze the cue ball on the cushion. If you do land the cue ball too close to the rail, your opponent will often give you the shot. It's much harder to execute a shot with the cue ball frozen on the cushion.

Rolling Out to a Jump Shot

As you learned in chapter 5 on critical shots, the jump shot used to be a rare shot indeed, and a very strong move for those players who could do it well. This was quite a safety and rollout maneuver for these players. They would roll out to a jump shot and their opponents were usually glad to hand it back. With the advent of today's myriad of jump cues, this is no longer the case. Lots of players can jump balls quite proficiently. Nevertheless, if this is one of your strong areas, it's worth a try. If your opponent opts to give it back, you've now learned that you can use the move again in the match, since she's obviously not fond of the shot. If she does elect to take the shot, and fails, you still have the option of using the move. The next time it comes up, your opponent, now lacking confidence, may opt to give you the shot back. And that will be to your advantage.

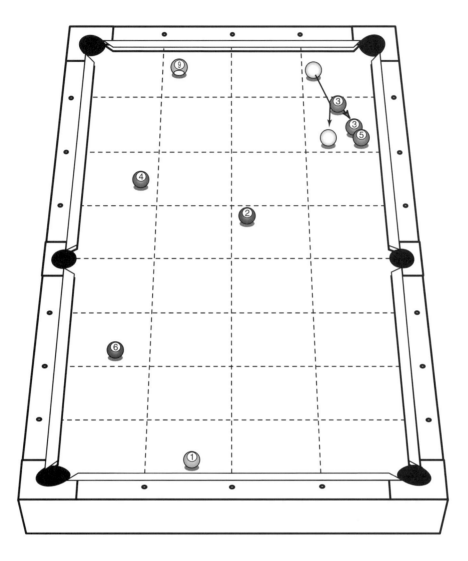

Figure 8.3 Another good rollout maneuver, creating clusters.

Rolling Out to a Kick Shot

Rolling out to a kick shot presents a similar scenario. Many of today's players are quite adept at kicking at balls. If your opponent is strong in this area, chances are he won't just kick to legally hit the ball. He will attempt to hit the hidden ball on one side or the other, driving it away from the cue ball and leaving you with a safety in return. Those same accomplished kicking artists will roll out to kick shots themselves. If you're not good at kicking balls, you're going to have to give up that shot to your opponent. It's therefore worthwhile to improve your skills in this area. If you cannot execute a kick shot with any degree of efficiency, you're in big trouble because you'll have to give up the shot, hoping your opponent makes a mistake and lets you back to the table.

Finally, if your opponent is weak in the rollout game and rolls out to a position where you have a difficult but makable shot, exercise the option to do so. The shot may be tougher than what you feel you can handle, but plan ahead. Play the shot so that if you do miss the ball, you will not sell out the rack. If you make it—great. If not, you will leave your opponent a very difficult shot or put her into a tough

Top ranked WPBA pro Ewa Mataya-Laurance using a jump cue.

position where she won't be able to see the ball and will have to play a miraculous shot of her own. This is commonly referred to as a free shot, since you have a great deal to gain and nothing to lose should you miss.

USING FOULS TO YOUR ADVANTAGE

A foul means scratching the cue ball or not contacting the proper ball or group of balls first. In Nine Ball and some Eight Ball league rules, a foul by your opponent allows you to place the cue ball anywhere on the table when you take over the table. It's a great advantage, to be sure, but even greater are the tactics behind fouls: how to cause them and how to capitalize on them, even if no runout opportunity exists.

Three-Foul Rules

Just like the rollout, another rule that more players should take advantage of is the three-foul rule. Three consecutive fouls by the same player is loss of game. This comes up most often, again, in the game of Nine Ball, though it's also applicable to Eight Ball in many sanctioned leagues and tournaments, and applicable in One Pocket. You have to pay attention to the actual game situation at all times to take advantage of the three-foul rule. In pro competition, it is required that you tell your opponent he is on two fouls in order to have his third foul count as a loss of game. Local and regional tournaments sometimes do not have this rule in place. In these instances it is considered proper etiquette to inform your opponent that he is on two fouls before he approaches the table for his next attempt at a legal hit. Since your opponent may not return the same measure of respect for you, pay attention to your own game, too, and do your best to avoid being put in this position. For example, you won't want to take an intentional foul if you know you are already on one foul and if there are plenty of places your opponent can hide the cue ball to foul you a third time and win the game.

Now that we've explained the defensive aspect of the three-foul rule, we'll focus on ways you can capitalize on the offensive strategies involved in the game. We'll begin with the break. If your opponent scratches on the break, or the cue ball leaves the bed of the table during the break, you will have ball in hand. A scratch on the break usually gives you one of three excellent options. First and most obvious is a runout. If the balls have spread well and you have the advantage of cue ball in hand to plan the ideal run, by all means do so. Second, having ball in hand may present you with a combination situation, if the lowest numbered ball on the table is close to the 9-ball and in reasonable proximity to a pocket. Third, if neither of these two options look promising, you have the three-foul option. With most or all of the balls still on the table, it should be pretty easy to play an excellent safety and cause your opponent to foul again. Now she's on two fouls, you have her under pressure, and there are still plenty of places to hide. Again, remember to tell her that she is on two fouls before she approaches the table for her third attempt at a legal hit. Figure 8.4 and figure 8.5 illustrate an example of a ball in hand situation after the break and the two consecutive safeties that will most likely result in a three-foul game win. In the first illustration, you are sending the 1-ball toward the right corner pocket (near the 3 and 8 balls), while hiding the cue ball in the 5-6 cluster. If the player gets no hit, you simply send the 1-ball back toward the 5-6 cluster, hiding your cue ball in the 3-8 cluster! By planning your safeties ahead of time, you will be able to better capitalize on the three-foul rule.

By now, you should realize that having ball in hand gives you no guarantee of running the table. If you have two or three clusters on the table, even with ball in hand you won't be able to tackle them all. It's usually wise in this case, especially with your opponent already on one foul, to play another safety and let him try the kick shot! Even better, with ball in hand, you can often strategically place the ball he will be kicking at near one of your problem clusters. Whether or not he makes a legal hit, he's bound to break up one of your problem areas, possibly allowing you to then plan a runout.

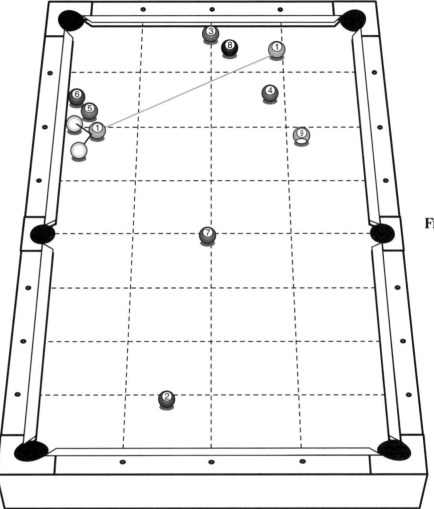

Figure 8.4   First safety in a three-foul strategy.

Intentional Fouls

Sometimes you may be better off taking an intentional foul of your own. If the balls already look problematic for your opponent, it's probably not prudent to try an impossible kick and risk loosening up the table layout for him. In figure 8.6, we've shown you such an example in a game of Nine Ball. The 2-ball and 4-ball are tied up, along with the 5-ball and 6-ball. Even with ball in hand, your opponent will not be able to win the game in the next inning. He'd have to open up two clusters and leave you safe at the same time! In this situation the strategy would dictate that you give your opponent cue ball in hand by simply shooting away, or picking up the cue ball and handing it to him.

Remember to resort to the intentional foul only when there is not a legitimate shot present that will allow you to open up the balls and still get a decent shot on the next ball. This is the only time that you will be much better off giving your opponent ball in hand instead of trying to do something difficult. Trying the difficult shot will probably give your opponent cue ball in hand anyway, but you risk disturbing the balls and allowing him an easier runout.

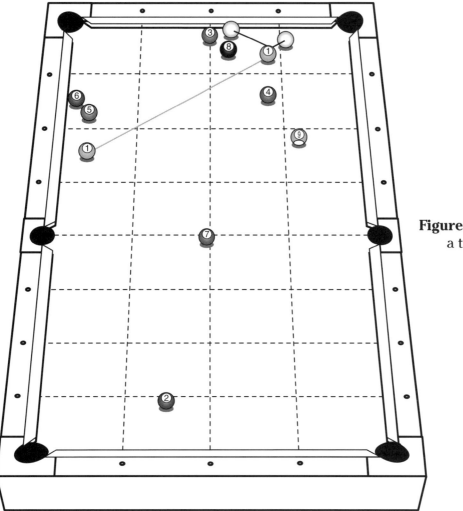

Figure 8.5 Second safety in a three-foul strategy.

Here's yet another way to prevent your opponent from running out even if he's left you in a predicament. Let's say you are left with a very difficult safety; you are well hooked and you have little or no chance to hit the ball. Apply what you learned about creating clusters in the section on rollouts! Attempt to create a cluster with another group of balls, so that even if your opponent gets ball in hand, he won't be able to run the table in the next inning. Remember to try to place the lowest-numbered ball of the group you are tying up closest to the pocket, making it more difficult for him to break up the cluster.

TEAM STRATEGY

Hundreds of thousands of players compete in sanctioned league competition each year, in addition to hundreds of independent leagues operating across the nation. Team league competition is such a big part of today's recreational cue sports, yet very little has been written about team play, and, more importantly, team strategy. The teams who win the big-purse amateur competitions aren't always the best

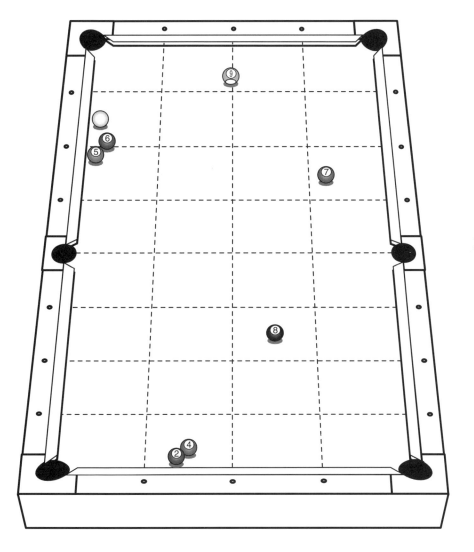

Figure 8.6 Taking an intentional foul.

players, but they are the best teams. They know how to capitalize on their strengths and minimize their weaknesses. Careful strategy goes into making them winners, just as in any professional franchised team sport.

The first things to consider in team strategy are the number of players you compete with on a team, what game you are playing, the format of the league, and who you will be playing against. Typically, teams are made up of three, four, or five people. In most cases, you may list additional players on your team roster, though they often must be declared when your team signs up. Have an understanding among your teammates, before the season begins, that each of you remains committed to completing the league season. It is frustrating, especially in sanctioned league competition, to lose a key player before qualifying for larger-purse regional and national events.

The majority of league play is Eight Ball, though Nine Ball leagues are picking up steam in some areas of the country. In Eight Ball leagues, because of the strategy involved, if you're trying to put together a winning team, you'll want good strategy players, not just great shotmakers. Remember, though, that your first consideration should be to have fun, and to be a team! Picking up a good player who doesn't normally associate with the rest of your team socially will sometimes bring down team moral, rather than improving the skill level of the other players.

Now it's league night, and you are in charge of the player lineup. Most often, a lineup will be dictated by who the opponents are in each individual match. There are two different schools of thought on creating a line-up. Some believe your stronger players should start, guaranteeing that they will play more games. The remaining players are ordered according to decreasing skill, with weaker players playing last.

Others believe your stronger players should play last, figuring that when it's crunch time they will have a much better chance of winning the match, particularly if it comes down to the last one or two games. We'd tend to side with those who believe that it's wiser to put the stronger players first, simply because you don't want to take the cue out of their hands. In other words, if you're playing on a five-person team and are down to three or four games left and already far behind, your better players become useless to the point that even their wins cannot pull you out. If both teams are packed full of great players, it really doesn't matter what you do. Just keep in mind that the playing level of your players can often determine the best team strategy.

As we've illustrated in this section, there are plenty of tactics and strategies involved in the cue sports, especially at the competitive level. Extensive knowledge of these requires practice and keen attention when you do compete. Always ask yourself, especially when you're in a tough spot, if there's a more clever option than the obvious first choice. The more you experiment, the greater number of tactics you will develop to improve your game, and more options will become second nature to you.

Chapter 9

Mind-Body Toughness

Think for a moment about why you want to play better pool. The reasons may be many and varied, but chances are they center around one of three primary motivations. You may play for the competition aspect, to beat an opponent. You may play for financial gain (e.g., tournament or league competition). Or, you may play to play the table; in other words, you play for the sheer beauty of the game and all its intricacies.

Option #3 is definitely the best reason to play and compete. Playing the table will make you the best player you can be. If there is any one concept that should be ingrained into the brain of a newcomer to the sport, this would be it. By continually learning and exceeding your own goals for your developing skill on the pool table, everything else will naturally follow.

This chapter deals specifically with attaining and exceeding your goals of high-performance pool playing through mental and physical training. You will learn to concentrate, to develop your skills of mental imaging (crucial to position play), and to improve your physical skills with increased power and coordination.

MENTAL TRAINING TECHNIQUES

Playing great pool involves a complex web of mental and physical coordination. According to Dr. Robert M. Nideffer in the *Athletes' Guide to Mental Training* (1985):

As a sport, billiards is much like archery in terms of both attention demands and the demands for control over muscle tension and coordination. A typical attentional sequence involves assessing the situation, including position of the balls on the table, game score, skill level of the opponent. Then, information is analyzed and a shot is planned. Next, attention is directed internally as the shot is rehearsed and as tension levels are adjusted and breathing controlled. Finally, attention narrows and becomes focused on the point that allows the player to stroke the ball in the desired manner. The athlete's analysis must allow the ability to think several shots ahead. (p. 139)

All of the mental and physical control required for the cue sports demands attention, concentration, and the use of mental imaging to produce the best performances. Haphazardly swatting at balls without a plan or attention to all the details set before you will prove suicidal in competition.

But, overfocus can be equally damaging. You may have heard a player say, after a match, "I thought too much" or "I overthought that shot." Too much attention to detail will produce mechanical body actions, unnatural rhythm, and second guessing in your pattern play and shot selection. You won't be allowing your body to let go and just play the game. It can be compared to picking up the phone and dialing a well-known number. You do it automatically, without conscious effort. Yet, someone can ask you the number, and you stare at the keypad, dumbfounded. So it is with pool. As your skills increase, your body develops muscle memory. When faced with a particular shot, your mind can successfully "dial the number" or remember the shot from a hundred times before.

Your focus, therefore, needs to be not on every little detail, but rather on letting your mind and body flow naturally through a game or match, while shutting off outside distractions.

Concentration

So how, you ask, can you concentrate and not concentrate, all at the same time? Well, if there were a magical formula for this, athletes would pay in spades. Nevertheless, concentration, by its definition, is attention to a specific *object*. You will need to learn to direct your attention to the proper *object* in pool to achieve complete concentration. That object is the task at hand—the game or match you are playing. Not each shot, not the crowd, not the clothes you are wearing or the tip of your cue, not self-reminders about stroking through the ball and not hitting a shot too softly. It is all these little details of our particular sport that can wreck your concentration on the task at hand.

You may have witnessed a match where a player plays an unbelievable game or series of games, seemingly effortless in their execution. Afterward, the player could honestly not tell you much about the match, or the crowd, or the room he just played in. It's often referred to as a trancelike state. The player's concentration was so honed, his attention to the task at hand so focused, that outside distractions literally disappeared, allowing him to completely utilize the knowledge he had gained through practice of his skills, without conscious thought or analysis. If you haven't yet experienced this in pool, or doubt that such a state exists, consider a simple example you probably have encountered, like driving home from work. Your mind can wander, and yet you arrive at your destination just fine, often not remembering specifically how you got there.

Again, we refer to the wise words of Robert M. Nideffer:

You are reacting so automatically that you do not have to consciously direct your body; you are simply letting it do what it has been trained to do. . . . Masters of karate and aikido refer to the special state of concentration where everything occurs automatically as "making your mind like water." When you

Courtesy of Pool & Billiard Magazine

ESPN Ultimate Nine Ball Champion and top ranked pro
Roger Griffis studies the table.

are in complete control of your mind, you are able to keep your own anxiety as well as external distractors from interfering with concentration. (pp. 6-7)

Think back to a time where you played a match, whether in a tournament or league, after not having played for a time. Chances are, you started out playing well; your mind forgot all the little commands and reminders that could interfere with your concentration. As the match progressed, it's also likely that you began to think more. Reminders and self-doubts started to creep into your head and you fought them with extra effort that was in fact needed for your focus on the game. Toward the end of the match, you became uncomfortable; your rhythm was off; you were having a more difficult time concentrating on the task at hand. Your mind began telling you all the things you should be doing and second-guessing all your moves. Your play was no longer natural or flowing; it became a series of little steps and actions, diametrically opposed to the ideal flow of an athletic performance.

Total concentration requires freedom from such internal, as well as external, distractions. If your mental and physical response to the task at hand is not automatic, your attention will scatter. Your brain will begin a searching for an answer to what you should do next; your attention will turn from the match to inward thoughts and often self-doubt.

Preparation

Now that you understand what concentration is, we can work on a few methods to improve it. First, you must come to your practice session, tournament match, or league night prepared. What do you use to prepare yourself for competition in other areas of your life? Many of these same things will help your pool game. For example, if you prepare for a big business meeting by dressing up to boost your self-image and confidence, you should take this theory with you to your pool game. We don't expect you to wear a three-piece suit to league night! What we are referring to is your comfort at the table. Play in clothes (and shoes) that make you feel comfortable and confident; this will be one less thing to think about. Before you work out, you should have a routine for stretching your muscles, which promotes better muscle action and relaxation. This should be no different than when you prepare for a pool workout! (See our section on page 222 about stretching target areas for the pool player.) You also should make sure to eat a light, healthy meal before engaging in any sport activity. Pool, again, is no different. Just because you may not work up a sweat during a long match, you will exert a tremendous amount of both physical and mental energy. If your body hasn't been fueled, your energy will run low, resulting in poor performance. Conversely, a huge meal will weigh you down and make you uncomfortable at the table. This commonsense guide to preparation is the first step in maximizing your concentration.

Relaxation

The second step is relaxation. In pool, if you are keyed up or anxious, you are sunk. Because of your natural flight/fight reaction to tense situations, your body will produce extra adrenaline to physically prepare it for the battle at hand. While this may be a nice feature for sprinting or bullfighting, the touch and finesse required in pool will surely suffer from too much power in your stroke! And, across the board, coaches in virtually every sport promote relaxation for their athletes through deep-breathing exercises. For example, the various martial arts demand its use, and for good reason. Deep breathing clears both the mind and the body, allowing calm focus on the task at hand.

There are dozens of deep-breathing methods recommended from almost every authority on mental training in sport. If this is a subject that interests you, there are a variety of books devoted to just this topic. In a favorite book of ours, *Mental Training for Peak Performance* by Steven Ungerleider, PhD (1996), an entire chapter is devoted to breathing exercises. According to Ungerleider, "the most important single aspect to staying focused in sport is breathing. Without proper breathing, even the best-conditioned athletes can get easily winded and fatigued and perform poorly" (p. 22).

This is actually great news for us pool players! Deep breathing is something we can do not only before a match, but each time we are sitting in our chairs waiting for our next opportunity at the table. The anxiety normally caused by waiting for your opponent to miss can be immediately conquered by concentrating on your breathing while in your chair. Try this. Take a deep breath through your nose, visualizing as you inhale that the air is being drawn into the very center of your body. Do this for 8 counts. Hold the breath for 2 counts, then slowly release it for 16 counts through your mouth, visualizing as you do that all the tension, anxiety, and self-doubt is exiting with that breath. Some people add to this visualization by using colors. When breathing in, visualize the color blue. When breathing out, visualize the color red. Blue is said to be a relaxing color, while red equates with anxiety. Therefore you are taking in relaxation and releasing anxiety. Players will often tell you that a few minutes of breathing exercise before they play will actually enable them to feel lighter, more ready to play, more focused, and that the table and balls even seem clearer and brighter in their vision.

Once you are prepared and relaxed, your focus and concentration will allow you to make your own mind like water and turn in your own peak performance. But one further step is necessary, and that is shutting down those external, or outside, distractions. Though pool is often compared to an activity like chess, or to a sport like golf, the crowds and patrons of tournaments, billiard clubs, and lounges usually don't know or respect the kind of concentration required for our sport. It's rude, but not uncommon, for a waitress or customer to walk in front of your line of sight as you pull the trigger, and only the most focused players can avoid these kinds of distractions. On the other hand, athletes in many fields must conquer the same distractions. Picture the gymnast, who, while competing on the balance beam, must deal with the sudden burst of applause directed toward a performance on the uneven parallel bars mere feet from where she is completing her own routine. You are not alone, and you can make use of advice given to these same athletes in similar situations.

First, relaxation is paramount and, again, best achieved through deep breathing. Second, chances are good that your concentration, like that of other athletes, is deteriorating while you are not actually playing, but as you wait for your next match, or your next turn at the table. You begin to hear the voice of the rather boisterous fan behind you, cheering on your opponent. You notice the waiter who seems determined to walk in front of players as they shoot, and you anticipate that he will do the same to you. You notice someone kicking her leg back and forth off the edge of her stool. The music is too loud, someone just dropped a glass—the list goes on and on. By the time you reach the table, your nerves are frayed. Like a scared rabbit, the least little movement caught from the corner of your eye will cause you to jump off your shot. Your concentration has shifted from the game to everything else but the task at hand.

Professional players are well aware of the potential hazards of outside distractions and have come up with several little tricks that keep them "dialed in." The following are a few of our favorites:

• Keep your eye on the cue ball while you are sitting in the chair. Don't watch how your opponent is playing, or try to predict what he or she will do next. Don't try to anticipate what shot you may have to take next. Just watch the cue ball. This keeps your mind and attention on the table. The last thing you want to be doing in the middle of a match is losing your focus by watching your opponent, or second-guessing what your next move will be, often becoming disappointed if your predictions do not come true. Keeping your eye on the cue ball will allow you to be ready to shoot when it is your turn. Your attention will not have to shift—you are already "zoned in" to where you need to be.

• Develop a rhythm or tempo in your mind. Establish what your own rhythm for shot execution is at the table. For example, if you bend, execute two regular warm-up strokes, then a short stroke, then back and into your execution, your "beat" may be bum, bum, bum, be, bum, buuum. When you find this particular rhythm, you can repeat it over and over in your mind, even when you are not shooting. It's similar to a chant or mantra in meditation, where the sound of your own mental rhythm completely takes precedence over anything occurring around you.

• A variation of the above is to pick a favorite tune, something that matches the rhythm of your own playing style (hard rock not advised!) and hum it to yourself throughout the match. Many players find they actually play better with music in the background, as this allows them to lose themselves in that sound and forget other distractions.

• Also keep in mind that you need to distance yourself emotionally from these distractions. They are what they are. For example, that waitress and waiter are just doing their jobs, probably not realizing they're in the way. If an athlete gets too caught up in the "why is this happening to me?" syndrome, bad luck will surely prevail.

Mental Imaging

When you get to a certain point in your physical pool game, your mental game will make the difference between winning and losing. By mental game, we refer not just to the memory of runouts and proper strategy, but to three key mental elements used extensively in athlete training today: visualization, mental practice, and mental imagery. While they may sound the same and the terms often become interchangeable, it is important to know a bit about each, how they differ, and how you can utilize these simple concepts to further develop your pool game. From visualizing your shot and position-play selection, to mentally rehearsing shots, games, matches, and even entire events, to complete mental imagery, honing your mental imagination and focus will prove valuable to any player. Again, there have been entire volumes devoted to the practice and execution of different forms of mental imaging. A few of our favorites are listed on page 242.

Visualization

You're probably using visualization, in one form or another, in your pool game already. Players first learn to use visualization to pocket balls. Then they learn to expand their visualization techniques to position play. Thinking three balls ahead is a great example of this. If you are thinking three balls ahead (as we have strongly encouraged you to do!), you are already visualizing where the cue ball will have to be on the next ball to get to a visualized spot on the table for the third ball.

Here's a suggested sequence for utilizing your own visualization skills. First, set up a simple Nine Ball runout on your own table with which to practice. Begin by looking at your first shot. Visualize the object ball to be pocketed. See it in your mind's eye rolling crisply into the corner pocket. Then look for the position, or the angle, you want on the next object ball to get to the third object ball. As you visualize the shot in its entirety, narrow your focus to just the ball in the pocket and the resulting cue ball position. From there, step into your stance and execute the shot, allowing your mind to calculate all the things you have already taught it: cue ball speed, direction, spin, and so on. As you try this the first few times, keep in mind these "Do Nots": Do not consciously think of all the processes the cue ball must go through to get to the next ball! Do not just jump down on the shot after you visualize the object ball going into the hole. In other words, don't even step into your stance until you actually see the cue ball coming to a stop on the table. This will allow you to visualize the entire shot, not just pocketing the ball, which is really only a job half done.

Now let's see if you can take your visualization skills a couple of steps further. We have already mentioned how important it is to always have in mind a destination for your cue ball. But what happens when you are shooting at the game ball, like the 9-ball in Nine Ball or the 8-ball in Eight Ball? Visualization can be a powerful tool in these instances. Say you are shooting the 9-ball into the corner pocket. You know the cue ball can stop anywhere, so long as you do not scratch, and you will win the game. The danger in this thinking is that your mind can actually stop at the edge of that last ball. There's no extension or natural progression to the next ball and your mind has a tendency to just stop at contacting that ball. This is a predominant reason you see so many game balls missed in competition. But, if you always have a destination for the cue ball, your mind cannot stop or become lazy; it must complete the shot. Now, with this knowledge, use your visualization skills to imagine a 10-ball a couple feet from your game 9-ball. Again, visualize the entire shot—pocketing the 9-ball and arriving in position for the imaginary 10-ball—before executing. You do not have to imagine difficult position on the imaginary 10-ball. Locate it near the 9-ball, pretending, for instance, that shape on the 10-ball will require a crisp, firm stop shot.

Visualization can even work to improve your break shot. Have an ideal position for your cue ball visualized before you break, along with picturing a ball (e.g., the corner ball in the Nine Ball rack) flying into a pocket, and even ideal position to shoot at the next ball! When you get strong enough mentally, you will be able to visualize all of the various scenarios in your pool game and confidently picture yourself straight to a win!

Mental Practice

Mental practice is the next step after visualization. While visualizing involves seeing a shot situation at the table, mental practice goes one step further, allowing you to visualize a series of shots, games, or even a match, without being at the table. Many professional pool players will tell you they knew they were first hooked on pool when they began seeing runouts in their sleep, in their daydreams, while driving or watching television. Surprisingly, not many realize that this is the first step to mental practice. Fewer still realize that you can indeed practice your pool game even when a table is nowhere to be found. Mental practice can be achieved through using your internal memory, recalling your own performances and practice situations, and through the memory of external experiences, recalling the talents and moves of others to improve your own skills.

Jean Houston is the director of the Foundation for Mind Research (Pomona, New York), and has authored several books, including *Mind Games, Listening to the Body,* and *The Possible Human* (1982). The latter discusses at length the concept of kinesthetic body imaging—using the mind to practice body movements without actually moving the body part. This is a good reference, offering actual training exercises for developing your mental imaging. Such exercises can then be transferred to your pool game. Say, for instance, you are sick for a few days and cannot get out to practice. You can still imagine playing a game or match—imagining shots, runouts, pattern plays, and so on. Through the use of body imaging, you can even imagine the feeling of stepping into your perfect stance, swinging the cue smoothly, making contact with the cue ball, and having it cleanly pocket the object ball.

You can also draw on the talents and experiences of better players to improve your game. Houston refers to drawing on the talents of better athletes to optimize the use of your kinesthetic body for rehearsing sport skills:

For example, if you are rehearsing your tennis serve kinesthetically, you might want to imagine that you are Bjorn Borg, Tracy Austin, or whoever you admire. . . . With kinesthetic rehearsal we can make the identification between these ideal images and our own movement . . . allowing the expression of our stored imagery of more optimal performance. (p. 20)

Author Steve Ungerleider (1996) also refers to drawing on the talents of better athletes, citing how skills might be improved by taking mental pictures of the flawless performance of others: "our minds take snapshots of the skills and record them in a specific region of our brains. . . . Imagery is based on memory, and we constantly reinforce the internal process by a flood of new pictures from external experiences to our minds" (p. 32).

Perhaps this has happened to you. You could watch a performance by a great player on television or a videotape and the same day turn in a performance well above that of your usual capabilities. This makes a great case for watching professional players in competition, whether live, on television, or on videotapes for sale in the billiard clubs and supply stores. If you haven't yet experienced skill improvement in this way, it's time to give it a try. Do your best to pick a player who matches you as closely as possible in body type, gender, and so on; this usually makes it easier to emulate his or her style of play. Watch the player live, or on tape

Courtesy of Pool & Billiard Magazine

Winner of four major titles in 1998, Player of the Year Francisco Bustamante executes a power break.

(which often works easier as you can repeat certain sequences you particularly admire), and then go out to play.

As you play with these techniques for mental practice, you'll develop quite a few of your own, and will very soon discover that you can use your mind to travel beyond visualization and mental practice into the complete mental imagery arena.

Mental Imagery

Mental imagery can be defined in the following way: "Imagery can be described as an exercise that uses all of the senses to create an experience in the mind. . . . Visualization is just one part of this imagery experience. We can also feel, smell, taste, hear and touch in our imagery experience" (Ungerleider 1996, p. 32).

In other words, mental imagery differs from mental practice in that it involves *all* the senses to create a more complete mental picture. By utilizing all your senses in the focused mental rehearsal of your pool game, you can simulate competitive conditions, to the point of eliciting natural physical reactions from your body, such as increased adrenaline and heart rate. Try this. Picture yourself in an important match, playing the best player you know. Visualize the crowd watching the two of you compete. Hear the crowd and ambient noise in the background, and the sound of each shot as your cue contacts the cue ball, and the cue ball sends an object ball crisply to a pocket. Feel the cue stick between your fingers, and the fabric of the table underneath your hand. And, most important, visualize a positive outcome in the match! Top athletes, even when not in actual physical practice, continually rehearse and use mental imagery to project positive reinforcements in their mental performances that will translate to eventual physical performance. This constant reinforcement not only allows you to practice while not actually on the pool table, but also builds your confidence in your game for when you do come to a match.

Finally, you can use mental imaging to practice ideal emotional states surrounding your physical performance. Mentally image the aftermatch emotions of winning. Mentally create the win in your mind: accept congratulations from fans, and feel the adrenaline in your body slowly dissipate as the competitive rush slows down. Enjoy the positive response of your mind and body to these mental images and it will be easier to re-create them in competition!

DEVELOPING CONFIDENCE

Knowledge is power. Truer words were never spoken, but they refer not only to the knowledge in your mind, but the knowledge in your body. Knowledge can be described as a developed skill honed through practice. In the sport of pool, there is a great deal of integration between mind and body knowledge; practicing a skill until it is second nature for your mind and your body will immediately increase your confidence. The more you play, the more shots you will begin to let go of and just shoot the ball, without conscious thought or calculation. This will allow you to shoot with authority, knowing that you will make the ball and that your cue ball will go where you intended.

Of course you may already realize that, but now you must take that feeling and transfer it to every single shot! This constant mental imaging within your game will further develop your tempo. If you can begin to shoot every shot with the same tempo and the same rhythm, projecting the same confidence and executing with the same sense of authority, knowing you will make the ball and where the cue ball will go, more difficult shots will begin to find their way to the pocket. Little by little, more shots, more safeties, and more game situations will become second nature to you.

In pool, as in most athletic endeavors, fear is your greatest enemy. A friend once told us that she was very concerned about her son playing football, and cautioned him endlessly to "be careful, don't get hurt, protect yourself." The coach found out and told her that was probably the worst thing she could do. Fear of getting hurt could make her son overly cautious, hesitant in his actions, and a more likely candidate for injury. While you're not subject to injury of this type in a noncontact sport like pool, fear-based play can produce equally devastating results. Too much hesitation, too much caution, babying shots that need to be stroked with authority—these fear-based actions will all produce errors that can be avoided.

If you are afraid of the shot in front of you, the situation, the score, your opponent, or people watching you, how can you possibly make the shot? With fear, your flight-or-fight instincts kick in, which are exactly the instincts you do not want at the pool table. Extra adrenaline will produce unneeded strength and cause you to lose your sense of feel and timing.

Replace the fear with confidence. If you have faith in your ability, and confidence in the outcome of each shot, you cannot simultaneously fear the outcome. Confidence and fear cannot coexist. Have confidence in your ability to get out of a tough situation. Have faith that you can reverse a score not in your favor. Have confidence that the crowd will appreciate your prowess at the table.

Once you have built a base of confidence through practice and faith in your ability, you can move on to fine-tuning your confidence and self-image with effortless play and occasional self-analysis to make sure, at all times, that you are having fun!

Effort Versus Effortless

Pool is often referred to as a "thinking man's sport" because of the extensive strategy involved. The sport is even compared to chess in terms of strategic maneuvers and offensive/defensive moves. Unfortunately, too many "thinking" pool players extend thinking to a dangerous degree during the game. Remember, it is still a sport. Too much thinking doesn't allow your body to do what it is supposed to.

So how can concentration and focus be so important? In pool, these concepts become very easy to confuse. You must strike a delicate balance. Thinking too much about your execution is no good. What your concentration skills must focus on is allowing the body to do what it has been trained to do. Once a shot situation is analyzed, the body must take over to effortlessly make the shot. The difficulty of this can increase in the pool games, because pool is a nonreactive sport, meaning your body is not reacting automatically to a ball being hit or thrown to you as in tennis or baseball. The nonreactive nature allows time for the untrained mind to wander unnecessarily.

To combat this and increase your confidence, your match play should take on an air of effortlessness. If you are putting forth too much effort, you are not playing naturally, letting your mind and body flow through the game or match. Relax, enjoy what you are doing. You have already put forth your effort through long hours of practice in honing your skills. Now it's time to show off a little and let your body do what it was trained to do!

Have Fun

In any sport at which you choose to excel, you have to have fun! With an attitude that says "this is work" or "this is so hard," you don't get as much out of playing, you won't be having any fun, and you certainly don't learn anything. Why bother?

Instead, try to take something with you from each practice session and each match you play. Don't focus on what went wrong or what shot you should have practiced more. Instead, ask: What went right? What shots am I proud of? What shot or technique or safety did I develop a little more confidence in? If you obsess over every missed shot, every bad roll, or every lucky roll your opponent got, you will have gained nothing, except a headache. Pretty soon your head is filled with negative thoughts about everything that can (and thus will) go wrong, and you become a mess, completely lacking self-confidence and unable to shoot the easiest shots with any kind of authority.

We're not saying you shouldn't acknowledge your faults or try to improve what doesn't work in your game. But there's plenty of time for that. Once you've reviewed the good things about a match or practice session (even try writing them down sometime), then you can make a list of the shots you might have played differently. Allowing yourself a bit of praise first will make you more eager to attack your problem areas. You can then work on each of them to develop better abilities in these areas that will translate to more self-confidence the next time you play!

PHYSICAL TRAINING TECHNIQUES

Here's a quick list of the ideal physical qualities every pool player would like to possess:

1. Good cardiovascular health for optimal breathing and physical/mental endurance.

2. Good balance and posture for proper stance and execution at the table.

3. Excellent hand/eye coordination.

4. Flexibility to allow proper bending and stretching at the table and avoid muscle tension.

Happily, these are desirable items to possess in most aspects of your life; so if you're not already engaging in activities to improve each of these areas, you should be, and not just for your pool game! Let's briefly tackle each of these four ideal properties individually and target some immediate improvement.

Cardiovascular Health

If you are already in good physical shape, this will be easy for you. If not, it's time to get off the couch. (But finish reading this section first!) Endurance in pool is critical, especially in long matches. While you may not feel the immediate effects of your body tiring, a body in poor health will quickly become mentally soft, too. Best bets: cardiovascular activities such as brisk walking, jogging, swimming, jumping rope, aerobics, or the use of rowing machines, exercise bikes, stair climbing machines, and so on. Cardiovascular activities like these promote good circulation and build muscle tone. The added benefits include getting oxygen flowing to the brain and the disbursement of excess adrenaline in your system. Breathing and relaxation exercises become effortless with a regular program of cardiovascular activity.

Balance and Posture

Poor balance and posture at the pool table or away from it will cause you all kinds of problems: poor spine alignment, sore, tense, or cramped muscles, pinched nerves, and even poor digestion. Fencing, a sport where balance and posture are critical, requires its athletes to strengthen the back, abdomen, buttocks, and upper thighs—the center of the body. Increased strength and tone to the body's center allow one to center more properly, thus creating excellent balance. It is interesting to note that one of the top contemporary female players in the sport today, Austrian native Gerda Hofstatter, was the European Junior Fencing champion before she traded her foil for a cue stick!

Exercises to target your body center include any number of back exercises, crunches, knee bends, and so on. Health club personnel and good home workout books can advise you on spot training in these areas. As they will caution you: if you have physical challenges to any area of your body, seek professional medical counseling or physical therapy before embarking on any program of intensive exercise.

Sports that work your target areas as well as improve balance and posture include martial arts, bike riding, hiking, and in-line skating, along with the aforementioned fencing. Another activity gaining increasing popularity is the trampoline, which benefits both your balance and your cardiovascular health. Keep in mind, though, this is a high-risk sport. If you're really adventurous, we could suggest tightrope walking (but don't forget the net)!

Hand/Eye Coordination

There are plenty of theories about hand/eye coordination, and plenty of explosions of those theories as more and more medical and brain research produces new findings. Hand/eye coordination was once thought to be predominantly a genetic characteristic (either you're born with it or you're not), but studies have shown that much of it is learned in the early stages of life, along with a great many other physical and cognitive abilities. Depending on your age, most of you probably didn't have parents aware of these recent research findings. Don't despair. By no means does this mean you're stuck at your current level of hand/eye coordination skills.

As you learned in our section on vision enhancement in chapter 2, hand/eye coordination can be improved, no matter what your age. Juggling, archery, and tennis are all fine activities for developing hand/eye coordination, along with pool! Some claim video games are also excellent for this, but we would caution you that they tend to be nonrelaxing activities and produce unnecessary strain on your eyes.

Flexibility and Stretching

Like hand/eye coordination, flexibility can be improved at any age with proper stretching and exercise techniques. We've included a separate section in this chapter on stretching and warm-up suggestions specific to the needs of the pool player. We advise anyone who participates in any physical activity to learn and practice good stretching techniques. If muscles are not properly stretched on a regular basis, muscle tension can ensue. This, in turn, can result in muscle soreness, pinched nerves, pulled muscles, and even serious physical injury.

The benefits of flexibility to pool players, especially in the neck, back, and leg areas, are enormous. On larger tables, many shots require a stretch across the table. Almost every shot requires bending at the waist, and raising the head up from this bent position to see the table. Inflexibility will cause, at a minimum, errors in your game, and will likely result in discomfort.

Most aerobics and dance-type classes teach excellent stretching techniques to promote better muscle movement and flexibility, as do the various forms of martial arts and yoga, which teach the added benefits of proper breathing and concentration. Swimming, as mentioned in our section on cardiovascular health, is also an excellent activity for flexibility, and provides nonimpact exercise for your entire body.

PHYSICAL TROUBLESHOOTING

Now that you know a little about what is optimal for your physical attributes as a pool player, you can work toward goals of improved physical health, strength, and agility. However, even the most athletic and strongest pool players encounter the occasional physical slump. Usually, this slump can be accounted for by bad body position of some sort, whether after a layoff from the game, an injury, or simply a quirk in one's stance or stroke. New equipment often results in physical changes, as can learning new concepts or skills. Your concentration on a new skill development may allow your body to lapse in a certain area. Perhaps you've even become lazy and your swing or mechanics have changed to a point where it simply throws off your entire game.

There's nothing more frustrating than trying to get out of a physical slump, especially when you don't know its origin. When this happens to you, immediately do a check of your fundamentals. If you have the advantage of playing with a teacher, coach, or good friend who knows your game very well, you might have them watch you to see if they notice any difference in the way you are approaching the shot, standing, or swinging the cue. If you do not have someone to watch your game, you might try videotaping yourself practicing. You may notice something you might not otherwise feel at the table. If this does not help, you will need to go through a step-by-step analysis of your physical game. Re-read chapter 1, and, as you attempt different shots, try to feel what is different or uncomfortable.

No matter your particular difficulty, there is a solution. However, don't rush into correcting something that doesn't need fixing, or you could complicate matters even further. And, thanks to the myriad of problems we have experienced in our own games, and seen other students and fellow professionals experience, we

Stretch Your Game

Most players just assume they can execute a solid swing without any form of warm-up. We disagree. You should engage in some form of stretching exercise prior to actually playing. Stretching will increase your mental and physical relaxation, reduce tension in your muscles that can lead to soreness and injury, help you develop better body awareness, and optimize your practice and performance sessions.

When you relieve as much tension as possible from your body, you can swing the cue more loosely, producing that much desired fluid movement. As has been mentioned before, excess adrenaline in pressure game situations will tighten up your muscles. That in turn will result in extra power that you just don't want in a "feel" game like billiards. It throws off speed control and kills the fluidity of movement.

For the most comprehensive set of stretches, our favorite book is *Sport Stretch* by Michael J. Alter (1990). Our favorites include stretches that target problem areas for pool players, including knees, hamstrings, quadriceps, abdomen and hip flexors, lower back, posterior neck, lateral neck, anterior neck, biceps, triceps, and forearm flexors.

(Ease, don't bounce into each stretch. Bouncing will increase, rather than decrease tension, and could cause injury.)

Here are a few of our own favorite stretching techniques:

• Toe touches: good for stretching the back muscles and hamstrings. Spread your legs shoulder-width apart and slowly touch your fingertips to the floor. Bend your knees if you need to, working toward a straight-leg position and bending merely from the waist.

• Windmills: This exercise is excellent for loosening up the muscles in the arm, shoulders, and neck area. Put your arms out at your sides and begin with small forward circular motions (arms straight), gradually working into larger and larger circles. Then, reverse the motion, moving the arm backward in ever-decreasing circles.

• Finger Push-Ups: These are excellent for stretching out the tendons in your fingers and wrist. Simply put your hands together, spreading the fingers apart as wide as possible. Use pressure to push against your opposite hand, stretching the fingers backward. This is particularly helpful when playing pool, since your grip hand is always in a cupped inward position. By stretching this seldom-worked area, your grip hand won't lock up or tighten in tense situations, which might otherwise cause you to punch a ball (not follow through) or overstroke a shot.

• Neck Stretch: This exercise will gently stretch your neck, shoulder, and arm muscles, and can be performed even while playing in a match to relax your body and your nerves. Sit straight on your chair or low stool, with feet in front of you, touching the floor. Hold onto the edge of the chair with your left hand. Gently allow your body to pull away from your left arm, tilting your head to the right side for the maximum stretch in your neck and shoulder area. Hold the stretch for a few seconds, then switch arms and repeat.

• Neck Rolls: In a sitting or standing position, roll your neck clockwise four times around, stretching it in all directions. Repeat this exercise counter-clockwise. This also can be done often to relieve neck tension, whether playing pool or working in an office. The first few times, you may hear a funny crackling sound—testimony to the fact that you can use a good stretch!

Feel free to refer to other books and classes on the subject of stretching, or watch how some of the more astute professionals warm up before a game. We guarantee you that a sound program of stretching will provide you with better performances on the pool table and overall better health.

can offer you a possible shortcut. The following are typical problem areas encountered by the pool player, and their symptoms. These will also provide you with a good checklist to run through in analyzing your physical game.

Foot Placement

Incorrect placement of the feet, predominantly the back foot, is a common problem, especially among players forced to play in smaller spaces or clubs without adequate room around the table. If you are not properly spaced from the edge of the table, your hand/eye coordination will be thrown off kilter. Standing too close will throw off your aiming ability because you don't have enough room for a free swing. When the swinging arm is cramped into too tight a space, the cue stick will naturally cross over through your shot, caused by your subconscious trying to make the ball even though you are not on it correctly. The crossover stroke results in mishits and unwanted english.

The reverse is also true. If you are standing too far away from your shots, you may be stretching too much. Your posture and balance will suffer, and your arm will be trying too hard to push through the shot, rather than swinging naturally from the proper distance. In either case, go back to your fundamentals and check on the placement of your back foot.

Finally, check to see that your feet are not too close together. This will result in awkward posture and bending, and will effect your balance and your swing. Chances are, if your feet are too close together, you are either crowding your swing, or standing to the side too much. Keep the stance open and comfortable.

Grip Position

Poor position of your back hand or grip hand can cause myriad difficulties. Let's begin with a grip that is too far forward. The simple mechanics of a grip that is too far forward dictate that you will not be able to follow through completely. What happens is that you run out of cue on your follow-through, causing you to bring your entire shoulder into play. The shoulder and elbow drop farther than normal to compensate for the short, punchy stroke. Not only will you have swing problems, but the extra body movement will cause excessive difficulties in your delivery and aiming ability.

If, on the other hand, your grip has slid too far back from its natural position, your timing will be thrown off. When the grip is moved back too far, you will hit the cue ball before you are supposed to for your particular swing. The distance won't be what you anticipate and you often end up with an uncomfortable and unnatural hesitation in your swing. You will be lined up perfectly, and won't understand why you are missing balls.

Bridge Difficulties

The bridge is the focal point of your swing. If your bridge hand is not in the right position or you've changed to a closed bridge, this could definitely throw off your stroke. Bridging too far back from the cue ball will allow less control. Bridging too far forward results in more control, but less follow-through and power. Make sure also that your bridge hand is in alignment with the rest of your body and not too far to the right or left of your shot. This is why, even though it is more difficult to achieve control over it in the beginning, we recommend the open bridge. Even a slight margin of bridge placement error in the closed bridge will result in poor aiming ability and crossing over the shot in your swing as, again, the body tries to compensate for the poor placement.

Too High, Too Low

If you're not getting down low enough over your shot, you may be having balance, swing, or follow-through difficulties, since, again, you are not allowing the arm its natural path for a swing (much like standing back too far from the shot). A head or back position that is too high will likely also cause physical discomfort, as you are forcing your body into an unnatural position.

Likewise, if you are too far down over your shot, you may be hampering your swing and, as a result, your ability to follow through and achieve pinpoint position. When you stand too low, your body will have to raise up in your follow-through to allow the arm to stroke through the shot. Always remember, moving any part of the body besides the arm is a big no-no.

Jumping Up

Which brings us to another common ailment of pool players—jumping up off the shot. Its causes include trying to watch the result of your shot, taking your eye off the object ball, and rushing your game. Some causes are mental, others physical, but the result is the same. To combat this, exaggerate the time you spend down on the shot after contact. Stay down on the shot until the cue ball comes to a complete stop. If this is very difficult for you to do, chances are you are getting up too quickly, anyway.

Improper Head Alignment

Perhaps you've picked up the very bad habit of moving your head to one side or the other, or tilting your head in your stance. While some players can get away with this (and indeed, some must because of vision limitations) the proper head placement, especially for anyone who does not play four or more hours a day, is directly over the cue stick—chin over cue, cue bisecting the eyes. Without centered placement of your head over the cue, you will have an improper perspective of the shot in front of you and your aiming will suffer.

Finally, if you do find yourself in a physical slump, don't panic. Run through your checklist; go back and check your fundamentals. Experiment. Give yourself time to sort it out. The worst thing you can do is try to change everything at once, or work yourself into a state of anxiety that tightens up every muscle in your body.

You're mentally ready to excel. You're physically ready to win. The only thing left standing between you and pool excellence is a bit of time and energy devoted to practice. Yes, that sounds like work. But, as you'll learn in our next chapter, practice can be fun and interesting, especially with the use of several creative practice games and a routine you can customize to your own needs and abilities.

Practice Made Fun!

Practice makes perfect. You've heard that before, but what makes practice perfect? Anyone can bang balls around the table for an hour. Will you learn anything?

By including a chapter specifically devoted to practice, our intention is to give you the keys to more efficient, more interesting, and more amusing sessions at the pool table. The biggest reason that most players, even when given all the knowledge they could ever use, don't achieve better results in their own games is a lack of practice. Let's face it: practice can be boring in any sport. Pool, when practiced alone, can get tedious very quickly if you don't have a good routine. You have to keep it interesting, keep it fresh, and make the best use of your skills in the allotted time you have to hone them.

This chapter will maximize your practice sessions, and the knowledge you take from other chapters will be integrated into your game sooner and last longer. We've included pertinent information on goal setting, sample practice menus, and interesting practice games. Use these concepts as a springboard, then mix them with your own ideas to come up with a practice routine that is tailored to your needs. As any professional player will tell you, a solid practice routine is all that remains between you and your quest for peak performance at the pool table!

GOAL SETTING

You may have read about goal setting in other sports or self-improvement books you've come across. You may have even been to a seminar or two in which, invariably, the topic turns to setting goals and keeping them. If you haven't heard any goal-setting lectures lately, we'd be surprised. We live in a goal-oriented society; we prioritize our lives based on goals. Accomplish one goal, and we're already building up to the next one. Guess what? In this respect, pool really is like life! And, like life, it can be tough to stick to your master plan. Nevertheless, it's easier to map your progress with a plan than to aimlessly knock balls around the table.

As in any activity, in your desire to be a better pool player, you can set short-range goals and long-range goals, monitor your performance, and build consistently toward a better game. How much you progress and how fast is up to you.

The only constant we can guarantee you is this: you won't ever completely master the cue sports. No one ever has; we expect no one ever will. And that's the real beauty of the sport; no matter your age, no matter your knowledge of the game, you'll always have something to learn.

Let's begin with your primary (or long-range) goal for your game. What do you want out of pool? Do you want to:

- Get good enough to win world championships?

- Compete on the pro tour?

- Win a little money in local or regional tournaments?

- Be the best player in your club?

- Play well enough to beat a few of your friends?

- Be able to make a few balls on your home table?

It doesn't matter to us; one goal is no better or worse than another. It's what you want from the game; so answer the question honestly.

Once you've determined the primary goal for your own game, assess your current skill level with the same honesty. The answers you give to these two questions will allow you to gauge the distance you'll need to travel from the player you are to the player you want to be.

Your goals can be played out in a casual group game

Your primary goal will determine the length of time you will invest in your short-range goals, which will fall into three main categories:

1. Improving your mental skills (concentration, confidence, and mental imagery)

2. Improving your physical skills (swing, touch, critical shots, etc.)

3. Improving your knowledge (pattern play and strategic skills)

Once you've determined your practice schedule, try to divide your time, whether daily or weekly, equally into attention on each of the three above areas. This will ensure your progress as a well-rounded pool player. If you concentrate on just one area, you will end up with weaknesses in your game that will affect the area in which you excel.

Finally, if you are a beginner or amateur player, start out slowly and build your practice sessions. You'll find it's easier to give 100 percent to three one-hour sessions than to one three-hour session, until you build up your mental and physical endurance for the game.

TWELVE PRACTICE GAMES

Practice routines will get stale very quickly with strictly drills and setup shots (though never discount their use for your game). To combat this, presented here are a dozen different games to play and/or unique exercises to perform to practice certain skills under game conditions:

1. Three Ball

Objective: To consistently run the 7, 8, and 9 balls after your "break."

Skills Worked: Cue ball control, position play, safeties.

Line up the 7, 8, and 9 balls in a triangle on the head spot. Break open the balls, paying particular attention to controlling your cue ball on the break. You may not take ball in hand after the break, so you will really want to try and keep your cue ball close to the center of the table. (For more on this, refer to Power Breaks on page 71.) Attempt to run the three balls.

If you don't get a decent shot on the 7-ball, attempt to execute an imaginative safety, hooking your "opponent" or leaving a difficult shot. (If desired, beginners may take ball in hand on the 7-ball after breaking.)

Once you become fairly proficient at this exercise, turn the "game" into Four Ball. Add the 6-ball and rack the balls in the shape of a small diamond. Three- and four-ball pattern practice will quickly have you recognizing patterns valuable to your Nine Ball game.

2. Phantom Eight Ball

Objective: To consistently run the stripes or solids in a phantom game of Eight Ball.

Skills Worked: Eight Ball power break, cue ball control, and pattern play.

Begin by racking all the balls as if you were going to play a real game of Eight Ball. Break open the balls. Look at the resulting table layout and decide which group (stripes or solids) you would choose. Then, remove the other group of balls from the table. This will help you begin to see your patterns for Eight Ball. It's easier to visualize the lay of the table more quickly without the clutter of seven extra balls. Phantom Eight Ball will speed development of your pattern-play knowledge. Again, beginners may choose to take cue ball in hand after the break.

3. No Rails

Objective: To run the balls without the cue ball contacting any cushion on the table.

Skills Worked: Cue ball control, speed control, and pattern play.

Throw six or seven balls out randomly onto the table; then place each one a minimum of 6–10 inches from the rail, with no balls touching each other or close together. Study your resulting table layout and, with cue ball in hand, anywhere you want to start, run the balls, without any object ball or your cue ball contacting a cushion!

There are actually a multitude of ways to run these balls without hitting a rail. This exercise is an overall great skill developer for pattern play, stop shots, and tightening up your cue ball control. It works both your mental and physical skills.

4. Safety Nine Ball or Eight Ball

Objective: To hook your opponent or imaginary opponent on every shot.

Skills Worked: Cue ball control, speed control, safety play, and kicking.

Begin with a Nine Ball rack. Break the balls and take cue ball in hand on the first ball. Play safe by either hiding the cue ball from the object ball, or vice versa, or hide both balls. If you are successful, you must now attempt to kick at the 1-ball. If you are not, you may pocket this ball and play another safety, or, if you think you can, run out. When playing with a partner, the partner typically must play safe unless he has a clear shot to a pocket, in which case he can pocket this ball and play safe on the next ball.

For variation, try playing Eight Ball the same way. If you are shooting first at the striped balls, try to hide your cue ball from any clear shot on a solid ball, and so on.

5. Frozen Six Ball

Objective: To pocket all six balls without banking or combinations.

Skills Worked: Frozen-to-the-cushion shots, speed control, and pattern play.

Set up the balls as indicated in figure 10.1. Place the cue ball in the area shown, and attempt to run all six balls. You must shoot them straight into the pocket without the use of caroms or combinations, and must attempt to run them all without taking cue ball in hand. This is an excellent test of your speed control and pattern-play decision making, and will hone your ability to make balls that are frozen to the rail.

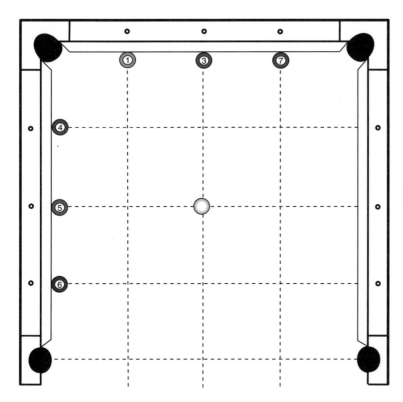

Figure 10.1 Attempt to run all six balls after setting up as shown.

6. Olympic Nine Ball

Objective: To achieve a 10-frame score, as in bowling, with 10 games of Nine Ball.

Skills Worked: Developing a runout mentality, cue ball control, pattern play, and power breaking.

Rack the balls exactly as shown in figure 10.2. Initially, rack them the same way each time. This will help you to recognize what is happening with your Nine Ball break in 10 consecutive racks. Later, you can rack them like any Nine Ball rack, making sure just the 1-ball is at the head and the 9-ball is in the center.

Break the balls. Whatever balls you pocketed stay down, as in a real Nine Ball game. With ball in hand (after the break only), attempt to run the table. Each ball you make is worth one point. Make a Nine Ball combination at any time during the frame and score 9 points. Break and run all nine balls and you get a bonus point, making the frame worth 10 points. Play 10 consecutive racks this way (also a great practice game to play with a partner: you shoot a frame, rack for him, he shoots a frame and racks for you, etc.). The maximum score is 100 points.

This will help you to develop more of a runout mentality. You will quickly see whether a runout is possible and how to go about getting there. It is also great for keeping track of your progress, since you walk away with a score that you can compare to your performance in subsequent practice sessions. Keep in mind that as fun and addicting as this particular game can be, it works only on your offensive game and does not take into consideration strategy or defensive (safety) skills. However, it works as an excellent counterpart to Safety Nine Ball!

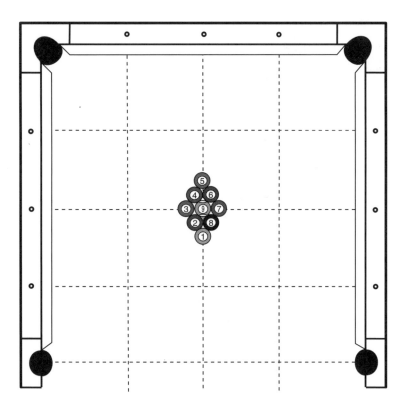

Figure 10.2 Rack the balls exactly as shown to learn more about your break.

7. Philadelphia

Objective: To run the rack of object balls, pocketing each ball off the cue ball.

Skills Worked: Cue ball control, speed control of both the cue ball and the object balls, caroms, and angle knowledge.

For more information on the game of Philadelphia, refer to page 119. Rack the balls as shown in figure 10.3. The cue ball is placed where the 1-ball would be, and you may use the 1-ball as your cue ball. Break the balls and attempt to pocket any ball by caroming it off the cue ball. You may use any object ball as your cue ball throughout the game. This will help you to see angles of balls as they come off other balls and develop your judgment of where to hit the ball to have it carom correctly off the cue ball. This is also an excellent exercise for controlling both the cue ball and the object ball. Hint: To string together runs of balls together in this game requires a bit of patience and creativity. You should notice immediately that a carom off the cue ball into a pocket is made easier when the cue ball is closer to the pocket. In other words it's in your best interest to pay attention to the speed of the cue ball. If it gets away from you, it may be several shots before you can maneuver it back toward a pocket. This game can be played by yourself or with a partner. You can play for who takes a majority of the rack, or to a set number of points.

8. Zigzag

Objective: To play a rack of 15 balls without making anything straight into the pocket.

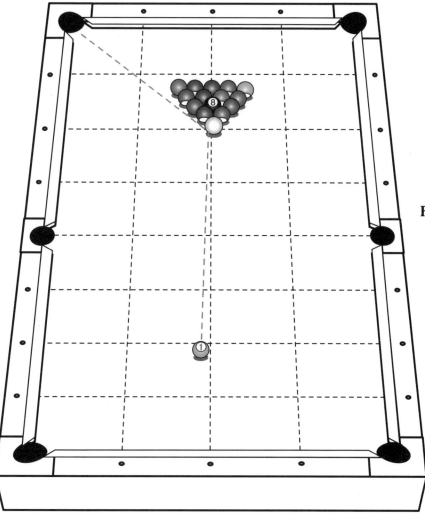

Figure 10.3 In Philadelphia, the cue ball is placed in the rack and you break with an object ball as shown.

Skills Worked: Cue ball control, banks, kicks, caroms, and combinations.

This game can be played alone or with an opponent. Rack all 15 balls and execute a power break to spread the balls as much as possible. You may shoot at any ball on the table, but you cannot shoot it directly into the pocket. You can bank it in, carom it in off another ball, kick it in, or play a combination. This will allow you an excellent opportunity to work on your critical shot skills.

9. Make Tracks

Objective: To pocket a series of balls, utilizing only two-rail banks.

Skills Worked: Aiming and banking.

Place the balls along the right side of the foot spot out to the long rail as shown by figure 10.4. You will be attempting to pocket each of the object balls into the corner indicated. This is an excellent shot for your repertoire, and is especially valuable in the intricate game of One Pocket. Begin by taking cue ball in hand and placing it behind the 2-ball, then the 5-ball, and so on, and try to stop the cue ball upon contact. Once you become proficient at this—when you can see the tracks

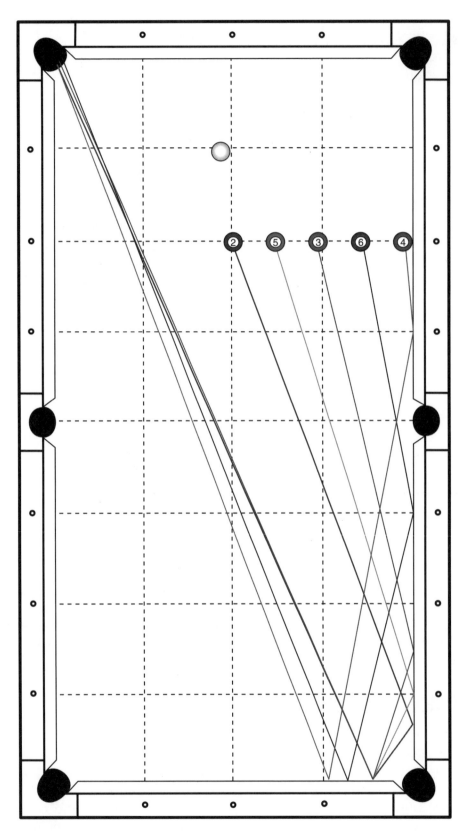

Figure 10.4   Set up the table as shown and attempt to make
the object balls in the corner.

to the pocket, and know where to aim on the first rail to get you there—increase the difficulty of the exercise. Simply change the angle of the cue ball as it attacks the angle of the object ball. You'll notice right away how this will alter the path of the object ball. This exercise is challenging!

10. Expand Your Limits

Objective: To discover just how many places your cue ball can arrive after pocketing an object ball and to be able to properly visualize a shot and have your cue ball arrive on the spot you have predicted.

Skills Worked: Cue ball control, speed control, follow, draw, english, and visualization.

This is a never-ending exercise, as there are few limits to where your cue ball can travel on any given shot (though preferably you will want to keep it on the surface of the pool table!). Set up the balls as shown in figure 10.5. Place your cue ball on the foot spot. You will execute your first shot with a center-ball hit, medium speed. Before you shoot at the first ball, however, you must visualize exactly where your cue ball will arrive. How did you do? Did the cue ball come short or long of where you visualized it should? Try the shot again. Once you have mastered the shot and resulting position with a medium hit, center ball, play it with draw, then follow. Now add spin—low right, high right, low left, high left. If you like, add and reduce speed. Just remember that in each case, you must first visualize where it is you will be placing the cue ball.

Once you become proficient at the combinations of shots for each of the five balls, move the exercise to work the right corner pocket. Place the cue ball back on the spot each time, so you are working with a constant.

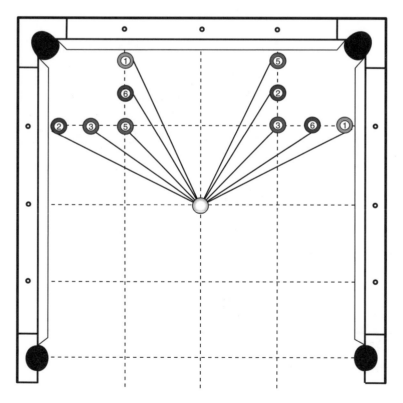

Figure 10.5 Before shooting each shot, visualize exactly where your cue ball should arrive.

This exercise will teach you better than any other the wide variety of position plays you can execute, depending on the shot with which you are faced. By visualizing both making the ball and your resulting cue ball position, you will quickly develop a feel for where the cue ball is going and just what you need to do to get it there!

11. Mississippi Nine Ball

Objective: To run a predetermined pattern in a Nine Ball rack.

Skills Worked: Cue ball control, pattern play, using the entire table.

Place the balls as shown in figure 10.6. Balls near the rail should be about a ball's width from the cushion. Take cue ball in hand anywhere in the shaded area shown. Then, run the rack! Seems simple, but this rack has been specially designed to make you travel back and forth, and not come too far one way or the other. Get out of line once and you'll see just how difficult it is to finish the rack!

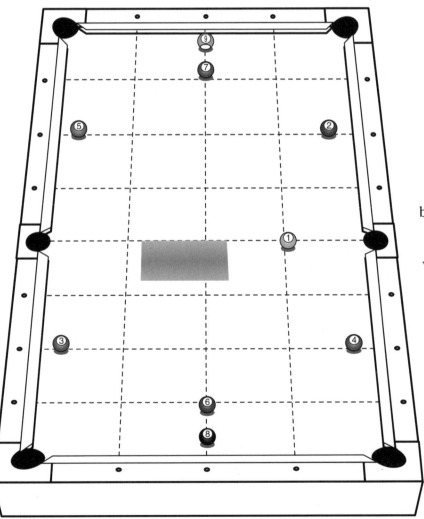

Figure 10.6 Set up the balls exactly as shown. This exercise is harder than it looks and requires advanced planning and working the cue ball back and forth.

This is an excellent practice tool to see patterns and hone your cue ball control. Miss, and you must start over. By trial and error, you will soon learn on which side you must be for each subsequent object ball to get shape on (arrive in position for) the next. If you are anything less than an accomplished player, don't expect to get this one right on the first attempt!

12. Rotation

Objective: To run all 15 balls in order.

Skills Worked: Advanced pattern and position play, cue ball control, critical shots like banking, caroms, and combinations, and power breaking.

There's simply no better way to really learn to work all your skills than Rotation. Rack all 15 balls as shown in figure 10.7, smash them open, and attempt to run all the balls in sequence. This is a great training aid for Nine Ball. Let's face it: if you become proficient at pocketing 15 balls in numerical order, 9 balls will seem like child's play! This will also work your advanced Eight Ball skills: when you run the first 8 balls, you will in fact be playing the solids, in rotation! This exercise is not for the faint of heart. If you are a beginner, achieve a little proficiency at the other exercises before attempting this!

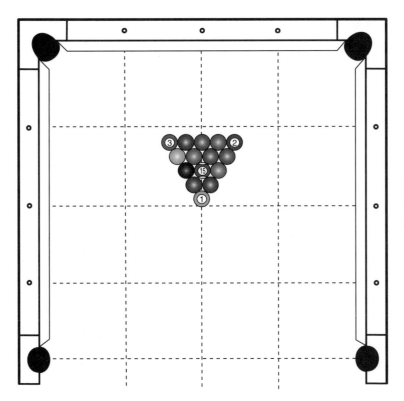

Figure 10.7 The rotation rack. This game allows you to work lots of cue skills.

Getting Past Frustrating Plateaus

Nothing can be more frustrating than when your game hits a brick wall. Suddenly, after measured improvement in your pool game for some period, you seem to be running in place. In some cases, it will even feel as though your skills have deteriorated. You don't know if it's physical or mental. You don't know if you even want to play anymore.

Don't panic! This happens to everyone, even the pros. The very first step you may need to take toward getting past a plateau in your game is simply to take a break! Take a week or two off from your game—entirely off! Try different things during the times you normally play: a round of golf, video games, bowling, a movie. Pool is a sport that requires time to learn and patience to improve. We all get so into learning and wanting to progress at a faster rate that impatience itself can hamper our progress. Forget about pool during your mini-vacation. When you come back to the table for the first time after your break, play just for fun. Put no pressure on yourself to perform.

What most people find is that even a short break will give them a fresh perspective and a greater desire to play the game. Often this alone will get you over the hump and sometimes even provide a minor breakthrough, as you play fresh and without added pressure on yourself.

Step #2 is to go back to the basics and work on your mechanics. Review your swing and your delivery, check your head and foot placement, adjust your grip. Try to concentrate on feeling what you are doing as you are doing it. You may simply need to get your body and your mind in tune with each other again. Whether or not you are experiencing a plateau, this is something every player should do once in a while to keep his game at a peak and avoid slipping into bad physical habits.

You may also want to change your choice of game for a while. For example, if you play Nine Ball consistently, maybe your routine has become stagnant. Try playing Straight Pool, an excellent game to build your confidence, see patterns, and refresh your interest. Or maybe play some Eight Ball, or Banks, or One Pocket. Some establishments have billiards or snooker tables. If your club possesses either, try one of these games for some variation. Playing games other than those in which you normally participate helps you to see different shots, tracks around the table, how the balls react, and other phenomena that you may have become anesthetized to in your basic routine. While searching out new games, you might want to take the opportunity to visit a new location. Often a change of venue is equally good for building lost interest and getting away from your usual game plan.

Finally, you might want to alter your routine itself. If you are used to playing with a partner, try playing by yourself for a while. Maybe you just need some time to work on your game and your thought processes without interruption. Practice different areas of your game on different days—for example, kicks on one day, banks and caroms on another. Sometimes getting the basic concept of a new shot down works wonders for your game and your confidence. If you already play alone, find a new partner to match up with on occasion.

Above all, don't take your game too seriously. Often, you find that you can't execute a particular shot and you become quickly frustrated, feeling that your game is slipping away. It won't. The knowledge you have will always be with you; it may just need a little prodding to resurface! Play the table and have fun. If you're not having any fun, you've probably lost sight of why you took up pool in the first place!

SEVEN-DAY POOL WORKOUT

Finally, to set you well on your way, what follows is a sample one-week practice menu, offering variety and interest to your practice routine. Where applicable, we have indicated the chapters you should reference for further discussion or explanation of the practice item listed. You may not have the time to include each of these items. That's okay. We've presented a great deal of information crammed into one week to provide a complete selection. This is meant only as a guide to represent all the areas of the game you will want to enhance. Take from this list, and develop your own daily or weekly menu of practice items that hold your interest and improve your skills. Prepare your own schedule as a teacher or coach might prepare homework assignments. Write your schedule down, and have a place where you can record your progress. Note what is practical and what is not. If you have only an hour to play, it's unrealistic to expect to work on seven different areas of your game. If you can or want to play only three days a week, that's fine too. Again, this is shown only as an example. If you do practice seven days a week and find that such a routine is frustrating to you, taper off to four or five days or less. Remember, the object is to have fun while you improve!

Don't be afraid to regularly revise and update your schedule. For example, if you begin with a lot of work on a proper stance and follow-through, eventually these skills will become second nature. At that point, you will want to replace some of the time allotted for those skills with time spent practicing another skill or technique, such as breaking or safety play.

Note: Each day's practice schedule already assumes some form of stretching before your pool workout. Refer to page 222 for areas of the body you should stretch before practice. You should also begin to incorporate eye exercises into your routine; these are found in chapter 2 and can be done at practice time or any time during the day.

We have designed each day of practice to work multiple areas of your game. Each daily practice session begins with a warm-up, followed by three exercises, followed by a cool-down period during which you will work on your mental imaging skills. The practice session can take anywhere from 45 minutes to a couple of hours, depending on the time you have and how long you can maintain your focus on the exercises presented.

Congratulations! You now have all the building blocks necessary to build a solid foundation for a precision pool game. As with all endeavors, undoubtedly there will be a few stumbling blocks along the way. Have patience. If you're tired of playing, take a break. The most important aspect to developing your pool game is to have the *desire* to become an accomplished player. Without it, you simply go through the motions of banging the balls around the table. If you find your desire waning, you need a vacation!

Take special care to check your physical fundamentals often, as this is where players most often falter. When you do learn a new skill, enjoy your mastery. The more skills you learn and make your own, the more you will want to learn. Experiment with the ideas we've given you. The possibilities for shot situations, creative safeties, position and pattern plays are endless. Spend time on both your mental and physical skills, as the integration of these is so important in the cue sports.

And of course, in keeping with the spirit of the sport we love, we leave you with the final two most important words: *Have fun!*

Seven-Day Pool and Billiard Practice Routine

Monday

Warm-Up: Throw out a few racks of balls and play with your eyes closed to get a feel for your stroke and follow-through. Play two or three racks this way.

Exercise #1: Throw a rack of nine balls out on the table. Shoot them with a closed bridge. Throw another rack out, shooting each shot with an open bridge. On the third rack, take cue ball in hand on each ball to set up a shot where the cue ball is on the rail. Use a rail bridge to execute. Throw out a fourth rack and take cue ball in hand to make each shot difficult enough to reach so that you must use the mechanical bridge.

Exercise #2: Play two to three games of Philadelphia. (Refer to Practice Game [PG] #7 in this chapter.)

Exercise #3: Break at least five racks of Nine Ball and, no matter what the resulting lay of the table, roll out to a position where your imaginary opponent has no shot, but where you can play a safety to hide the opponent. Play the safety, rerack the balls, and repeat the exercise.

Cool-Down: Sit quietly. Breathe deeply a few times, and imagine yourself running a rack of Nine Ball (or Eight Ball) if this is your game of preference. Begin with the break. See all the balls as they come to rest on the table. Plan your strategy, and mentally run the rack. This exercise should take about 10 minutes.

Tuesday

Warm-Up: Perform the center ball chalk exercise (chapter 3, page 51).

Exercise #1: Play a few games of Olympic Nine Ball (PG #6).

Exercise #2: Follow up exercise #1 with a few games of Safety Nine Ball. Refer to chapter 7 and PG #4.

Exercise #3: Tighten up your game with a few rounds of Frozen Six Ball (PG #5).

Cool-Down: As on Monday, sit quietly, breathe deeply, and mentally image two racks of Nine Ball or Eight Ball.

Wednesday

Warm-Up: Throw out a few racks of balls, executing each shot as a stop shot. (Refer to chapter 5, page 91.)

Exercise #1: Play a few rounds of Make Tracks (PG #9).

Exercise #2: Follow this up with a few racks of Zigzag (PG #8).

Exercise #3: Tighten up your game with a few racks of No Rails (PG #3).

Cool-Down: Another mental imaging exercise. This time, imagine you are in a match and the score is hill-hill, meaning you and your opponent each need one game to win. Watch your opponent shoot, and miss the first ball of the rack. Step to the table and find yourself hidden on the 1-ball. Execute a kick/safety and leave her hooked. Watch her kick at the ball and leave you a shot. Then run out the table!

Thursday

Warm-Up: Throw out a couple of racks and play each shot to bring your cue ball back to the center of the table. (Refer to the chapter 6 sidebar on page 157.)

Exercise #1: Play a few racks of Phantom Eight Ball (PG #2).

Exercise #2: Follow this with at least five rounds of Four Ball (variation of PG #1).

Exercise #3: Tighten up your game with a try at Mississippi Nine Ball (PG #11). Try to work this until you can get at least halfway through the rack.

Cool-Down: Mentally image a run of at least 16 balls in Straight Pool. Imagine the table is open and you've chosen your break shot. Run the rack leading up to the break shot, shoot this, and spread a few of the balls from the rack as you do so, enabling you to continue your run. You may mentally continue the run as long as you are able to without losing the mental picture.

Friday

Warm-Up: Throw out a couple of racks of balls and attempt to shoot each shot toward the pocket, but without actually pocketing the ball. This works your object ball speed-control skills.

Exercise #1: This is the only exercise you will focus on today. Play Expand Your Limits (PG #10), using just the left corner pocket.

Exercise #2: If time allows, repeat Exercise #1, this time using the right corner pocket.

Cool-Down: The above exercise has continually used your powers of visualization. Rather than mentally imaging something new, sit quietly and review the exercise in your mind, seeing all the resulting cue ball positions as you played them.

Saturday

Warm-Up: Throw out a few racks of balls and attempt to execute each shot with your resulting cue ball position at least six inches from any cushion on the table. (Refer to Shrink Your Table, page 171.)

Exercise #1: Play five rounds of Three Ball (PG #1).

Exercise #2: Expand your practice with a round of Olympic Nine Ball.

Exercise #3: Further challenge your runout abilities with a game or two of Rotation, attempting to run all 15 balls in order.

Cool-Down: Imagine running a rack of Rotation, from the break to the 15-ball!

Sunday

This is "Dealer's Choice" day! You may pick any exercise for a warm-up, followed by three of your favorite game or drill exercises, followed by a half-hour mental imaging session. Imagine any game situation you like, even if it's playing the best player on the planet for the World Championship title!

Glossary

ball in hand: When a player fouls, the opposing player may place the cue ball anywhere on the table for their first shot.

bad hit: When a player fouls the cue ball by not making a legal hit on their intended object ball. Typically, the incoming player is awarded ball in hand.

bank shot: Refers to an object ball contacting one or more cushions before being pocketed.

bar box: Nickname for a coin-operated pool table, typically a 3½ by 7 model found in taverns and lounges.

billiard: A shot in which the cue ball contacts an object ball before contacting and pocketing the intended object ball.

break: The opening shot of any pool game.

bridge: The support formed by the front hand on which, or in which, the front of the cue stick rests.

butt: The lower half of a cue stick (in a two-piece cue, from the joint down to the bumper).

carom shot: Shooting an intended object ball off an object ball to pocket the intended object ball.

cinch shot: When the emphasis is placed on making a shot, without regard to resulting position of the cue ball. This can be a difficult shot, used when it is important to place all the attention on pocketing the ball, or when the next shot is so close to a pocket it doesn't matter much where the cue ball comes to rest.

combination shot: Shooting an object ball into an intended object ball to pocket the intended object ball.

double elimination: A tournament format in which players are paired on a chart and must continue to win each match to progress through the winner's side of the chart. The first loss a player incurs results in that player being moved to the loser's side of the bracket. Another loss results in elimination. The winner of each bracket plays in the final match.

draw: Achieved by hitting below center on the cue ball, draw will cause the cue ball to reverse its forward roll after impact with an object ball.

duck: A slang term for hiding the cue ball or intended object ball with a safety shot.

ferrule: Usually made of hard plastic or ivory, the ferrule is found at the front end of the cue shaft. The cue tip is glued to the ferrule.

foot spot: Midway between the long rails and two diamonds up from the short rail, the foot spot is used as a reference for racking the balls. The front ball in any rack, or an object ball returned to the table after a foul, is always placed on the foot spot.

grip: Refers to the back hand position on the cue stick.

head spot: Opposite the foot spot, the head spot is usually not marked by a spot, but falls midway between the long rails and two diamonds up from the head (breaking) end of the table.

hooked: When the direct path between the cue ball and object ball is blocked by impeding balls (or, in the case of corner or side hooked, by the edge of the rail cushion). Also referred to as being snookered.

inside english: This can be right or left english placed on the cue ball, depending on the angle of the shot. When cutting a ball to the right, inside english refers to right english. When cutting a ball to the left, inside english refers to left english.

joint: In a two-piece cue, the joint is where the butt and shaft screw together. Joint materials are usually composed of steel, plastic, or ivory.

jump shot: Accomplished by elevating the butt end of the cue stick and shooting down on the cue ball, the jump shot forces the cue ball to bounce into the table bed and over an obstructing ball or balls.

kick shot: When a direct path to the intended object ball is obstructed by another ball or balls, the cue ball can be shot (kicked) into one or more rails in an attempt to make a legal hit.

lag: Used to determine who will break, players each shoot an object ball from behind the head string toward the opposite end of the table and back. The object ball that comes to rest closest to the head rail wins. The player winning the lag can elect to break or pass the break to the opponent.

legal hit: The intended object ball must be contacted by the cue ball, and either the cue ball or the object ball must then contact a cushion. In a frozen ball shot, the cue ball must contact the cushion after contacting the frozen object ball, or the object ball must be driven to another rail.

massé: An extremely elevated stroke of the cue stick on the cue ball (the cue stick is usually perpendicular or nearly perpendicular to the table surface). A massé shot will allow you to send the cue ball forward, whereupon it will grab the cloth and come straight back.

mechanical bridge: The mechanical bridge has the appearance of a cue stick, with a stable, grooved attachment at the end on which the front end of the cue can be placed to guide its path. It is used when a shot is too far away to bridge with the hand. Also referred to as bridge or rake.

miscue: When the cue tip slides off the cue ball on attempted contact. Causes of miscues include lack of chalk, lack of a scuffed tip, or a poorly stroked shot.

outside english: The opposite of inside english, outside english (also called running english) can be right or left english placed on the cue ball, depending on the angle of the shot. If cutting a ball to the right, outside english refers to left english. When cutting a ball to the left, outside english refers to right english.

pilling: This term refers to bits of fabric fibers that loosen from the fabric on the table bed, usually when the cloth is newer. Pilling causes erratic movement of the balls across an otherwise smooth surface.

rollout: Also referred to as a pushout, this shot occurs when the player elects not to attempt contact on his intended ball and shoots the cue ball to a different position on the table. The incoming player may elect to shoot the shot left by the player pushing out, or ask the player to shoot again, at which point the player must make a legal hit.

round robin: A tournament format in which a player plays every other player in the tournament, or every other player in a bracket. Players with the best win/loss record in each bracket then advance to a single- or double-elimination playoff.

running english: *See* outside english.

safety: A defensive shot in which the goal is to leave the incoming player without an offensive opportunity.

scotch doubles: A two-person team format, usually male/female. Scotch doubles often feature alternating shots at the table, rather than alternating turns.

scratch: Pocketing the cue ball or jumping it from the bed of the table. A scratch is a foul, with the incoming player receiving ball in hand or the appropriate penalty for the game being played.

scuffers: A variety of tools that are used to scuff the cue tip, providing a rougher surface to which chalk may adhere, increasing friction between the smooth leather tip and the surface of the cue ball.

shape: Synonymous with position; you play position for the next shot, or to get shape on the next shot.

shaft: The upper half of the cue stick (in two-piece cues, from the joint up to the cue tip).

single elimination: A tournament format in which players are paired on a chart and must continue to win each match to progress through the chart. A single loss eliminates the player.

snooker: A cue discipline using a larger table (full-size models are 6 by 12), with smaller pockets and smaller balls. This game is very popular in England and British Commonwealth countries, garnering hundreds of hours of live television coverage each year.

snookered: *See* hooked.

stroke/swing: The motion of the arm that causes the cue stick to contact the cue ball.

tip tapper: A tool that is tapped against the cue tip to form a rougher surface to which chalk may adhere, increasing friction between the smooth leather tip and the surface of the cue ball.

wrap: Found on the butt of a cue stick, the wrap is most often made of nylon, linen, leather, or cork. Partly decorative, partly functional, the wrap provides a less slippery surface than polished wood for which to grip the cue.

Bibliography

Alter, Michael J. 1990. *Sport Stretch*. Champaign, IL: Human Kinetics.

The Billiard Congress of America. 1992. *Billiards—The Official Rules & Records Book*. New York: Lyons & Burford.

Chaney, Earlene. 1991. *The Eyes Have It: A Self Help Manual for Better Vision*. New York: Instant Improvement.

Franklin, Eric. 1996. *Dynamic Alignment Through Imagery*. Champaign, IL: Human Kinetics.

Houston, Jean. 1982. *The Possible Human: A Course in Enhancing Your Physical, Mental and Creative Abilities*. New York: The Putnam Publishing Group.

Kubistant, Tom. 1986. *Performing Your Best: A Guide to Psychological Skills for High Achievers*. Champaign, IL: Leisure Press.

Nideffer, Robert M. 1985. *Athletes' Guide to Mental Training*. Champaign, IL: Human Kinetics.

Ungerleider, Steven. 1996. *Mental Training for Peak Performance*. Emmaus, PA: Rodale Press.

Index

About the Authors

Gerry "The Ghost" Kanov and **Shari "The Shark" Stauch** combine an unprecedented wealth of professional pool experience and talent to create this book. Both are staff members of *Pool & Billiard Magazine*, the top publication for the sport. They have played and worked with virtually every top professional pool player and instructor in the world.

Kanov has been playing professional and amateur pool since 1968. He has dozens of local and national Top 3 finishes and championships, including two national team championships as a player/coach. He is an instructional editor and technical advisor for *Pool & Billiard Magazine* and writes the "Ghost" column.

Kanov also is a touring professional on the Camel Pro Billiard Series and a coach for several top players. He also has a screen credit; he portrayed a referee in the motion picture *The Color of Money*. Kanov lives in Downers Grove, Illinois.

Stauch has been on the Women's Pro Billiard Tour since 1980. She has been consistently ranked in the top 32 and is a former Illinois and Wisconsin State Nine Ball Champion. She is the owner and editor of *Pool & Billiard Magazine* and has performed dozens of exhibitions for a variety of clients, such as ESPN/ESPN2 and Gordon's Gin and Vodka.

Stauch is the founding president of the Billiard Education Foundation, which conducts youth billiard national championships and provides scholarships. She serves as the Public Relations Director of the World Confederation of Billiard Sports, an international federation that succeeded in getting pool recognized as an official Olympic sport. Stauch was also involved with *The Color of Money*, serving as a consultant. She lives in Summerville, South Carolina.